The Education Mayor

American Governance and Public Policy Series
Series Editors: Gerard W. Boychuk, Karen Mossberger, and Mark C. Rom

The Education Mayor

Improving America's Schools

Kenneth K. Wong
Francis X. Shen
Dorothea Anagnostopoulos
Stacey Rutledge

Georgetown University Press
Washington, D.C.

As of January 1, 2007, 13-digit ISBN numbers have replaced the 10-digit system.
13-digit   10-digit
   Paperback: 978-1-58901-179-3   Paperback: 1-58901-179-1

Georgetown University Press, Washington, D.C. www.press.georgetown.edu
©2007 by Georgetown University Press. All rights reserved. No part of this book
may be reproduced or utilized in any form or by any means, electronic or
mechanical, including photocopying and recording, or by any information
storage and retrieval system, without permission in writing from the publisher.

Library of Congress Cataloging-in-Publication Data

The education mayor : improving America's schools / Kenneth K. Wong . . . [et al.].
   p. cm. — (American governance and public policy series)
   Includes bibliographical references and index.
   ISBN 978-1-58901-179-3 (alk. paper)
   1. School management and organization—United States. 2. School improvement
programs—United States. 3. Educational change—United States. 4. Education,
Urban—United States. 5. Mayors—United States. I. Wong, Kenneth K., 1955–
   LB2805.E282 2007
   379.1'530973—dc22
   2007007018

∞ This book is printed on acid-free paper meeting the requirements of the American
National Standard for Permanence in Paper for Printed Library Materials.

14 13 12 11 10 09 08 07   9 8 7 6 5 4 3 2
First printing

Printed in the United States of America

Contents

Tables

Preface

FROM NEW YORK AND BOSTON TO CHICAGO AND Washington, D.C., a new style of big-city mayor has emerged over the past decade. These mayors are no longer content to sit on the sidelines and watch as their cities' schools struggle to educate their cities' young people. These new-style mayors believe in a straightforward, yet unconventional, idea of urban governance: City government should be held accountable for city schools. When city hall and the school district are jointly under the leadership of the mayor for accountability and management purposes, the new institutional arrangement may be characterized as "integrated governance."

Though straightforward, holding the mayor accountable for school performance challenges our conventional understanding of educational governance. Citizens have traditionally looked to their mayor and city government to maintain a fire department, supply police protection, provide public works, and maintain the city's parks. But citizens are not used to looking to their mayor when they think about their city's schools. For public education, one thinks first of the school board and the district superintendent. In this book, we challenge this conventional paradigm. For citizens of large American cities who are dissatisfied with the state of their cities' public education, it may be time to look beyond the school board and superintendent to the mayor's office for a new style of educational governance and management.

The movement toward mayoral involvement in big-city schools restructures existing governance and politics. Few city hall officials have been intimately involved with the workings of the local school district. Beyond an annual budget allocation or occasional liaison meeting, city school districts typically operate in isolation from the rest of city government. Separate statutes, buildings, personnel, accounting, and leadership maintain thick barriers between the two local institutions. In this book, we propose that it may be time to break down those barriers—time to understand public education not as a separate entity but as part of a comprehensive set of services and institutions that improve the overall quality of life for city residents. Where urban school districts are underperforming, in particular, it may be time for the mayor and city government to leave the sidelines and to work with their city's schools to create the conditions and provide the resources for systemwide school improvement.

Whether mayors should increase their involvement in urban education, however, depends not on rhetoric but on *results*. In this book, we focus on results—in particular, on the results in cities that have turned to mayor-appointed school boards as a reform strategy. This "first wave" of districts has emerged over the past decade, led by high-profile mayors in Boston (1992), Chicago (1995), Cleveland (1998), and New York (2002).

As we will discuss, mayor-appointed school boards are not for every city. Detroit (1999–2004) and Washington (2000–4) both experimented with mayoral control during this first wave but ultimately returned to more traditional school governance. Like virtually all governmental reforms, mayor-appointed school boards alone cannot entirely erase severe systemic inequalities.

Clearly, parents, policymakers, and researchers are all keenly interested in the relationship between mayoral leadership and city school performance. Some analysts have pointed out that there are not enough data yet for proper evaluation. Others have speculated that it may simply not be possible to connect governance reforms to district improvement. For policymakers faced with real-time decisions, however, these justifications are not sufficient. This study is motivated by a desire to take the best available data, whatever their limitations, and to produce the best possible empirical analysis of the pressing question: What impact does mayoral control have on school system performance?

To address this question, we conduct a mixed-methods analysis of the effects of mayoral control of big-city school systems on four critical areas of school district performance:

1. productivity (for example, student achievement)
2. management and governance (for example, financial and organizational operations)
3. human capital (for example, characteristics of teachers and leadership)
4. building public confidence (for example, public awareness and opinions about the school district)

There are many ways to analyze these four areas, but ours is the first to engage in large-scale, cross-district empirical analysis. We distinguish ourselves from existing studies in two primary ways. First and foremost, we focus on school district performance as measured by student achievement on standardized tests. We complement our empirical analysis with qualitative investigation of the macro–micro linkages between school governance and classroom practice. Second, we conduct a statistical analysis that allows us to directly compare educational outcomes utilizing a database that includes achievement, financial, governance, socioeconomic, and demographic data for a nationally representative sample over multiple years.

Our sample includes every large-city school district that is coterminous with its home city. We include 104 school districts located across forty states, and we synthesize achievement data from thousands of schools. This study also recognizes that it is important to understand why mayoral control may be linked to achievement improvements. We therefore explore the macro–micro linkages, examining the relationship between a governance shift and the resulting changes in classroom practice.

In addition to student achievement, mayor-led integrated governance promises to bring about improvements in fiscal management, a more efficient allocation of human capital resources, and improved public confidence and awareness about the city's public schools. Examining the relationship between mayors and management and finances provides us with a better understanding of the broader organizational outcomes mayors can set out to improve.

The evidence we present in this book suggests that integrating city and educational governance under a mayor-appointed school board can bring about significant, positive changes in a school district. Mayors can use their political capital to buy time for professional educators to implement long-term programs in the school district. Mayors can foster a "politics of partnership" with state and federal officials to allow for more local control and funding. Mayors can reallocate resources to reduce the achievement gap between high-performing and low-performing schools and to focus the system on improving teaching and learning in classrooms across the district. Mayor-appointed school boards can contribute to the ultimate goal of every school reform: higher student achievement.

Acknowledgments

THIS RESEARCH PROJECT HAS RECEIVED GENEROUS financial support from the U.S. Department of Education's Field Initiated Studies Program, the Joyce Foundation, the Spencer Foundation, the Broad Foundation, and the Laboratory for Student Success. We received additional institutional support from Brown University's Urban Education Policy Program and its Department of Education, the Annenberg Institute for School Reform, Harvard University's Program on Inequality and Social Policy and the Harvard Government Department, Michigan State University's College of Education, and Florida State University's College of Education. For instructive comments on and reviews of earlier findings, we thank Terry N. Clark, Robert Crowson, Robert Dreeben, Fritz Edelstein, Jeffrey Henig, Rick Hess, William Howell, Richard Hula, Mike Kirst, J. D. LaRock, Douglas Kriner, Laurence Lynn, Gregory McGinity, Marion Orr, Paul E. Peterson, Herbert Walberg, and Marcus Winter. For valuable research assistance, we thank Jennifer Blaxall, Claudia Edwards, Arif Lakhani, Danielle LeSure, McCall Lewis, Zoe Savitsky, and Ted Socha. For excellent editorial review and advice, we thank Karen Mossberger, Mark Rom, and Gail Grella and the rest of the staff of Georgetown University Press. Francis wishes to recognize that all his work is *Ad Maiorem Dei Gloriam*. All of us would like to thank the school district leaders, principals, teachers, and students at our study sites, especially Chicago, who welcomed us into their districts and classrooms and provided valuable insights into their everyday lives in urban schools.

Mayoral Governance in Education Gains Prominence

THE 1990S SAW THE EMERGENCE OF A "NEW STYLE" OF mayor interested in taking a strong leadership role in their city's school system. Two mayors, Chicago's Richard M. Daley and Boston's Thomas Menino, have been at the forefront of this ground-breaking movement. On October 25, 1996, Mayor Daley visited Boston and made a joint appearance with Mayor Menino. The topic was public education. Both mayors made it clear where they stood on the mayor's role. "As president of the U.S. Conference of Mayors, I believe that education is the greatest challenge facing our cities today," Daley said. Menino agreed: "Mayor Daley and I share a very important philosophy. Neither one of us is willing to wash our hands of public education. We refuse to let our schools fall by the wayside and join the chorus of politicians saying the failure of the schools isn't their fault. No, Mayor Daley and I believe that when it comes to educating our kids, *the buck stops in the mayor's office*" (Brown 1996).

More than a decade has passed since Mayor Daley and Mayor Menino made these proclamations. In that decade, nearly a dozen U.S. mayors have followed suit by stepping up their role in public education. Some cities, such as Cleveland and New York, have adopted the Chicago–Boston model and have granted the mayor the power to appoint a majority of the city's school board members.

The spread of mayoral control raises new questions about the structure and consequences of governance for our nation's city schools. What does school governance look like under the new-style mayors? How does mayoral control affect what happens inside schools and classrooms? How does mayoral control affect school and student performance? This book addresses each of these questions. Drawing on both large-scale, quantitative data and qualitative case studies, we describe how mayoral control is currently organized in cities across the country, how it operates within schools and classrooms, and its consequences for student achievement. Our findings indicate that mayoral control and the model of integrated governance to which it has given rise can improve student performance, increase and sustain fiscal discipline, and raise the profile of public education in our nation's cities. Mayors occupy a central institutional place in the urban political economy. When done right, integrated governance can help restore confidence in and commitment to our city schools.

WHEN THE SCHOOL SYSTEM IS INTEGRATED WITH CITY GOVERNMENT

The new-style education mayors have helped to produce a new form of governance for our nation's urban schools: integrated governance. Within an integrated governance framework, school district governance is no longer isolated from but is incorporated into the governance of the local municipality (or, as in city–state hybrid models, with the governance of both the city and state). Unlike the traditional bureaucratic model, integrated governance, as exemplified in Chicago since 1995, focuses on student outcomes, policy coherence, and greater accountability. It is "driven by a focus on student performance and is characterized by district-level capacity and willingness to intervene in failing schools" (Wong et al. 1997, 148; Wong 1999). Integrated governance represents a marked shift from an older style of mayor leadership that emphasized patronage in jobs and contracts and a lack of performance accountability. Under integrated governance, new-style mayors are more likely to encourage fiscal discipline and remain open-minded to innovative practices that blend bureaucratic and market approaches on outcome measures.

The mayor's role in an integrated governance framework can be difficult to isolate in a multilayered educational system. In such a system, policy decisions and activities can be differentiated by levels of analysis, institutional roles and functions, and the kinds of constraints that actors face and the resources they command at a given level. Explaining the nature of mayoral production in the policy organization thus requires a differentiated approach that fully appreciates the constraints, nature of resource allocation, and appropriate role of a given unit in the policy system.

A differentiated approach also makes clear from the start that integrated governance reform is not simply a recentralization of authority, nor can it be fully understood by focusing only on the issue of school board appointive powers. Instead, integrated governance redefines the responsibilities and enhances the capacity of districtwide leadership. Given its strong focus on raising student performance, integrated governance legitimizes systemwide standards and policies that identify and target intervention at low-performing schools. In effect, it aims to create the institutional pressure and support necessary to address a key limitation of decentralization, namely, that organizational change at the school site is not a sufficient condition for academic improvement systemwide.

CITY SCHOOLS AND CITY ECONOMIC DEVELOPMENT

Integrated governance has emerged in a climate in which policymakers have placed a greater emphasis on building human capital as a form of economic development. Schools are increasingly seen as critical to attracting businesses and retaining middle-class families in the city. From a fiscal perspective, public schools constitute one of the largest local employers. For example, the Chicago Public Schools ranks as the second largest public employer in the state. Further, education dominates the local budget. Though it is not a part of the city budget in most cities in a technical sense, education expenses range anywhere from 25 to 35 percent of total city expenses. Schools' heavy reliance on local property taxes highly affects a city's taxing and spending capacity. In the 1990s, mayors demonstrated their fiscal prudence and initiated administrative reforms to improve city government performance. Consequently, in addition to viewing the schools as crucial to their cities' economic growth, mayors began to see their cities' school systems as their next key challenge for service improvement (Wong, Jain, and Clark 1997).

Mayoral interest in education also reflects an increased focus on quality-of-life issues among the American public. Urban politicians have become increasingly willing to allocate funds to build up schools as community centers for local activities, such as after-school and summer recreational programs. Local schools are important neighborhood institutions. This is particularly true in high-poverty neighborhoods. Schools can serve as social buffers that create opportunities for children and parents of low-income backgrounds to connect to the social and economic mainstreams. In neighborhoods marred by constant warfare among rival gangs, schools offer signs of stability and provide an accessible safe haven for the local students. Improving city schools is thus critical to addressing crucial quality-of-life issues for city residents (Wilson 1987).

FORMAL AND INFORMAL ROLES FOR MAYORS

During the past two decades, city mayors have taken on a range of roles in relation to city schools. Integrated governance in the form of a mayor-appointed school board is a formal reform. By "formal," we mean that in this reform model, there is a *legal change* in the governance arrangements; the mayor's relationship with the school board and with other stakeholders is changed by statute. Short of a formal, legal change, however, there are many ways for mayors to become involved in education informally. Long Beach mayor Beverly O'Neill, for instance, describes a different approach: "Involvement can take many different forms. . . . In Long Beach, we have promoted a model that involves not control, but conversations, cooperation, and collaboration." Columbus mayor Michael B. Coleman has established the Columbus Office of Education with the purpose of "extending and enhancing both educational and developmental opportunities for all citizens of Columbus." In Denver, the school board notes that Mayor John Hickenlooper "has pledged powerful and clear support." The mayor of Springfield, Illinois, created its first-ever education liaison (LaRock 2003a).

One of the most visible education mayors without formal authority has been San Jose mayor Ron Gonzales. In a *New York Times* op-ed article titled "10 Ways a Mayor Can Help Improve Public Education," Gonzalez (2003) described how he worked with the nineteen different school districts operating within his city's borders. Recognizing that he does not "have the option to take over schools the way some of [his] mayoral colleagues have done," he tries to "work with our schools and education leaders to build partnerships that encourage excellence in the classroom and build neighborhoods that support academic success."

Other mayors have used creative means to influence school district performance. Some, such as the Seattle and San Diego mayors, have introduced nontraditional leadership.[1] In Saint Louis, the mayor brought in nontraditional leadership in the form of a corporate turnaround team. In Indianapolis, the mayor has gained the power to allow new charter schools. In Los Angeles, Mayor Riordan (operating with no formal authority over the board) attempted, in 1999, to make himself an "education mayor" by pushing forward a slate of school board candidates. One estimate guessed that Riordan, with backing from philanthropist Eli Broad, spent "about two million on [that] year's four school-board contests" (Blume 1999).

Given these informal options available for mayors, the question can be asked: Do the channels of communication between the city and the school district need to be formalized? In leading theories of urban politics, informal powers dominate the discussion. Stone (1989) emphasizes the selective incentives that a mayor can employ. Peterson (1981, 129) argues that "where politics are at a low pressure informal channels of communication substitute for formal ones." In the context of urban education, Paul Hill and his colleagues emphasize the need for citywide partnership, but they focus on the creation of a civic reform oversight group (Hill, Campbell, and Harvey 2000). This is an informal group, relying on indirect civic and economic incentives to function (e.g., members want to help their city schools, or members believe that with stronger city schools the economic fortunes of the city will improve).

Given the different types of involvement mayors can have in city schools, we seek to understand how integrated governance, as a formal structure, compares with school districts where an elected board insulates schools from formal mayoral influence. By including both integrated governance and elected school boards in our analysis, we can put the formal-versus-informal debate to an empirical test.

CHALLENGES TO MAYORAL CONTROL

In addition to presenting our evaluation of mayor-led integrated governance and specifying the options available for mayors, we also address these challenges to mayor-appointed school boards: (1) Mayoral control is undemocratic, (2) mayoral control is a power grab, and (3) mayoral control is the same as a "state takeover." These challenges represent the main grounds on which citizens and various interest groups, as well as scholars and policy advocates, have contested mayoral control.

The First Challenge: Mayoral Control Is Undemocratic

A common criticism of mayor-appointed school boards is that they are undemocratic because they are replacing an elected school board with an appointed one (Chambers 2006). In reaction to the proposal in 2005 of mayoral control in Albuquerque, for instance, the school board president described the proposed system as "taking away the rights of citizens to vote for people they want on the board" (Siemers 2005). Similar sentiments were expressed in San Diego, where a school board trustee argued in 2005 that "if you believe in local control, you believe in school board elections" (Sutton 2005). Viewed differently, however, mayor-appointed school boards may actually allow for more public participation in education.

The traditional urban school board has become increasingly frustrating to many stakeholders and observers. On the basis of a 1998 survey, the National School Boards Foundation (1999, 12) found that "there is a consistent, significant difference in perception between urban school board members and the urban public on a number of key issues." Though 67 percent of the urban board members rated schools in the A and B categories, only 49 percent of the urban public rated the schools similarly. Whereas three out of four board members rated the teachers as excellent and good, only 54 percent of the public agreed. More recently, concerned civic groups have identified urban school boards as needing significant improvement. The Broad Foundation, for instance, has established the Broad Institute for School Boards at the Center for Reform of School Systems (McAdams 2002).[2]

For many reasons, school boards as presently constituted may not have the political incentives necessary for significant reform. From an electoral perspective, the national average for school board election turnout appears to be around only 18 to 20 percent (Shen 2003). Those who do vote may likely be voting out of special interest and not necessarily for the overall health of the city. Terry Moe (2005) conducted interviews in 2000–3 with over 500 school board candidates in California and found that unions exert significant influence in local school board elections.

Placing accountability for the schools in the hands of the mayor can address the problems of low voter turnout and issues of representation. Democracy, within an integrated governance framework, is achieved through mayoral elections. A broader electorate voting on overall quality of life, rather than a school-board-specific electorate, is less likely to be captured by a particular education interest. When New York City mayor Michael Bloomberg accepted control of the city's schools, he recognized this democratic impulse as the cornerstone of the new arrangement: "The Mayor should have sole control over the appointment of the Schools Chancellor, and the Chancellor should report directly to the Mayor. That establishes democratic accountability—and if democracy can be trusted to safeguard our social services, police forces and other essential services, why wouldn't it work to protect our most precious resource, our children?" (Bloomberg 2002).

Critics of integrated governance make the argument that "local control" is being sacrificed. This line of argument tends to conceptualize democracy as "street-level democracy" or school-level democracy (Fung 2004). In the 1960s, the push for local control in many urban districts meant taking power away from a centralized school board and giving it to neighborhood groups. The use of the term "local control," however, can be misleading here. Relative to state authority, integrated governance provides cities with local control because mayors are given authority to make policy that is in the best interests of their locality. To be sure, integrated governance remains in tension with a system of decentralized, shared decision making. There is good reason for this tension. In the context of large, urban school systems, shared decision making is challenged by powerful, entrenched interests. The mayor may have both the most at stake and the most capacity to establish a governing coalition among diverse interests that can be focused on systemwide school improvement (Cronin 1973; Fantini and Gittell 1973; Lopate et al. 1970; Wohlstetter and McCurdy 1991).

The Second Challenge: Mayoral Control Is a Power Grab

Early in the twentieth century, as we discuss at greater length in the next chapter, mayors wanted power over the schools to use them for patronage. These mayors, whom we term "old style," saw the schools not as an integral part of quality of life but rather as a political tool they could leverage for their advantage. There is a concern that twenty-first-century mayors will adopt the same old-style posture once they gain control over the school district. We argue, however, that new-style mayors follow a dual strategy of "accountability and control." The emphasis on accountability distinguishes them from a previous regime of mayors who sought to dole out school jobs without public scrutiny.

When mayors describe their approach as "the buck stops here," it is easy to envision mayoral control as a mayor walking around hallways with a big baseball bat (Bloomberg 2002). This image, however, does not accurately describe mayoral control. Mayor-appointed school boards operate in the context of a partnership between the mayor *and the professional educator brought in to run the district.* The mayor can provide the professional educator with the political buffer he or she needs to enact meaningful reform. This type of partnership has been seen in Boston. Cuban and Usdan (2003, 44) find that in Boston, the mayor "has been willing to expend his political capital to provide a buffer allowing the superintendent to establish the infrastructure for student improvement." A politics of partnership operates similar to a division of labor. To reduce the pressure on the superintendent, the mayor uses political capital to produce quick results at the expense of sustained growth. In return, the superintendent focuses attention on redirecting resources and designing interventions, being less burdened by the adverse pressure of local politics.

A politics of partnership should also exist with teachers' unions. Unions may be wary of mayoral control out of a concern that mayors' push for management efficiency will result in less favorable bargaining conditions for teacher compensation. Mayoral control, however, need not be associated with more hard-line union bargaining. Just as the mayor must find common ground with other labor unions providing services to the city, so must the mayor find common ground with teachers' unions about how best to educate city students, while providing teachers with sufficient compensation and resources.

Anecdotal evidence from mayor-controlled districts suggests that successful mayors are adopting a "politics of partnership" approach with both superintendents and unions. In Chicago, Mayor Daley and Paul Vallas had a very productive partnership. Vallas's replacement, Arne Duncan, has also enjoyed a good relationship with Mayor Daley. For Harrisburg mayor Stephen Reed, mayoral control of the system works because of the partnership he has with his superintendent, Gerald Kohn. Commenting on Kohn, Reed says "I have someone who's qualified, and who I'm comfortable with."[3] In the case of unions, Mayor Daley has negotiated multiyear union contracts that ensure labor peace for a sustained period. Detroit, a counterexample we discuss later in the book, illustrates the potential negative consequences when teachers' unions are not made a part of the new mayor-led regime.

The Third Challenge: Mayoral Control Is the Same as a "State Takeover"

A related, but distinct option for reform is state "takeovers" of school districts. States have intervened in local government, whether education related or not, when they have seen local finances in disarray. In assessing districts, states rely heavily on indicators, rather than identifying underlying structural problems. Most states have had provisions for a state takeover of local school districts, but states rarely invoke them, except in cases of clear financial mismanagement or illegal activity. With the introduction of the federal No Child Left Behind (NCLB) legislation, states are paying greater attention to academic accountability as the basis for direct intervention, including taking over schools. NCLB includes takeover as one type of corrective action to turn around persistently low-performing schools. Even when intervening, states often refrain from entirely dismantling the local school district administration, such as the school board and the superintendent. A majority of state takeover laws allow state administrators to influence decisions behind the scenes in a more limited fashion in academically troubled districts, first giving schools or districts an opportunity to improve before more drastic measures are taken (Kleine, Kloha, and Weissert 2003).

Mayor-appointed school boards are often characterized as the same type of reform as the state takeover of school districts. In the current era of NCLB, policymakers often mention "takeover" as an intervention strategy without specifying the governmental level of policy initiation. In an earlier study, we compared the two types of takeover. In this study, however, we focus solely on mayors. Mayoral control differs from state takeover in that state takeover imposes an outside authority on the district, whereas mayoral control emanates from local interest. This policy difference has political consequences. Unlike state-appointed superintendents, mayors are politically accountable to their local constituents. If parents and residents are unhappy with the progress of educational reform, they can choose to vote the mayor out of office. When state-appointed officials are put in charge, however, it is sometimes difficult to see who is accountable if the district does not improve.

Another important difference between city and state takeovers is the balance of revenue coming from city-versus-state sources. State-takeover districts

are likely to be more accountable to the state than city-takeover districts because states are funding a greater portion of total district revenue in the state-
takeover districts. In city takeovers, there is greater accountability to the local
taxpayers because they are funding a majority of the district's revenue (Wong
and Shen 2002).

PLAN OF THE BOOK

In the following nine chapters, we further specify what we mean by integrated governance, presenting analyses of it in a range of cities to identify its
consequences for school and student performance. In chapters one and two
we place integrated governance into the broader context of urban school reform. When compared with other reform initiatives, integrated governance
maintains a stronger focus on systemwide accountability and enables the
school district to apply incentives and sanctions to improve schools. We further discuss the important historical shifts in urban public education leading
to mayoral control. Because mayoral governance varies across cities, we provide contextual details on the similarities and differences of these institutional
arrangements across urban America. We also analyze the legal and political
context in which mayoral control operates.

In chapter three we make the transition to our empirical research. Chapters
three through five focus on student achievement, and chapters six through
eight examine other institutional and organizational effects associated with
mayoral governance. In chapter three we discuss our design for our study of
104 school districts, including sample selection, methodology, and the nature
and scope of the data. We also describe our approach to measuring mayoral
control and account for a series of competing explanations. In chapter four
we explain this research design and examine the relationship between mayoral control and student achievement. We present results from a series of fixed-
effects regression models examining standardized student achievement from
1999 to 2003. In chapter five we build on this analysis by examining the gap
between high- and low-performing schools. We examine the gap between the
lowest and highest quartiles of schools, and we also give the results of regression analyses of inequality ratios in our sample of school districts.

In chapter six we turn to macro—micro linkages in an effort to explain the
mechanisms that may account for the relationship between mayors and classroom performance. We focus on the challenge of instructional improvement
in low-performing high schools and present a case study of Chicago school-
level responses to mayoral control in the late 1990s.

In chapter seven we expand our analysis beyond achievement and look at
the relationship between mayoral control and fiscal outcomes. We present the

results from our fixed-effects regression analysis of revenue, expenditure, and staffing data in the sample of cities. In chapter eight we draw together data from diverse sources to explore the relationship between mayors and public support for education. We examine recent State of the City speeches and public opinion data from some mayor-controlled school districts.

In chapter nine we conclude the book by looking at the possibility of expanded mayoral leadership in urban education. We link our empirical findings to policy directives and provide cautions along the way. We emphasize the importance of proper timing and partnerships in designing an optimal institutional role for the mayor to lead systemwide improvement in education. Due to space limitations in this volume, we have also created an online supplement that contains a host of additional data tables.[4]

CHAPTER ONE

The Historical and Political Context of Integrated Governance

THE RECENT TREND TOWARD MAYORAL CONTROL OF school boards represents a historic shift in urban school governance. Since the turn of the twentieth century, city schools have been separate and insulated from city hall. The emergence of new-style education mayors who have advocated for and gained expanded formal power over city schools has given rise to integrated governance. Driven by mayors concerned with reinvigorating their cities in the face of major economic, social, and cultural shifts, this integrated governance places city schools at the center of efforts to improve the quality of life of city residents.

In this chapter, we first delineate the contours of integrated governance by contrasting it with three major competing reform options. We then locate the emergence of integrated governance in its historical and political contexts, in particular discussing its relationship to the rise of accountability in education governance. In a climate dominated by the politics of accountability, city mayors are in a unique position to build systemwide capacity for improvement and to meet the challenges of a multilayered system. We especially consider how integrated governance can address the urban-specific problems of entrenched school boards, changing racial dynamics, and efforts to develop civic capacity in our nation's cities. We start from the same premise from which all political scientists who study education policy have begun: "Educational reform does not take place in a political vacuum" (Stone et al. 2001, 20).

DEFINING INTEGRATED GOVERNANCE

The emergence of mayoral control has been facilitated by three types of legislative processes: (1) state legislation that grants authority to the mayor to replace an elected board with an appointed board (e.g., Chicago); (2) state legislation that grants authority to the mayor to appoint the school board but then calls for a citywide referendum on whether to continue this grant of authority (e.g., Boston, Cleveland, and Detroit), and (3) voter approval of changes in a charter that allow the mayor to appoint school board members (e.g., Oakland).

Within each of these three general types, state legislatures have much flexibility to specify the formal arrangement of power. For instance, when the state legislatures grant a mayor authority to appoint the school board, they may attach a sunset provision. In New York, the 2002 legislation that allowed New York City's mayor to appoint a majority of school board members includes a provision that unless there was additional state action before 2009, the mayor's school board appointment powers will expire that year. A similar scenario has played out in Washington, where there was a sunset provision calling for the mayor's appointive powers to expire in 2004.

Legislatures also have much flexibility in the number of board members the mayor appoints, relative to the overall number of board members. In some cases, like Chicago, the mayor appoints all board members. When mayoral control was in operation in Detroit, however, one state-appointed member was present on the board in addition to the mayoral appointees. In Oakland, the mayor appoints only three out of ten school board members. The state legislature may also put additional checks and balances in place in the form of oversight or nominating committees. In many mayoral control cities, the mayor appoints the school board members from a slate of potential candidates determined by a city nominating committee. In some districts, there is further oversight through a committee that monitors the board and its progress in managing the district.

As this discussion suggests, mayoral control largely centers on the appointive powers granted to mayors over school boards. We locate mayoral control within a broader framework that we refer to as *integrated governance*. Though we use the terms "mayoral control" and "integrated governance" interchangeably throughout this book, integrated governance encompasses more than mayoral control. In addition to formal mayoral authority to appoint school board members and district administration, integrated governance is characterized by a strong political will to improve the operations of the city's school system; partnerships between city hall, the schools, teachers' unions, and civic groups dedicated to systemwide improvements; a focus on systemwide standards and performance outcomes; and district leadership committed to using a mix of intervention and support strategies to meet the challenges faced by urban schools.

To further delineate the contours of integrated governance, it is useful to contrast it with three competing models that have come to dominate the reform of urban school districts in recent decades: (1) efforts aimed at redefining power and authority over key systemwide institutions, such as the school board and the central school bureaucracy; (2) shared governance that grants parents, local community members, and school-level educators authority over hiring and resource allocation; and (3) consumer-driven programs, such as state-funded vouchers and charter schools that rely on market-like efficiency to improve student performance. These reform models are not mutually exclusive and are often implemented simultaneously within a district. In table 1.1, however, we present an analytical scheme that helps to distinguish the reforms along two conceptual dimensions, the level of analysis and the primary focus of their efforts.

First, the reforms can be differentiated in terms of the level of analysis, that is, whether they empower the capacity of systemwide institutions or shift power to the school and community levels. Reforms aimed at redefining institutional power and authorities share a systemwide focus with the mayor-led integrated governance model. This contrasts with the school- and family-level focus of shared governance and consumer-driven reforms, respectively. Second, the governing paradigms can be distinguished by their relative focus on accountability. Reforms that seek to alter existing forms of institutional power and authority and shared governance reforms are designed to improve accountability in the policymaking process. Thus, they are process-oriented reforms. Integrated governance and consumer-driven models, in

Table 1.1   A Typology of the Politics of Urban School Reform

Level of Analysis	Primary Focus of Governing Paradigm	
	Access to Policymaking Process	Outcome-Based Performance
Systemwide	(A) Institutional power and authorities redefined	(C) Mayor-led integrated governance reform
School-community	(B) Shared governance or site-based empowerment	(D) Consumer-driven programs, e.g., choice, charter schools, private schools

contrast, are outcomes oriented. They focus on improving performance outcomes.

These differences in level of analysis and primary focus make available different reform strategies. Table 1.2 identifies the different types of reform strategies likely to be enacted under each of the four governance models. The table illustrates the range of strategies available under integrated governance. Because integrated governance employs a systemwide level of analysis in combination with a primary focus on school-level outcome-based performance, a much wider range of reform strategies is available under this model than under the other three. Integrated governance facilitates reforms aimed at building district political capacity, increasing central administration efficiency, and directing instructional and school improvements through systemwide curricular efforts and school-level sanctions and support policies. None of the other three models promotes such a wide range of reform strategies capable of addressing the myriad challenges that city schools face across the multiple levels of the school system. In this way, integrated governance allows for a differentiated policy approach that more closely reflects the organizational and political complexity of city school districts.

THE HISTORICAL CONTEXT OF MAYORS AND SCHOOLS

To explain the nature of integrated governance as a reform model and its emergence at the start of the twenty-first century, we need to look at mayors and schools at the start of the twentieth century. Though mayoral control represents a break with past education governance models, it is a model with roots in the shifting nature of school and city politics in the twentieth century.[1]

Urban school governance in the twentieth century was dominated by reform efforts that kept mayors and other political leaders from interfering in public schools. During the past eighty years, school governance has gone through three phases, each of which can be broadly differentiated by the degree of mayoral control. The Progressive reform of the 1920s was designed to use "scientific management" to keep partisan (mayoral) politics out of the school sector. By the 1960s, school boards and superintendents allied with the mayor to manage intense conflicts over educational issues, many of them further complicated by racial and income inequities in big cities. The emergence of accountability-based reform during the 1990s created a new set of political realities that made possible a more active mayoral role.

The progressive-corporate governance paradigm dominated the reform phase that roughly spanned the period from the 1920s to the mid-1960s. During the first quarter of the twentieth century, urban centers were growing rapidly as the manufacturing and industrial sectors created job opportunities for waves of working-class immigrants. The new model that originated in the Progressive Era continues to dominate many districts even today. The main features traceable to the reforms of the 1920s include a citywide, nonpartisan, elected board in charge of appointing the school superintendent as its professional chief executive; an administrative hierarchy and delivery of services led by a professionally credentialed school superintendent and his or her professional cabinet; personnel policies codified in details to guard against political interference; schooling services (e.g., instructional time) organized with age-specific grade levels and subject matter knowledge; and a taxing authority autonomous from city hall. The result was a school system insulated from city hall. In 1969, Gittell (1969, 158) observed that "the most significant trend in education in New York City has been the isolation of school administration from city government."

To be sure, it is not the case that every city saw a formal separation of powers immediately. As noted by Diane Ravitch (2007), from 1898 to 1969, the New York City mayor appointed all members of the school board. In Chicago too, mayors have a long history of involvement in education (Peterson 1976). It is also not the case that mayors did not turn to informal avenues to exercise influence on the schools system. Instances of informal mayoral influence are scattered, for example, throughout Jeffrey Mirel's history of the Detroit school system (1993).[2] In the 1930s, when facing a fiscal crisis, the mayor created a committee to specifically address how to reduce teacher salaries. In 1932, the mayor "met informally" with school board members to gain their support for the budget cuts. Detroit's example illustrates how, in a system where the mayor had little institutionalized power over the school board, he or she had to rely primarily on informal means of influence. Within this context, insulated city school systems were able to build and maintain their own institutional rules, enforcing their autonomy from city hall.

Changing urban school politics created new opportunities for mayors to mediate competing demands throughout the 1960s, 1970s, and 1980s. The main factors contributing to heightened school conflicts were racial tension over the pace of desegregating schools in the wake of *Brown v. Board of Education*, taxpayer dissatisfaction with the local property tax burden, the readiness of teachers' unions to strike when collective bargaining failed, and the declining political influence of the urban population in state legislatures. These challenges outmatched the capacity of an independent school board and its professional superintendent. As a result, mayors found themselves in a new role in relation to city schools, namely, crisis managers. Mayors began to re-enter the realm of school governance during this second politically contentious phase of reform.

Table 1.2 Institutional Characteristics of School Governance Models

	Reform Strand			
Reform Strategy	(A) Institutional Power and Authorities Redefined	(B) Shared Governance or Site-Based Empowerment	(C) Mayor-Led Integrated Governance Reform	(D) Consumer-Driven Programs (e.g., choice and charter schools)
Build political capacity				
Use political capital to shield school district	–	–	+	–
Expand intergovernmental efforts	–	–	+	–
Build public confidence in school system	+	+	+	+
Management				
Corporate management (e.g., chief executive, information networking)	–	–	+	–
Leadership with diverse expertise	–	–	+	+
Reform in financial administration and labor contract	–	–	+	+
Restructure human resource practices	+	+	+	+

	Col 1	Col 2	Col 3	Col 4
Standards				
Systemwide academic standards	+	−	+	−
Alignment of curriculum and assessment	+	+	+	−
Performance-based accountability (e.g., academic promotion policy)	−	−	+	−
Capacity building				
Sanctions on low-performing schools/students	−	−	+	−
Support for low-performing schools/students	−	−	+	−
Instructional improvement policy	+	+	+	−
Efforts to narrow achievement gap	−	−	+	+
Incentives for school self-governance				
Site-based recruitment of principals and teachers	+	+	−	+
Support charter schools	−	−	−	+
Options to contract services with alternative suppliers	−	−	+	+
Strong parental preferences	−	−	−	+

Note: + denotes that the reform strategy is likely; − denotes that the reform strategy is less likely.

By the 1990s, big-city mayors began to see public education as an important investment in improving the city's overall quality of social and economic
life. Mayors, often working with the business community, saw schools as a
key to improving overall city performance.[3] They saw efforts to improve
schools as part of a broader agenda aimed at enhancing safety, parks, and recreational services for the city's families. Mayors became increasingly keen to
implement policies that could turn around declining schools and depressed
neighborhoods. Under their leadership, the 1920s model of insulating school
governance from mayoral influence came to be significantly revised.

THE POLITICS OF ACCOUNTABILITY

Although big-city mayors, in particular, moved to the forefront of urban
school reform in the 1990s, an important contributing factor to the rise of
mayoral control is the broader climate of accountability in public education.
The policy and politics of accountability that became increasingly potent
during the 1990s gained increasing relevance with the passage of the federal
No Child Left Behind Act in 2002. This act, which was modeled after the
accountability reforms enacted in big-city school districts such as Chicago and
Houston, tied federal money to measurable outcomes and introduced sanctions for low performance. Concurrent with the federal government's focus
on holding districts accountable, the public, policymakers, and organized interests have increased their demands for improvement in district-level governance as well as student performance across all fifty states. These demands,
coupled with various institutional responses, have gradually redefined the
politics of education at the local level. Local city schools are increasingly vulnerable to state and federal intervention. In this climate, mayoral control becomes an attractive option. It makes available citywide resources to leverage
school improvement. In addition, it extends responsibility for school improvement to city hall, placing accountability squarely on the shoulders of the
mayor.

The new politics of accountability constitutes a hybrid of choice, standards, sanctions, and incentives. This new politics has gradually replaced the
existing paradigms that rely on a strong central bureaucracy or "materialist-
oriented" interest group politics. In its place, various types of reform politics
have emerged to move districts to rearrange power and authority both at
the systemwide and school site levels. At the systemwide level, reformers have
tried to mobilize and engage a broad coalition to promote human development issues. At the site level, a sense of "ownership" among faculty, parents,
and community members is seen as a viable force to improve school
performance.

The rise of accountability-based school politics challenges our current understanding of how politics shapes educational issues. Accountability has created new political demands for popularly elected political leaders, such as mayors and governors, to exercise more direct control over the central bureaucracy in education. At the same time, it also raises questions as to whether interest groups are able to conduct business as usual without losing credibility and public support. An increasing number of parents, particularly in low-income minority neighborhoods, are supportive of choice-based programs that promote competition in the educational sector. In other words, we have entered a phase of institutional transition, where the politics of the status quo is subject to mounting pressure to incorporate the new rules of accountability. Some experts have observed that in this climate, "the power curve in large urban systems is leaning toward mayoral control, as down-ballot, low-interest school board elections and stricter campaign finance laws combine to produce employee-dominated governance structures" (Bersin 2005). The office of the mayor, representing the city's electorate, is in a unique position to address the challenge of systemwide accountability.

CONFRONTING ENTRENCHED SCHOOL BOARDS

During the past two decades, reformers have begun to call for a rethinking of city school boards. Urban school boards carry a heavy burden. They are charged with stemming years of decline associated with broader economic, social, and cultural shifts, and with improving long-failing schools. In the 2003 Charlotte School Board elections, for example, the local newspaper reported that "many say the next four years will determine whether the community locks in a strong, stable public school district or allows it to begin a typical urban decline" (Helms 2003). City school boards face these demands in a period of continuing decline in public participation and an increase in special interest control in school governance matters. Although we sometimes think about elected school board members in the same way we think about other elected officials, this view is not supported by research or present observations. In New Orleans in 2004, for instance, the school board race attracted few candidates. One former Orleans Parish School Board member observed that "the problem is that they are nonpaying jobs, few people run, there's low voter turnout and it's dominated by special interest groups and contractors" (Thevenot 2004).

Research going back thirty years suggests that this observation is not unique to New Orleans. Writing about his venture into the study of school boards as a political scientist, Zeigler admits that he "brought to the enterprise the traditional biases of political science. Namely, I assumed that since (in most cases) school board members are elected public officials, they should be 're-sponsive.'" Zeigler makes a distinction between organizations that serve the general public and those that serve a specialized public. Zeigler argues that school boards are there to serve a specialized public—the students—and there-fore we must adjust our expectations for "responsiveness." Specifically, Zeigler (1975, 3–5) argues that although "many people seem to believe that since board members are supposed to be the representatives of the local voters, they should respond automatically to the loudest voices in the community, . . . sometimes those voice are misinformed—and wrong."[4]

Echoing Zeigler's initial impressions, in his study of fifty-seven urban school districts between 1992 and 1995, Hess found that school board elections brought out few voters. Instead, these elections served as stepping stones for board members' political ambitions. Hess's (1999, 63) descriptions of these elections sound familiar: "Members are elected in sparsely attended elections; the central issues are often undefined and the candidates' positions unclear." But contrary to other studies, Hess finds that urban school board members are "surprisingly ambitious." His findings suggest that "school boards are a starting point for those entering community politics" (pp. 66–67). In other words, school board members maintain a strong sense of electoral interest.

In addition to the political interests of their elected members, city school boards have also become dominated by teacher union interests. Taebel's theory of constituent voters and clientele voters is helpful to understanding how this influence shapes city school politics. According to Taebel, constituent voters are theorized to be those who are "direct beneficiaries of local government," for example, government employees. Clientele voters are those whose benefits from local government "are generalized in nature." In his study of a 1974 school board election "in a moderately sized city in the Southwest," he (1977, 157) finds that "out of 55,000 registered voters, only 2,525 voters actually cast ballots, . . . for a voter turnout rate of 4.6%." But his most interesting finding is the disproportionate representation of constituent voters in the elec-tion. Using voter surveys, he finds that only 68.8 percent are clientele voters. In other words, even though teachers and public school employees are not 32 percent of the electorate, in this election they were. His conclusion is that "elected officials would be well off if they merely attain the support of the constituent voters."[5]

Mayoral leadership through an appointed school board offers an alter-native to traditional board elections. Relative to board elections, mayoral elections are higher profile and are not single issue. These two factors make it difficult for single-issue interest groups to have undue influence on the election. Using Taebel's terminology, the percentage of "constituent voters" will be greatly reduced in mayoral elections with a much broader citywide electorate. As a result, the mayor's education policy should promote citywide interests, not just the limited interests of a particular group or section of the city.

In addition to school boards, teachers' unions are often at the center of discussions about urban education reform (Loveless 2000). Though often perceived as in opposition to teachers' unions, integrated governance can facilitate partnerships between city hall and unions. To date, the relationship between organized labor and mayor-controlled school districts varies. In Chicago, under mayoral control the school board successfully negotiated two four-year contracts with the teachers' union that included substantial raises for teachers. These actions brought both financial and labor stability to the system. In Detroit, however, union antagonism was an important factor in the vote to eliminate mayoral control. In some cases, union support can be won over time. In Cleveland, the teachers' union was initially against mayoral control, but in 2002 it supported the referendum. Moving forward, this strand of governance may also draw on "reform unionism," with the question being whether or not teachers' unions can serve as partners in school reform.[6]

THE RACIAL DYNAMICS OF MAYORAL CONTROL

A new century has not eliminated race from the center of urban politics. Clotfelter (2001) found that "white flight" persists and is linked to interracial contact in the schools. Orfield (2001) has highlighted the phenomenon of "resegregation," which challenges the ability of urban school districts to hold on to their top students. Despite its centrality to urban politics and education, as Henig and Rich (2004, 15) point out, "proponents of school reform in general and mayor-centric reform in particular have shied away from race when discussing their ideas." Portz (2003) has shown how language used in Boston school reform efforts has also remained race neutral. In this section, we hope to more clearly address the relationship between mayoral control and racial politics.[7]

Henig (2004, 198) suggests that the push for mayoral control can be understood as one of two narratives: "In one version, race plays little or no role; the account centers on governance structures. In the other, race is the dominant subtext." Thus far in our discussion, we have focused only on the first version, emphasizing governance structures. The second narrative, however, with its emphasis on racial dynamics, must also be taken into account.

The key distinction between the two narratives is that in the second narrative, the school district is understood by the African American community as more than just a producer of student outcomes. As Henig and Rich (2004, 18) point out, "Some within the minority community see efforts to put mayors in charge as an assault upon a valued institution and therefore rally around the status quo even if they are disappointed in the objective performance of the schools." The reason is that the school district is seen for its "both real and symbolic roles as a springboard for local self-rule and an important source of jobs and status within the Black community."

It is also important to recognize, as Thompson (2005, 305) has, that "there is no simple 'black' demand" in urban communities. Rather, "the term 'black' is shorthand for diverse and internally conflicted communities." In this context of pluralistic values, Thompson argues that a mayor must listen and acknowledge difference:

> Building trust among deeply conflicted groups in cities and regions and creating a sense of fairness and political consistency is only possible when mayors (and other powerful leaders) recognize that some groups have radically different standards from others for judging the fairness and effectiveness of rules, political decisions, and political platforms. Mayors should acknowledge these different perspectives in order to shape rules and make political decisions that are equally acceptable to both powerful and weak groups. (p. 306)

This split within the African American community is important to recognize because it suggests that the tensions surrounding mayoral control may at times be less about the skin color of the mayor and more about the centralization of authority. The racial dynamics of mayoral control also involve other ethnic minority groups. A host of emerging non-English-speaking immigrant communities may make new demands on the city school system to which politicians will have to respond. Mayoral leadership and school politics is and will continue to be shaped by these pressures.

It is also the case that simply sharing the same skin color will not cure institutional conflict. Henig and his colleagues find that a transition to a black mayor does not necessarily make school board politics easier:

> Black mayors seem no less likely than white mayors to squabble with black school boards; black educators seem no less likely than white ones to use their positions of authority to co-opt parental initiatives. Furthermore, race does not become the defining cleavage in black-led cities. Black stakeholders seem no less likely than white ones to see education problems as severe; black officials and white business leaders join in partnership arrangements intended to bring about systemic change. (Henig et al. 1999, 276)

In the context of new-style mayoral control, both black (Dennis Archer, Michael White) and white (Richard Daley, Thomas Menino, Michael

Bloomberg) mayors have taken the helm of their city school districts. In chapter eight we explore how support for their reform programs has varied across racial populations within the city. For both mayors and schools, a question must be kept in mind: Does improving school district efficiency and productivity come at the expense of minority opportunity for advancement?

A related, and equally important, question is whether the drive for test score improvement and fiscal efficiency dampens minority political participation. The best research on this question has been conducted by Stephanie Chambers (2006). In examining the effects of mayor-led governance in Chicago and Cleveland, she finds that community responsiveness and participatory democracy both decreased after the mayor-appointed school board was put in place.

CIVIC CAPACITY AND INTEGRATED GOVERNANCE

During the late 1990s, the Civic Capacity and Urban Education Project (CCUEP), headed by Clarence Stone, assembled a team of political scientists to study school politics in eleven cities. To improve the quality of school governance, Stone and his associates called for various sectors, both public and private, to work together, systemwide, on human development issues. For instance, Stone argues that schools should look beyond their own walls and partner with community development issues. "Civic capacity," argued Stone and his associates, "involves mobilization by a broader array of community interests to remove policy-making authority from subperforming policy subsystems" (Stone 1989, 7). None of the eleven cities, however, attained a systemic level of civic mobilization. Among the structural barriers were functional insulation of the school administration from other policy domains, a culture of preserving jobs in the context of "employment regimes," and interest group politics that were reinforced by union power (Stone et al. 2001, 7).

Efforts to build civic capacity are likely to be affected by how interest groups articulate their concerns and are organized. In this regard, the analytical lens that differentiates "materialist" and "postmaterialist" values is useful in understanding the political tension surrounding accountability issues (Inglehart 1990). Though the former is associated with jobs and tangible benefits, the latter is closely associated with democratic values and quality of life. Although interest group politics is central to our pluralist system, "materialist-oriented" organized interests can become autonomous power centers that undermine the organizational capacity of the school system. A major "materialist-oriented" interest group is the teachers' union.

Grimshaw's study of Chicago's teachers' union suggested that the union has gone through two phases in its relationship with the city and school administration. During the formative years, the union largely cooperated with the administration (and the mayor) in return for a legitimate role in the policy-making process. In the second phase, which Grimshaw (1979, 150) characterized as "union rule," the union became independent of both the local political machine and reform fractions. Instead, it looked to the national union leadership for guidance and engaged in tough bargaining with the administration over better compensation and working conditions. Consequently, according to Grimshaw, policymakers "no longer are able to set policy unless the policy is consistent with the union's objectives" (p. 150). Others have noted that the aging of union organizations can lead to the problems of "mature institutions," wherein union leaders have to mediate trade-offs between quality and supply of labor (Cooper and Liotta 2001). Still others see a new trend in school competition, observing the need to replace "collective bargaining" with "reform bargaining" (Johnson and Kardos 2001).

Countering the materialist values are the postmaterialist politics that have emerged in American cities. Clark and his associates note the rise of the "new political culture" in city hall and argue that hierarchical structures, such as the traditional patronage-based political machinery, no longer play a key role in mobilizing citizen concerns (Clark and Hoffmann-Martinot 1998; Wong, Jain, and Clark 1997). In urban centers, union membership in the manufacturing and service sectors has declined. Ideologically based groups, on both the left and the right, seem to have lost much of their reputations in city councils, state legislatures, and the nation's capital (Berry 1999). Instead, citizen actions are increasingly realigned with postmaterialist concerns. They have become more focused on "quality-of-life" issues, such as a lower crime rate and better schooling and park services; less organized along rigid class lines; and more pragmatic about governmental and market solutions to address educational and social problems at the local level. To the extent that the postmaterialist regime persists, racial and class categories will become less predictive of how citizens view and decide on educational policy issues.

There are many similarities between the approach of the CCUEP and our own study. We are in agreement that "it takes a city," and that civic capacity is an important means of achieving long-lasting student achievement. At the same time, Stone and his CCUEP colleagues (2001, 164) are "sympathetic to the new emphasis on mayoral leadership," and "believe that civic capacity demands a central place for politics and formal governmental authority." Where we differ with the CCUEP researchers is in our belief that mayoral control can be an important first step in bringing together a fragmented city. If CCUEP provides the road map for reform, we believe that mayoral control becomes the institutional "jump start" to begin the journey. Civic capacity "is about various sectors of the community coming together in an effort to solve a major problem," and integrated governance is about one sector of the community (the mayor) taking a clear, forceful lead (Stone et al. 2001, 4).

The ability of integrated governance to jump-start civic capacity is illustrated by the success of mayors, such as Richard M. Daley in Chicago, in developing partnerships with teachers' unions. As we noted above, this partnership brought both financial and labor stability to the school district and allowed for an intensified focus on issues of teaching and learning.

Further, because the new-style mayors have tended to incorporate school reforms into a larger quality-of-life agenda, integrated governance can initiate the creation of a broad coalition of interests across racial and class lines aimed at improving the schools systemwide and connecting school improvement to neighborhood development. It is important to note, however, that whether such a coalition emerges under integrated governance or whether racial divisions merely get papered over by a citywide perspective is as yet unclear and will undoubtedly vary considerably according to each city's political and economic contexts.

The civic capacity view conceptualizes mayoral control differently—as an outcome of civic capacity, not a precursor. For instance, Shipps (2004, 60) argues that "Chicago's adoption of strong mayoral control is one of the several *outcomes* of building civic capacity for reform, not itself a cause of civic capacity or reform." For Stone and his colleagues (2001, 164), "the question is not mayoral leadership or not. The real question is whether the mayor's leadership is part of a substantial civic coalition." For us, the question is whether mayoral control may change the political dynamics in ways that make it more likely for a coalition to form. We believe mayoral control may be able to do just that.

Mayor-appointed school boards offer a way to bypass the difficulty of building up a political regime, as the state legislature gives power directly to the mayor. The mayor's bargaining position with the rest of the regime is now shifted. The mayor is no longer in the middle of a complicated web of interests but is sitting somewhere above those interests with more power than he or she has enjoyed before. The mayor can use that power to shield the school district from additional political encroachment.

One recent piece of research utilizing the CCUEP survey focused directly on mayors, and it tends to support this view that the mayor expends political capital as a buffer for the school district. Marschall and Shah (2005, 165) looked at the role of mayoral influence in the CCUEP cities. In describing the difficulty of overcoming the collective action problem to achieve civic capacity, they recognize that "given the complexity of urban education reform, the larger number of potential stakeholders, and the diverse incentives, we should not be surprised that overcoming the collective action problem has been difficult." They use data from the CCUEP survey as well as local media sources to look for contrasts in levels of consensus on agenda across eleven cities. After a cross-district analysis, they find that the "evidence suggests that mayors might be one of the crucial components needed to move cities from conflictual to consensual politics within the domain of education policy" (p. 174). This evidence is consistent with our theory that mayoral control of schools can be a way to overcome collective action problems. Mayoral control in this view is an important factor leading to greater civic capacity.

BROADER IMPLICATIONS FOR THE SIGNIFICANCE OF INSTITUTIONAL GOVERNANCE

Nancy Burns (1994) has shown persuasively how institutional structure shapes policy and debate within cities. Studying how local government boundaries are determined through state, local, and national politics, she concludes that "if we want local politics to be about different issues, then we must redefine the institutions—change the parameters in which local government operates—which will, in turn, redefine the character of the interested parties" (p.115). The broader point made by Burns is that boundaries institutionalize values. When those values are racist or motivated by private gain at the expense of others, the institutions that arise from them can be harmful to local democracy and the overall health of the city. We believe, however, that when institutional change is driven by a desire to reduce achievement inequality and improve all public schools, the results can be beneficial to the city.

Although we recognize that other institutional designs (e.g., school choice) and school-level management affect the productiveness of a school system, we reject the notion that school district governance does not play a role in school system success. We argue in this book that school district governance arrangements create the enabling preconditions that are necessary for schools and teachers to successfully complete their core activities. It is a necessary, if not sufficient, condition to turn around inner city school systems. We agree with Portz (2003, 112–13) that "governance arrangements are best viewed as enabling. They provide a context within which resources are more—or less—effectively brought to bear in support of student learning." Mayors can set the stage for educational improvement by providing adequate resources properly distributed throughout the district, safety, technical assistance, public support, and labor agreements. Our empirical analysis enters the debate over governance reform by testing the proposition that governance changes are linked to student and financial outcomes.

Finally, scholarship in the politics of education directs our attention to how educational governance is organized, the distribution of power in the decision-making process, the nature and management of conflict, and the outcomes and impact of policy decisions. In considering institutional features, a starting point is Peterson's *School Politics, Chicago Style* (1976), which provides a systematic analysis of how Mayor Daley balanced the interests between his political machine and the reform faction on the Chicago school board during the 1960s and the early 1970s. Peterson's discussion of pluralist versus ideological bargaining remains an original contribution to the politics of education.

In the framework presented by Wilbur Rich (1996), these systemwide interests may take the form of a public school cartel. He defines this cartel as "a coalition of professional school administrators, school activists, and union leaders who maintain control of school policy to promote the interest of its members" (p. 5). He argues that these cartels establish and maintain "preemptive power" that allows them to maintain control despite changes in governance structure. Using Cleveland as an example, Rich and Chambers (2003, 179) argue that "the Cleveland [cartel] has remained intact despite state and mayoral takeovers." To the extent that a cartel is effectively operating within a city, changes in governance structure such as the introduction of mayor-appointed school boards should not be expected to produce changes. The reason is that, in this view, mayors are not really in control but are bound by informal bargaining they must do with the cartel.

The distribution of authority and power between school and other governing institutions is disrupted when a formal legal change is made, allocating more power to the mayor. The move is toward a unitary or integrated system of control versus a dispersed or fragmentary system. Our study provides a test of whether a more integrated system is related to improved district outcomes (Wong, Jain, and Clark 1997; Wong and Sunderman 2000). The next chapter describes how integrated governance works in practice by analyzing different paths to mayoral leadership in twelve different cities. As we will see, integrated governance looks quite different across a variety of urban settings. We will see how different cities and mayors have wrestled with the institutional tensions we have discussed in this chapter.

CHAPTER TWO

The New-Style Education Mayors

IN THE 1990S, CHICAGO'S MAYOR RICHARD M. DALEY and Boston's Mayor Thomas Menino represented the vanguard of a new style of education mayors that put education performance at the forefront of their agendas for economic growth and civic renewal. Over the course of the past decade, mayors in Cleveland, New York, Providence, and several other cities have taken over leadership of their cities' schools. Other mayors have identified education as a central issue. In Ohio, the Ohio Mayors' Education Roundtable has expanded from the eight to the twenty-one largest districts in the state (Edelstein 2005). In the 2005 Minneapolis mayoral race, education was at center stage, with the challenger, Peter McLaughlin, saying he "would have an Education Cabinet and seek a nonvoting mayoral appointment to the School Board" (Russell 2005). Education was a major issue in the 2005 New York City mayoral race as well. Mayor Bloomberg used education to launch his campaign against his opponent (Cardwell and McIntire 2005). Education was also at center stage in the 2005 mayor's race in Cincinnati (Pierce 2005). During the race, one of the candidates (a sitting Ohio state senator) introduced a bill in the state senate to allow for mayor-appointed school boards in Cincinnati.[1]

To be sure, not all mayors are interested in taking on education as a top priority. Constitutional tradition and statutory limits tend to maintain institutional separation between city hall and the school board. Political considerations also displace education from the mayor's core focus. Even in a city like Baltimore, with its long tradition of mayoral control, Martin O'Malley focused more on public safety and improving city services during his first term (Orr 2004; see also Cibulka 2003, Orr 1999). This serves as a caution that "contemporary mayors do not necessarily have to construct a school-focused electoral coalition or governing coalition" (Orr 2004, 29). But even if mayors are not initially interested in education, given the importance of schools to a city's economic, social, and cultural vitality, voters may begin to expect mayoral involvement. Mayors may have little choice but to confront the education question: "What are you going to do about the schools if you win in November?"

In this chapter we provide an overview of mayoral control as it has been enacted in twelve cities. Though other scholars have emphasized the informal roles that mayors play in their cities' schools, we focus on those cities whose mayors have been given legal control of their public schools. This type of leadership radically departs from the informal roles and partnerships that have long characterized mayoral involvement in urban education.

Table 2.1 presents basic demographic data about the set of cities in which mayors have gained legal control over the public school system. We locate each of these cities in one of three distinct categories. First, one set of cities moved from a traditional elected school board to either a full or partially mayor-appointed school board, and they continue to keep those mayoral appointments in place, as of 2005. This first group includes eight cities: Boston, Chicago, New Haven, Providence, Harrisburg, Oakland, Cleveland, New York, Jackson, and Trenton.[2] Second, two cities—Baltimore and Philadelphia—have moved from mayor-appointed school boards to a city–state joint-appointment governance arrangement. Third, two cities—Detroit and Washington—have tried mayoral control but have reverted back to traditional governance arrangements. In 2007 Washington once again moved to mayoral control. We discuss the cities within each category to gain a sense of the context in which mayoral control has taken hold and in which it has been combined with state governance or been abandoned. The discussion here is meant to serve primarily as background for the in-depth quantitative and qualitative analyses we present in subsequent chapters. For readers interested in more detail on a particular city, we have provided references to more detailed case studies.

THE FIRST GROUP: FROM ELECTED TO MAYOR-APPOINTED BOARDS

The first group of cities comprises those in which mayoral control has largely taken hold. Though mayoral control has been relatively recent in Hartford, most of the cities in this first group moved toward mayor-appointed school boards during the mid-1990s. Boston and Providence have the longest histories with this form of governance. Boston's mayor gained the authority to appoint school board members in 1989, and Providence's system of

Table 2.1 Characteristics of School Districts with Mayor-Led Integrated Governance

City	Start Date	End Date	New/Old Style	Mayor Appoints Majority of Board?	Mayor Appoints All of Board?	Mayor Has Full Appointment Power?	Enrollment	2003 U.S. Size Rank	Children Living in Poverty (%)	African American (%)	Hispanic (%)
Boston	1992	Ongoing	New	Yes	Yes	No	61,552	64	26	47	14
Chicago	1995	Ongoing	New	Yes	Yes	Yes	436,048	4	28	51	26
Baltimore[a]	1997	Ongoing	New	Joint Appointment with Governor			96,230	31	25	88	2
Cleveland	1998	Ongoing	New	Yes	Yes	No	71,616	45	29	71	7
Detroit[b]	1999	2004	New	Yes	No	Yes	173,742	12	31	91	5
Oakland	2000	Ongoing	New	No	No	Yes	52,501	80	24	43	22
Harrisburg*	2000	Ongoing	New	Yes	Yes	Yes	7,492	<500	26	78	14
Washington	2001	2006	New	No	No	Yes	67,522	52	29	84	10
Philadelphia[c]	2001	Ongoing	New	Joint Appointment with Governor			192,683	9	27	65	8
New York	2002	2010	New	Yes	No	Yes	1,077,381	1	29	34	27
Hartford*[d]	2005	Ongoing	New	Yes	Yes	Yes	22,734	289	36	40	54
New Haven	Pre-1990	Ongoing	New	Yes	Yes	Yes	20,329	346	31	56	21
Providence	Pre-1990	Ongoing	New	Yes	Yes	No	27,580	225	36	22	30
Trenton*	Pre-1990	Ongoing	New	Yes	Yes	Yes	13,231	<500	22	67	29
Jackson	Pre-1990	Ongoing	Old	Yes	Yes	No	31,529	187	32	96	1

Note: Demographic data are for 2003.

*As described in chapter three, these small and midsized districts are not included in our empirical analysis.

[a]Before 1997, the school board in Baltimore was appointed by the mayor. See the text for a discussion.

[b]The governance description for Detroit in this table refers to the period 1999–2004. As discussed in the text, Detroit reverted to an elected school board in 2004.

[c]Before 2001, the school board in Philadelphia was appointed by the mayor. See the text for a discussion.

[d]The governance description for Hartford refers to the period 2005–. Before 2005, the school board was appointed by a mix of mayoral and state authorities. See the text for a discussion.

mayoral appointment stretches back to 1980. As the brief descriptions below indicate, there is considerable variation across these cities in terms of the rise of mayoral control and the policies that the mayors have sought to enact. This reflects both the complexities of educational politics and the multilayered nature of the educational system. At the same time, common themes also emerge from across the eight cities. First, state legislatures have played a key role in initiating mayor-appointed school boards in most of these cities, with the courts providing further impetus in some. Some mayors in this group of cities have petitioned the state for expanded authority over their cities' schools, while in other cases mayoral control emerged after a state takeover of the district. Second, the mayors of these cities have been successful in establishing productive relationships with both business leaders and teachers' unions. It is important to note, however, that some mayors continue to face challenges from other organized interests in their cities. Third, though their educational agendas vary, the mayors in this group of cities have tended to emphasize districtwide standards, tying them to outcome-based accountability policies that place low-performing schools under district intervention and/or improvement plans. Fourth and finally, many of the mayors have also been able to use their expanded powers to address fiscal crises and launch capital improvement efforts to replace decaying infrastructures. It appears that this combination of legal and state legitimacy, coalition building, and an emphasis on systemwide educational reforms has contributed to the stability of mayoral control in these eight cities.

Boston

The Boston school community was highly polarized in the 1970s, largely due to the controversies surrounding efforts to desegregate the district through busing. Though Boston retained some very prestigious schools, such as Boston Latin, the school system overall was widely perceived as "too politicized" with declining quality. In this challenging context, Mayor Raymond Flynn, in 1989, supported the passage of a referendum, which was approved by a very narrow margin of 50.8 to 49.2 percent, that gave the mayor direct control over the city school system. As a result, Boston's mayor currently appoints a seven-member board as opposed to the previous thirteen-member elected board. The mayor selects board members from a set of candidates presented to him by the Nominating Committee.

Mayor Thomas Menino, Flynn's successor, is among a new group of mayors who have successfully reformed the management practices in city agencies. In 1992, Menino appointed seven members to the first postreform school board. Since then, he has proclaimed himself an "education mayor." He sees improving education as an important strategy in retaining middle-class residents in the city. His strong educational platform gained voters' approval in 1996, when 54 percent of the electorate opposed a referendum that called for a shift back to an elected school board. The 1996 election saw an unusually high turnout of 68 percent. The 32 percent turnout in 1989, when the reform was adopted, pales in comparison.

In his 1996 State of the City speech, Mayor Menino tied his political future to the success of the city's school system, urging Boston residents to "judge me harshly" if goals for schools were not realized. He has invested financially in the schools as well, adjusting the city's entire budget to ensure that educational reforms have priority. Since he took office, the School Department's operating budget has increased by $60 million. Its capital budget increased by $43.2 million, or 255 percent. Menino also appointed a former U.S. assistant secretary of elementary and secondary education, Thomas Payzant, as the school superintendent. Payzant worked closely with Menino on a five-year reform plan, and Payzant was one of the longest-serving urban district superintendents, in office for eleven years. The current superintendent, Michael Contompasis, the former headmaster of Boston Latin School, was appointed in 2006.

Menino has been able to garner support for his authority and for the school system, more generally, from a range of interest groups. The business community strongly supports him. Though the teachers' union initially opposed the move to mayoral control, they also have come to support him. His school board voted to end busing and moved the schools back to a neighborhood-based system.

Among the mayor's first accomplishments was a five-year contract with the teachers' union. Several neighborhood and minority groups, however, complained that they were not adequately represented as a result of mayoral control, and they have continued to oppose Menino's authority over the school system.

Menino has also begun to establish policy coherence. Since gaining control in 1992, he has focused on the implementation of districtwide learning standards and standards-based student assessments. In the fall of 1996, his administration launched a five-year Focus on Children plan, with strong accountability at the school and classroom levels. He also initiated a high school restructuring plan, and he has since placed an emphasis on ending social promotion, improving after-school programs, and wiring every school to the Internet. In 2004, then-superintendent Payzant promoted comprehensive efforts to reduce the achievement gap between white and Asian students on the one hand and African American and Latino students on the other hand. These efforts seek to develop capacity across the district's schools by providing professional development for principals and teachers focused on analyzing student learning through state achievement tests, the Massachusetts Comprehensive

Assessment System, formative assessment and classroom work, demanding high expectations for student learning, and employing culturally relevant practices to raise achievement among the district's racial and ethnic minority and low-income students. They also include developing partnerships between schools, parents, and communities through the Committee Forums series and continuing and expanding partnerships with private corporations and foundations. The district was recognized as the most improved urban school district and awarded the Broad Prize for Urban Education in 2006.[3]

Chicago

The Illinois state legislature passed the Chicago School Reform Amendatory Act of 1995, granting Chicago's Mayor Richard M. Daley authority over the city's school district.[4] Like Boston's Mayor Menino, Mayor Daley considered quality public education essential to retaining the city's middle-class residents. A strong public school system, in his view, could also attract businesses to Chicago. Mayor Daley moved immediately, upon the passage of the reform law, to appoint Gery Chico as the new school board president, and Paul Vallas to the newly created position of chief executive officer (CEO). Both had served in Daley's administration; neither had an education background.

Chicago is frequently cited as an example of successful mayoral control. Since Mayor Daley took control of the schools in 1995, test scores have generally risen across elementary grades and a more rigorous academic curriculum has been implemented in the high schools. Former president Bill Clinton cited Chicago as a model in his 1999 State of the Union address, and Chicago is the model that many cities look to when they consider mayoral control. What is it about the Chicago experience that has gained so much national attention? It is useful to discuss several important features of mayoral control in Chicago.

First, mayoral control integrated authority systemwide. The 1995 Chicago School Reform Amendatory Act granted the city's mayor the authority to appoint a five-member school board and select a CEO to oversee the district's top administrative team, including the chief education officer; eliminated competing sources of authority, such as the School Finance Authority and the School Board Nominating Commission; and granted the school board powers to hold local school councils accountable to systemwide standards. The law also expanded the capacity of the district's new leadership to launch an educational accountability agenda aimed at systemwide improvement in teaching and learning. In particular, the law enabled the leadership to identify and place low-performing schools under district intervention, with the threat of possible closure.

Second, the newly appointed district leadership moved immediately to improve the district's fiscal management. Using expanded powers over financial operations provided by the 1995 act, the central administration improved capital funding, balanced the budget, and secured labor stability through a four-year contract with the teachers' union. The school board launched the first capital improvement plan in decades to address the deterioration of the schools' physical plant. The administration also improved management efficiency by waging a public battle against waste and corruption, downsizing the central office, and contracting out several operations.

Third, district leaders gained the support of the public and of the business community, while balancing needs of school-based autonomy. The district's management improvements garnered the support of the business community and improved public confidence in the school system. The reformed school board and district leadership also attempted to strike a balance between managing from the center and letting schools operate autonomously. The district's school-sanctioning policies garnered considerable attention throughout the 1990s. Though these policies allowed for district intervention into low-performing schools, other initiatives provided failing schools with additional resources and fostered principal and teacher discretion in program design. Further, the high school reform agenda, launched in the second year of mayoral control, promoted the expansion of options at the secondary level, such as career academies and the International Baccalaureate Program. These policies have remained largely in place, but they have been modified under the current superintendent, Arne Duncan, to include measures of progress on student achievement gains and, in the district's high schools, on dropout and graduation rates. The district has also continued its efforts to expand school choice within city neighborhoods and to develop schools as centers for community and parental involvement. Eleven years after taking control of the school district, Mayor Daley focused his 2006 State of the City address on the gains made by students in the district's elementary and high schools and linked the city's economic and social well-being to these gains.

Cleveland

In Cleveland, mayoral control followed earlier state intervention.[5] The state took over the school district administration in 1995, when the federal district court removed the powers of governance from the local elected Board of Education and placed the powers in the hands of the state superintendent of public instruction. The Cleveland city school district was in a "crisis situation." Of all students from the 1990–91 eighth grade class, only 33 percent actually graduated from high school in 1995. During this time, Mayor Michael White used his office to support school board candidates and to seek broader support from the business community.

Cleveland regained local administrative powers in 1998, when the federal court lifted the previous orders. An Advisory Committee on Governance of the Cleveland Summit on Education proposed a bill in 1997 that gave control of the district to the mayor. During the legislative session, Mayor White negotiated with a Republican governor and a Republican legislature to gain control over the schools. Seeing the potential for success in Chicago, the legislature granted Mayor White control of the Cleveland Public Schools in 1998. As a result, in 1999 White appointed a nine-member school board. That board hired an experienced school administrator, who served as interim superintendent for eight months. He was replaced by the New York City educator Barbara Byrd-Bennett in November 1998. Byrd-Bennett established her leadership in the school system and remained in office during the arrival in 2002 of a new mayor, Jane Campbell. The teachers' union, which had initially opposed the appointed board, also grew to support the new regime after successfully negotiating a new contract in 2000. In 2002, Cleveland voters had a referendum to decide on the continuance of the mayor-appointed school board. More than 70 percent of voters supported the continuation of the mayor-appointed school board that had been in place for four years. The city's current mayor, Frank Jackson, has strengthened the relationship between city hall and the schools through coalition building and the creation of the city's first cabinet-level education adviser. The district hired a new CEO, Eugene Sanders, in 2006.

Harrisburg

Faced with a city school system that was performing at very low levels, Harrisburg mayor Stephen Reed partnered with State Senator Jeffrey Piccola to develop an amendment to the 2000 Pennsylvania Education Empowerment Act, which we discuss just below (LaRock 2003a).[6] Part of this amendment would allow for a five-person, mayor-appointed school board if there was not significant improvement in the school system. The law was challenged in Pennsylvania State Court, but the Pennsylvania Supreme Court examined both the state statute and Harrisburg's own city charter, ruling that the state provision was not a special law for a single city, and that it did not violate the city charter.[7]

The broader Education Empowerment Act, which Pennsylvania governor Tom Ridge signed into law in May 2000, was designed to improve the state's lowest-performing districts. Under the act, the state designates "empowerment districts" and then works with the local authorities to "improve student performance, and the management and operation of the school district."[8]

Since gaining control of the schools, Mayor Reed has been able to begin implementing a comprehensive School District Improvement Plan, which outlines a number of new initiatives, including a standards-based curriculum across all grades (Harrisburg City Schools 2001). Implementation of the plan has led to increased enrollments and improved academic performance. The plan has resulted in a large suburban enrollment in the district's magnet school program. Mayor Reed also led the creation of universal three- to five-year-old prekindergarten programs, and he has been a leading player in the successful creation of the first new comprehensive university to be chartered in the state in a hundred years (Baker 2006).

Harrisburg differs from the other school districts we consider in this study because of its comparatively small size. With only fifteen schools and roughly 8,500 students, it is about the size of the smallest district that we will include in our quantitative analysis. We will discuss at greater length in chapter three why Harrisburg is not included in our empirical analysis.

New Haven

New Haven's city charter allows the mayor to appoint its seven-member board. Mayor John DeStefano Jr., who has been in office since 1994, believes that "a mayor should be responsible for the quality of his schools" (Collins 2002) and has worked to significantly reduce the high school dropout rate and increase education capital investments. He has also been an advocate for more school choice options in the district. Though challengers, such as 1999 opponent James D. Newton, have argued that New Haven's overall academic progress still lags behind and that the district's bureaucracy remains an impediment to success, under Mayor DeStefano's leadership, the city's magnet school program has grown to twenty schools of choice and draws students from both city and suburban families. The program has been nationally recognized for integrating schools in Greater New Haven across racial and economic lines. DeStefano's $1.5 billion school construction plan effectively leveraged the state's matching funds to reduce class sizes in New Haven.

Since 1992, the New Haven Public Schools have been under the direction of Superintendent Reginald Mayor. Mayor instituted a remediation program for low-performing students that included ending social promotion and provided additional instructional time for retained students through mandatory summer school and Saturday Academies.

Providence

Providence has a long-standing system of a mayor-appointed school board, governed by the Providence Home Rule Statutes from 1980. In 1993, following a recommendation by the 1991 Providence Blueprint for Education Report, a Providence School Board Nominating Commission was established by then-mayor Buddy Cianci. The commission "is comprised by each of the five (5) sponsoring non-profit organizations who nominate a Commission member" (Field 2002). Today, the commission conducts an annual search to replace three members of the nine-member board (Providence Schools 2005). The board presents a slate of potential candidates to the mayor, who then selects three to serve.

Providence mayor David N. Cicilline, who took office in 2002, has made school reform a top priority. He secured labor stability through forging a partnership with the Providence Teachers' Union. He also helped to redesign the city's four high schools. He "is focusing his leadership and involvement on establishing community schools and linking a broad range of services and programs to at-risk students. This does not necessarily require new school construction, but a vision of how to use existing buildings to create new and different learning environments, and coordinating the provision of selected city social services to the students at or near the schools" (Edelstein 2004). He has also promoted the development of a comprehensive after-school program that centers on the creation of "campuses" to play host to after-school activities with resources from the city's libraries, recreation centers, and schools. To support this program, the mayor and school district were able to secure a $5 million grant from the Wallace Foundation.

In 2005, Mayor Cicilline appointed Donnie Evans, from Tampa, as the new superintendent of schools. In 2006, Evans began implementing the Whole School Effectiveness reform program in Providence based on his experience raising the number of "A-rated" (high-performing) schools in Tampa from seven to eighty-seven.

Hartford

In 1997, in accordance with the Connecticut Special Act 94-4, the Hartford Public Schools were taken over by a state management team. The "State Board of Trustees for the Hartford Public Schools became responsible for the governance, management, and fiscal operations of the Hartford public school system" (Connecticut General Assembly 1999). This Board of Trustees was renewed, in Special Act 01-7, through December 2005. From 2002 to 2005, with the State Board still in place, management of the school board was under a State Board with four elected members, and three members appointed by the mayor, after consultation with the governor and General Assembly, and with the approval of the Hartford Court of Common Council.

In addition to the State Special Act, in 2002 the residents of Hartford voted to amend their city charter to (1) move from a council–manager to a strong-mayor form of government, and (2) change their school board from an elected body to a joint elected and appointed board, with five members appointed by the mayor and four elected. The amended charter, as provided by Special Act 01-7, did not govern until December 2005, when the mayor, Eddie A. Perez, made news by appointing himself one of the five Board of Education appointees. Allan B. Taylor, the chairman of the charter revision commission, observed that this was within the legal framework: "We set up a structure that in effect makes the mayor accountable for the school system. By putting himself on the board, the mayor makes that even more clear" (Gottlieb and Carmiel 2005).

Trenton

In 1978, the citizens of Trenton voted to implement a mayor-appointed nine-member school board. This makes Trenton one of the longest running mayor-led school districts. In describing his role with the schools, Mayor Douglas Palmer said in 2004 that he wants his school board and superintendent to "do what's best for these kids, [and] I'll handle the political weight" (Emanski 2004). Over the past decade the mayor's office and school district have worked well together. Two central office positions, the city and community liaison services coordinator and the director of curriculum, keep communication between the city and central office continuously open, allowing ideas and decisions from city hall to permeate the entire district.

Although the school board holds the right to hire the superintendent and maintains autonomy in decision making, the mayor has played a pivotal role in the selection of recent district leaders. In 1998, Mayor Palmer hired James Lytle as his superintendent. Over the course of Lytle's tenure, Palmer and Lytle met regularly to discuss Lytle's districtwide reform ideas and decisions. When Lytle took on the position of superintendent of schools, the district faced multiple challenges: a severe backlog of special needs and prospective special needs students who needed evaluation, reevaluation, and placement; an alarming dropout rate; increased competition with charter and private schools for students and funding; and a set of his public schools—including half the elementary schools and all the secondary schools—not meeting state performance standards. Through a weekend retreat in August 1998 and considerable interaction among Trenton's senior administrative group and the Trenton Board of Education, school communities, employee organizations, and the New Jersey Department of Education, Trenton came up with a strategy to turn the district school system into a more effective educational institution. Seven years later, when Superintendent Lytle announced his resignation, improvements had been made in district performance (Hanover 2005).

The selection in the summer of 2006 of new superintendent, Rodney Lofton, was designed to continue these improvements. Lofton's selection also illustrated the cohesiveness of the mayor and school board. The school board voted unanimously in favor of Lofton's hiring, and Mayor Palmer commented that the new superintendent "shares my vision of where we need to move the district. We are on the same page regarding student achievement and employee accountability" (Parker 2006).

In addition to working well with school district leadership, Mayor Palmer has been active in promoting long-term district reform. After an intense evaluation by the New Jersey Education Law Center (ELC), in June 2005 Palmer created the Coalition for Hands-On Achievement of Necessary Goals in Education to address the report's findings. He stated that "instead of sitting on a shelf, the ELC research will be our organizing framework. We will use it as a roadmap to improve educational opportunities. We will combine it with the priorities our parents identify and go to work together to specify the actions we need from our schools, our parents, and our students, so that our schools become more safe, thorough, and efficient" (Palmer 2005).

Oakland

If Chicago is recognized as a model for mayoral takeover governance, Oakland illustrates the problems with "mixed" appointed and elected boards.[9] Jerry Brown became mayor of Oakland in June 1998, inheriting a school system that "embodies the failure of public education" (Coburn and Riley 2000). Faced with the challenge of turning the Oakland Unified School District around, Brown established a Commission on Education, which issued a final report in 1999. In addition to Brown's commission, California's Fiscal Crisis and Management Assistance Team (FCMAT) performed a districtwide audit in 1999. The reports highlighted many areas for improvement, including better management and accountability, a more challenging curriculum, and more flexibility for schools to make their own hiring decisions.

Mayor Brown increased his authority through an amendment to the city charter that passed in 2000. The amendment increased the size of the school board from seven to ten members, with the three new members being appointed by the mayor. Because the governing board of the Oakland Unified School District has ten members, however, Mayor Brown did not gain majority control. Furthermore, some of the additional school board candidates that he has supported have lost their elective races. Facing strong institutional resistance, he has had difficulty in implementing any large-scale management changes in the school system. His strategy has been to "put people on the school board who push the superintendent" (California Department of Education 2003).

Mayor Brown's increased formal authority has in recent years been overshadowed by the Oakland Unified School District becoming insolvent in

2003, prompting emergency state funding and a state takeover of the district (California Department of Education 2003). Until finances can be squared away, the Oakland schools are being run by an administrator appointed by the state superintendent of public instruction. In this context, the school board (whether appointed by Mayor Brown or not) serves in more of an advisory capacity. FCMAT was brought in to produce a plan of action for the district. This type of "state takeover" is distinct from mayor-led integrated governance. The presence of outside state administrators has caused serious disputes with the Oakland Education Association, the teachers' union that represents teachers in the Oakland Unified School District. Nearly two years of tense contract negotiations finally led to a new contract in May 2006, but only after the union nearly engaged in a one-day walkout a month before.

In a climate of financial distress, political resistance, and possibly shifting priorities for the mayor, it seems unlikely that Oakland will go forward with such comprehensive reform programs as have been implemented in New York.

New York

The nation's largest school district has historically been the site of many education reforms and innovations. Talk of mayoral control of the city's school district had been heard for decades, and it grew louder in the 1990s as other cities successfully implemented mayor-led governance. In a 1999 speech on education, Mayor Rudolph Giuliani was clear in his intentions: "New York City needs to do what was done in Chicago, Detroit, and other major American cities: eliminate the bureaucratic Board of Education—meaning both the central board and the 32 community school boards, which sap resources and hinder student achievement—and replace them with a system that is accountable to parents and voters and directly focuses all resources and energy on improving schools" (Giuliani 1999). Mayor Giuliani's vision, however, was not realized until his successor, Michael Bloomberg, took office.

Mayor Bloomberg, elected in 2001, worked with New York governor George Pataki and the New York State Assembly to pass legislation in the summer of 2002 that restructured the governance of the New York City schools. Under the new governance plan, a thirteen-member school board was created, with seven members appointed by the mayor. The other six members are appointed by the five New York City borough presidents. In addition to handing majority appointive power to the mayor, the plan eliminated the thirty-two community school boards in June 2003. The new governance system, which will require reauthorization by the legislature in 2009, gives the mayor the power to appoint the schools' chancellor. In July 2002, the mayor made his first appointment, choosing the lawyer and businessman Joel Klein to run the schools. At the time, Klein was the chairman and CEO of Bertelsmann, Inc., and had previously been U.S. assistant attorney general in charge of the Department of Justice's Antitrust Division.

Working together for four years, reviews of the Bloomberg and Klein partnership are mixed. On one hand, the chancellor and mayor point out that test scores have been on the upswing. In a special 2005 report by the *NewsHour with Jim Lehrer* that looked at the New York City reforms, Klein pointed out that "our test scores have gone up in an unprecedented way. Our graduation rates are up; they're higher than they've ever been" (*NewsHour with Jim Lehrer* 2005). On the other hand, critics point out that community and parental involvement has suffered. Commenting on the reforms in 2006, the political scientist Jeffrey Henig observed that with reduced local control, "the parents and the community activists are upset. They're frozen out" (Mabeus 2006). The future of mayoral control in New York City may include an expanded use of private groups to run public schools. According to newspaper reports in the fall of 2006, preliminary discussions were being held to explore the expansion of private management options (Herszenhorn 2006). Such a move would complicate the relationship between Chancellor Klein and the United Federation of Teachers (UFT). Responding to these proposals, Randi Weingarten, president of the UFT, emphasized that "on an issue that is this transcendent there has to be a real public debate" (Heszenhorn 2006). Like mayoral control in other cities, the success of the reform is likely to hinge on a successful politics of partnership that both promotes innovative reform and invites many stakeholders to the table.

Jackson

In Jackson, the mayor appoints the school board with the approval of the city council. Though this appointive process puts Jackson in the first group of cities, it differs from the rest of the districts in that group. Unlike the other districts where new legislation has been required, long-standing Mississippi law allows districts such as Jackson to choose their own method of board selection.[10] Because the mayor's appointive power is historical and not part of a new wave of reform, Jackson does not fit as well into our category of "new-style" mayoral governance. The mayor also works in conjunction with the City Council, whose approval is required. In terms of accountability, then, Jackson may be more analogous to Baltimore's older mode of joint control under the mayor and state. The mayor's appointive power is also limited to *appointments* and does not extend to removal. Jackson mayor Frank Melton discovered this when, in July 2005, he asked all board members to voluntarily submit their resignations. His goal was to restructure and improve board performance, but he discovered that once appointed, board members could only be removed if they had committed a felony.

Despite these differences, we include Jackson in the first group because the current Jackson city government is increasingly focusing on management and improved student performance. In the summer of 2005, Mayor Melton attempted to exert more power over the school board because he was unsatisfied with school district performance. He identified the Jackson school board as underperforming, saying, "There are 32,000 students in the school system and 10,000 are not going to school. That's just unacceptable to me" (Joyner 2005). To the extent that the Jackson city government increases its emphasis on outcome-based performance accountability, it may begin to resemble the governance structure of other districts in the first group.

THE SECOND GROUP: FROM MAYOR-APPOINTED BOARDS TO SHARED CITY–STATE GOVERNANCE

The second group of cities includes Baltimore and Philadelphia, cities where mayoral control has given way to shared city–state governance. These cities illustrate, again, the critical role that states have played in relation to mayoral control. However, as we discuss, the state–city relationship is quite different in these two cities, a difference that has had important consequences for the type of roles that the mayors have played and the changes that have been enacted in the schools.

Baltimore

As noted by James Cibulka, Baltimore presents a "counter-example to [the] trend" of mayor-appointed school boards.[11] In Baltimore, the mayor had historically appointed the school board. The governance change was to move away from a school board appointed solely by the mayor and toward a system of shared power between the state and the city. Under the old regime, Baltimore's mayor enjoyed extensive administrative powers over the district. The school system, however, relied heavily upon state funding, and its repeated fiscal crises prompted repeated threats of a state takeover. Twenty percent of all state school aid goes to Baltimore, and the city receives 58 percent of its funding from the state government—it receives more state school aid than any other districts in Maryland.

In 1993, in an attempt to solve both the schools' fiscal and performance problems, Mayor Kurt Schmoke contracted out several of the city schools with an education management agency, Educational Alternatives, Inc. (EAI). As expected, the teachers' union was not supportive of his contracting-out efforts, and hence the EAI contract lacked teacher accountability. After the experiment failed, Schmoke began petitioning the state legislature for increased funding. The city sued the state, alleging that a lack of financial resources had kept Baltimore's schoolchildren from receiving an adequate education.

State officials, for their part, were frustrated with the district's dismal performance. In 1998, the city schools met state standards in only two of thirty-one areas of student performance measured by standardized tests, attendance, and other indicators. The dropout rate was among the worst in Maryland. In January 1999, state school superintendent Nancy Grasmick said that thirty-five Baltimore schools were performing so badly that they were eligible for direct state intervention and restructuring; only two other schools in the state were deemed eligible for such "reconstitution."

The state first recommended a complete takeover of the school district. In a political bargain in 1997 with Democratic governor Parris Glendening, Mayor Schmoke agreed to share power with the state legislature and the governor. In return, the state would allocate additional money to the district. The mayor and the governor jointly appointed a nine-member Board of School Commissioners to lead and execute reforms over a five-year period. The new city–state partnership made the schools' CEO accountable to the state legislature, instead of to local politicians. Working together, the New Board of School Commissioners and the State Board of Education created a four-year "Master Plan" for turning around the Baltimore City Public School System (BCPSS). This plan was first implemented in the 1998–99 school year.

Today, control of the BCPSS is a joint city–state venture. In selecting a school district superintendent, the state superintendent generates a short list of candidates. The mayor and governor then make a joint appointment. Once appointed, the superintendent remains a member of the mayoral cabinet and works for the mayor. Both the mayor and superintendent have changed since the arrangement was first implemented. Mayor Schmoke decided not to run for a fourth term, and in November 1999, at the age of thirty-six years, Martin O'Malley became Baltimore's youngest mayor. The superintendent position has also changed hands numerous times. Robert Booker replaced interim CEO Robert Schiller in 1999, but Booker ran into financial difficulties and was replaced in July 2000 by Carmen V. Russo. Russo left in 2003, and Bonnie S. Copeland was named as interim CEO. Charlene Boston is the district's current interim CEO.

The period since 2000 has been marked by extreme financial difficulty.[12] When Russo became the new CEO in July 2000, she found that Booker had run a deficit. School officials announced in September 2000 that they were facing a $5 million deficit from the previous year's overspending, and that they would have to do some budget trimming. Those problems have continued to the present day. The declining state of Baltimore's schools and what to do about it remain perennial issues in Maryland politics.

Philadelphia

In December 2001, Philadelphia mayor John F. Street and Pennsylvania governor Mark Schweiker announced a new partnership between the city and the state that replaced the old nine-member Board of Education (which had been appointed by the mayor) with a five-member School Reform Commission, with three appointees chosen by the governor and two by the mayor.[13] With the hiring of Paul Vallas, the former CEO in Chicago, Philadelphia began to make a series of important reforms in 2002 and 2003.

Among the key accomplishments in the Philadelphia schools during this period were establishing districtwide standards; implementing a "structured curriculum" and a more structured school day (120 minutes of reading and 90 minutes of math every day) for kindergarten through ninth grades, and enhancing the quality of curriculum choices in high school, including international baccalaureate programs at neighborhood high schools, and reform in career and technical education that meets industry standards. In addition, the mayor and CEO have pushed for extending instructional time, particularly for struggling students in low-performing schools.

To further build systemwide capacity, Philadelphia established the Office of Accountability, Assessment, and Intervention in 2002 to conduct quality reviews of low-performing schools, design steps to support school improvement, and implement a student promotion policy. Philadelphia has also introduced a system of sanctions and rewards. Schools that are not making "adequate yearly progress" (the state version of the No Child Left Behind) can be placed on "probation." In October 2002, the district administered its first TerraNova test to all students in grades three through ten (covering 128,000 public and charter school students) and provided schools with results in December so that administrators, principals, and teachers could use them to improve their practices during the second half of the academic year.

Under the mixed city–state governance, the district has implemented cost-saving measures, including workforce reductions that cut $25 million. At the same time, the district identified $44 million of waste and inefficiencies, and it launched a $1.5 billion capital plan to build new schools, modernize facilities, and reduce overcrowding. Philadelphia has also extensively contracted out services to private educational management organizations (EMOs). Edison Schools was hired as the "lead district adviser" to manage central administration (March and July 2002). Edison was commissioned by former governor Tom Ridge to conduct an assessment of the academic and financial position of the Philadelphia School District in the fall of 2001. Among the EMOs, Edison Schools manages the largest number of schools. Edison Schools founder and CEO Chris Whittle argues that "creating a healthy fresh look at private-sector partnerships in public education may prove to be one of Philadelphia's most historic outcomes" (Whittle 2005, 36). Not all EMOs, however, have produced strong results. In April 2003, the district terminated its contract with one EMO, Chancellor Beacon Academies, for lack of performance. And the status of Edison and Victory Inc. schools was cast in some doubt after student performance fell in these schools in 2006 (Dean 2006).

The state has continued its support for the direction taken by Mayor Street and CEO Vallas under now-governor Edward Rendell. Citing a fifth year of improvements in the district's scores on state tests, Governor Rendell actively supported renewing CEO Vallas' contract in 2006. Though a broad range of interest groups—including the School and Home parents' group, the Philadelphia Federation of Teachers, and the Greater Philadelphia Chamber of Commerce—supported the renewal, the School Reform Commission vote was split, three to two (Woodall 2006). Tensions between the district and the teachers' union also emerged in 2006 as the district faced continued budget problems, overcrowding in many schools, and a shortage of highly qualified teachers (Snyder 2006).

THE THIRD GROUP: FROM ELECTED TO MAYORAL CONTROL AND BACK TO AN ELECTED SCHOOL BOARD

The final group of cities includes Detroit and Washington. In these cities, mayoral appointment of school board members failed to take hold. Though the history of mayoral control differed considerably in the two cities, its failure to take hold was related to the inability on the part of both the cities' mayors and the school leaders they appointed to build the types of coalitions that have been critical to the success of mayoral control in other cities.

Detroit

Detroit provides an example of a city that never fully embraced mayoral control, tried to adapt to it, was not able to carry it out successfully, and ultimately returned to a traditional elected school board.[14] In 1997, Detroit mayor Dennis Archer strongly opposed Republican governor John Engler's proposal for the State of Michigan to take over the Detroit city school district. Governor Engler was frustrated with the city's low-performing schools and with the fact that the school district consumed a major portion of the state budget. The Detroit Public Schools received 64 percent of its revenue from the state, and 11 percent from the federal government. The state share and Detroit's education expenses were expected to increase under Michigan's restructured school finance system, which equalized funding across school districts. The school system was widely perceived to be in crisis; only half of Detroit's high school students graduated. Even basic supplies—from textbooks to toilet paper—somehow had trouble making it into schools. Teachers routinely walked out on strike.

In 1998, Mayor Archer offered to participate in a local reform plan that would have engaged a broad spectrum of the Detroit community, but the elected Detroit school board tabled the proposal. Seeing Chicago as a success story, the mayor negotiated with Governor Engler to gain greater control over the school system. Engler and the Republican legislature gave the mayor control over the Detroit schools in 1999. In April 1999, the mayor appointed six of the seven board members. The seventh member of the board was the state superintendent. Mayor Archer also negotiated several outcome-based accountability measures with the state legislature, including a proposal for reduced class size, mandatory summer school, substantive after-school programs, and technical training for teachers.

Detroit's initial experience with mayoral control was highly contentious. Though business leaders supported the mayor, the teachers' unions opposed him. Local community and civil rights groups were split, with the Detroit NAACP opposed to mayoral control but the Detroit Urban League supporting it. In May 2000, Kenneth Burnley was named the district's CEO. Burnley had previously served as a superintendent in Colorado Springs and promised that he was "not going to take a long time to start doing things" (*Detroit Free Press* 2000). His vision, however, never turned into sustained improvement. As a result of historical tensions involving both education and race, his layoffs and school closings brought heated criticism. At a January 2002 board meeting, it was reported that "at one point, about half of those attending the raucous Detroit Public Schools Board of Education meeting last Wednesday chanted: 'Burnley's got to go! Burnley's got to go!'" (James 2002).

Burnley did not initially receive help from the city's mayor. In 2002, Kwame Kilpatrick was elected Detroit's new mayor. Mayor Kilpatrick's inaugural speech demonstrated that he was not thinking about structural educational governance issues when he entered office:

> One of the things I learned at Mayor's school [at Harvard] was to focus on two things—to focus on two priorities. Today I'm here to tell you what the two priorities of the Kilpatrick administration will be. Number one, the police department. Before we can begin to work on economic development, we have to have public safety in order. We're going to undertake a major restructuring of the police department. We're

going to change the image and the culture and the quality of service provided. . . . My second priority is Mayor's Time. We talked about this all through the campaign. Mayor's time is from 3 p.m. and 8 p.m. after school, when eighty-two percent of juvenile delinquency takes place here in the city of Detroit. (Kilpatrick 2002)

It was not until 2003 that Mayor Kilpatrick became more active in education reform. He attempted, in December 2003, to get state legislation passed that would move up a vote on the elected school board from its originally scheduled date in November 2004 to March 2004. The vote was to determine if the city school board should remain under mayoral appointment or return to an elected body. In contrast to Chicago and Cleveland, where mayors had formed stronger working relationships with teachers' union officials, community leaders, and state politicians, Kilpatrick's political efforts were met with stiff resistance from the Detroit Federation of Teachers.

Unable to build political support or generate sustained academic improvement, mayoral control in Detroit was headed for a sound defeat when it was put to a vote in November 2004. If Proposition E passed, it would allow the mayor to appoint a strong chief executive on top of an elected board—further entrenching features of mayoral control. A "no" vote on Proposition E meant a return to an elected school board. The vote became a civil rights and racial issue for many in Detroit—as the NAACP; the Coalition to Defend Affirmative Action, Integration, and Immigrant Rights and Fight for Equality by Any Means Necessary; the American Federation of State, County, and Municipal Employees; and others all came out against the proposition. Some groups, such as Voices for Working Families, even put together get-out-the-vote campaigns specifically to oppose the proposition. With so much opposition, there was a very strong turnout. The proposition lost by a margin of two to one, and Detroit returned to an elected school board.

Washington

In 1995, Congress stripped the District of Columbia local school board of most of its powers and created the District of Columbia Financial Responsibility and Management Assistance Authority to run Washington's schools.[15] Governance was initially delegated to the Emergency Transitional Education Board of Trustees. But after a successful legal challenge (decided in 1998), the Board of Trustees was reduced to an advisory position, and the elected board was given a place at the table. The authority, in reaction to the ruling, stated that it remained "committed to the role of the Board of Education. We understand that the Board of Education and the Board of Trustees are engaged in helpful discussions regarding a cooperative relationship for their mutual participation and support in improving the quality of education in the District. We hope that these discussions are fruitful" (Brimmer 1998). The local school board, however, remained powerless in many aspects of the decision-making process.[16]

In 2001, Mayor Anthony Williams stepped in, as voters approved a measure that would allow him to appoint four members to the nine-member school board. Without a majority of appointees, Mayor Williams's ability to direct education policy was hampered. Conflicts with the school board president did not help matters. As City Council member Kevin Chavous observed, "You could initially see tension between those members who are elected and those who are appointed by the mayor" (MacPherson 2003). In 2004, the mayor tried to get the City Council to pass a measure that would transition from the hybrid board to a system where the superintendent reported directly to the mayor. The measure was defeated. The mayor's four appointees served until 2006, and a fully elected board began governing in 2007 (Cella 2004).

Then-superintendent Paul Vance had initially made some structural changes, replacing the deputy superintendent and two associate superintendent positions with a chief academic officer, chief operating officer, and chief of staff (Vance 2006), instead of a structure much like the one instituted in Chicago. In December 2002, the schools' Central Office submitted their proposed fiscal 2004 operating budget, and for the first time included performance-based budgeting reports from every unit in the Central Office. A major "culture change" was introduced in the Central Office, as staffing was reinvigorated with nontraditional and new leadership. But Vance left in November 2003, and the interim replacement, Elfreda Massie, served only until April 2004. She was replaced by chief academic officer, Robert Rice, on an interim basis, and in September 2004, he was replaced by Clifford B. Janey. With such administrative and governance shifts, administrators believe it was difficult to determine whether the new "transformational culture" Vance attempted to install while the district remained under mayoral appointment would lead to lasting improvements in student achievement.

Recent developments have moved Washington back to the path of mayoral control. In spring of 2007, the City Council approved Mayor Adrian Fenty's proposal to take over the school district and to turn the city's school board into an advisory body. The mayor's plan was supported by the teachers union but opposed by members of the elected school board. According to the District of Columbia Public Education Reform Amendment Act of 2007, the mayor will exercise direct control over the three "chiefs," the chancellor who runs the daily operation of the district's 140 schools, the deputy mayor who oversees the work of the State Office of Education, and a CEO who is in charge of facilities and capital improvement projects. Mayoral power, at the same time, will be checked by the City Council, which holds line-item budgetary authority. At the time of completing this chapter, the reform act is under consideration by the U.S. Congress. Because Congress has to approve the reform, it seems that Washington will offer a unique design in integrated governance.

CONCLUSION

The brief descriptions of mayoral control in several cities provided above illustrate the unique circumstances and educational politics that contributed to the rise, adaptation, and—in Detroit and Washington, D.C.—eventual demise of mayoral control. They also point to the range of policy options that mayoral control provides to district leaders. At the same time, though each case was unique in the conditions and politics that led to mayoral control, the cases also point out some of the factors that appear to be particularly salient to the viability of mayoral control.

First, the cases clearly illustrate the critical role that state legislatures play in mayoral control. Though some mayors gained authority over the city schools through changes in the city charter or city referenda, most were granted authority to appoint school board members by the state legislature. In addition, state takeovers led in some cases to enhanced mayoral control, though in others it resulted in a mixed, city–state model. The states' role in mayoral control reflects the expansion of state involvement in education policy that has occurred over the past three decades. This expansion has been particularly relevant to city schools. As city schools have faced continued budget concerns and persistent low performance, state legislatures, increasingly dominated by suburban constituencies, have pressured school leaders to institute changes and threatened state takeover. For many mayors, particularly those in the cities where mayoral control has been most successful, these tensions provided opportunities to expand their role in education and to enact strong governance and educational reforms. As the cases above suggest, these new-style education mayors formed productive partnerships with state legislatures and, in many cases, protected their cities' schools from state takeover. In the cities where mayoral control has been more contentious and less successful, however, such as Baltimore and Detroit, the relationship between the city and state has remained strained. It is significant that these latter districts have continued to face a worsening fiscal crisis while mayoral control in many other districts has brought a degree of fiscal stability.

In addition to the states' role, the cases also point to the critical importance of coalition building. The mayors who have been able to institute
mayoral control are those who have been able to garner support from both
the business community and the teachers' union. Moves to weed out corruption and an openness to outsourcing and other market approaches have
bolstered business support. The ability to negotiate long-term contracts with
the teachers' unions and efforts to strike a balance between centralized reforms and professional discretion have further gained, over time, teachers'
support for mayoral control. This is significant, given both the history of
labor unrest in city schools and that mayors depend, in large part, on teachers to produce improvements in student performance.

The cases also provide, however, some points of caution. Though business and teachers' groups have come to support mayoral control in many
cities, other community groups have remained suspicious if not resistant to
mayoral control. This resistance often falls along racial lines. Minority residents in inner-city neighborhoods may see mayoral reform as an attempt
to implement corporate management and cost savings. Though we have not
explored these tensions here, the cases point to the importance of building
coalitions across racial and ethnic communities, as well as among the city's
business and labor leaders, and addressing the needs of highly disadvantaged
groups within the city.

Third, the cases show that mayoral control can stimulate policy inno-
vation. Strong accountability agendas have been the hallmark of mayoral
control in many of the cities discussed above. Whether this necessarily follows from mayoral control or reflects the current policy environment,
many of the mayors who have gained authority to appoint school board
members have instituted policies that hold schools and students accountable for student outcomes. At the same time, the cases also show that
mayoral control has resulted in efforts to bring the schools together with
other city services to expand programs and provide more options for students and families. Mayoral control has further opened schools to more
controversial market approaches and restructuring, including outsourcing.
Though these approaches, like Philadelphia's move to open the district up
to EMOs, have produced mixed results, they reflect an openness to inno-
vation that characterizes many of the districts in which mayoral control
has persisted.

This chapter has described the political and policy context in which mayoral control has been enacted across a range of cities. It provides a picture
of how mayoral control has emerged and evolved as an educational reform
effort in a range of cities. In the chapters that follow, we examine the consequences of mayoral control for a range of factors, focusing on student out-

comes. The new-style education mayors have devoted significant political capital to efforts to raise student achievement, calling, as Boston's Mayor Menino declared, for voters to judge them by the success of their city's schools. We turn now to examine this record.

CHAPTER THREE

Evaluating the Effects of Mayoral Control

MAYOR-LED INTEGRATED GOVERNANCE OF URBAN SCHOOL districts is a policy reform aimed at many, multilevel systemic effects. Given such a diverse set of outcomes that mayors may affect, how can we properly evaluate their impact? How can we tell if mayors are making a difference?

There are many ways to evaluate and analyze the rise of mayor-led integrated governance. In this book, we employ a mixed-methods approach. Our quantitative analysis focuses primarily on achievement, financial, and staffing outcome variables that are measurable across districts. When such measures are not readily available, most notably in the high school context, we turn to qualitative case study analysis to draw inferences about the effects of mayoral control. There we draw on classroom observations and interviews in order to examine the complexity of organization dynamics and instructional practices. The detailed qualitative data collection methods will be provided in chapter six.

Our approach, which emphasizes governance–achievement links, distinguishes us from other studies of mayoral control.[1] Methodologically, these previous studies have primarily been small-N case studies, relying on interviews, surveys, and document analysis. Using this methodology, it is difficult to link governance changes to changes in student achievement and financial or management outcomes at a systematic level. The same problem of inference arises in single district studies, even when those studies are carefully executed. In 2003, for instance, the *Journal of Education for Students Placed at Risk* ran an entire issue on the city–state partnership in Baltimore. Though we learn much about Baltimore, we are left with questions about the generalizability of the findings.[2] For instance, is Baltimore's experience the rule or the exception? The only way to know is to consider Baltimore relative to a large number of other similar cities. In this study, we attempt to do just that.

We have designed an analytic approach to complement existing research by adding a new quantitative, empirical assessment to existing case studies. The hallmark of our analysis is moving beyond district-level summary statistics to conduct a more systematic intra- and interdistrict analysis. This chapter discusses the five steps we have taken to develop a rigorous study that will be able to assess the benefits and drawbacks of mayors leading urban school systems. Those five steps are (1) choosing a sample of districts to study, (2) determining how to measure outcomes in those districts, (3) developing a strategy to measure mayoral control in those districts, (4) allowing the model to consider alternative explanations, and (5) addressing criticisms of the empirical approach.

SAMPLE SELECTION

As emphasized by King, Keohane, and Verba (1994) in *Designing Social Inquiry*, the goal of social science research is inference. In our case, we want to make inferences about the impact of new-style mayor-led integrated governance in large cities, *relative to the old style of elected school boards* that would have been operating in its place. Because we are analyzing systemwide governance arrangements, randomized field trials are not an available or appropriate research approach. Given that random assignment is not an option, our methodological challenge is to develop a purposeful sample that will allow us to generalize to the population of interest.

In determining the population of interest, we can narrow our focus by recognizing that the first wave of mayor-led integrated governance has not provided a policy prescription designed for all U.S. cities. As we discuss in chapter nine, there may be an expansion of mayoral leadership in the coming decades to small and midsized cities in both suburban and rural areas. But to date the instances of mayoral control have been in large, urban districts. Mayoral leadership has also emerged in places where school district boundaries are coterminous with city government boundaries. This means that multiple school districts are not overlapping in the same city, and that multiple cities are not sending students to the same school district.

It is not a surprise that large, urban school districts have been the first to turn to mayoral leadership as an education reform policy. The political economy of large school districts tends to perpetuate the problems of fragmentary leadership, group competition for "private regarding" benefits, ineffective use of resources, declining public confidence, and persistently low academic performance. Integrated governance is designed to address these challenges by clarifying accountability and building the capacity for more effective delivery of schooling services. With this in mind, we took the following steps toward developing a purposeful sample of all such districts in the United States.

Decision Rules for a Sample of 104 School Districts

Using data from the National Center for Education Statistics' Common Core of Data (CCD), and a series of decision rules, we identified districts in the nation that (1) are not a component of a supervisory union, (2) primarily serve a central city of a Metropolitan Core-Based Statistical Area, (3) have at least forty schools, (4) receive at least 75 percent of their students from a principal city, and (5) send at least 75 percent of their city's public school students to the same school district.

The first three decision rules restrict our analysis to large districts serving big population centers. Supervisory unions typically provide services for groups of small districts or schools. Vermont is the state that chiefly uses supervisory unions, which are run by superintendents and extend over several nearby towns. Because these supervisory unions serve smaller areas and cut across a number of different political boundaries, they are distinct from those large, urban districts that have been the focus of the first wave of mayor-led reform.

To be sure, a new round of mayor-led governance may be emerging in midsize districts that we do not evaluate in this study. Some small and medium-sized cities now have mayor-appointed school boards. Trenton and Harrisburg—each considerably smaller than the rest of the mayoral control cities—are not included in our sample. The application of mayoral control in small- and medium-sized cities may be a policy gaining prominence in the next wave of reform, and in our conclusion in chapter nine we offer lessons that midsize districts may learn from our study of big city mayors. There can be, of course, some debate as to how "large" a city must be to be included in the sample. When looking at the size of school districts in the United States, we used New Haven (with forty-eight schools) as a point of reference. We established a floor at forty schools, to produce a sample of urban districts that are at least the size of New Haven. New Haven has the added benefit of being a central city in the study of urban politics.[3]

The last two decision rules are designed to address the requirement of a coterminous city/district boundary. As discussed in the first two chapters, mayor-appointed school boards are not an appropriate policy reform when the boundaries of the school district vary significantly from those of the mayor's city. To briefly summarize, this disconnect between district and city can arise in one of two ways. First, a single city may be served by multiple school districts. Dallas and Indianapolis are examples of this situation.

Second, a single school district may serve students coming from multiple cities. This is more common, as large city districts may also serve some smaller, surrounding municipalities. When the percentage of students in the district gets too small, the mayor may have less influence because the district will be listening to officials in those other municipalities as well. We chose 75 percent for each of these decision rules because it is generally accepted as a high, supermajority bar. Ratification by three-fourths of the states, for example, is required to amend the U.S. Constitution.

Implementing Decision Rules

We put our decision rules into action using the 2002–3 CCD, district-level database. In table 3.1, we present the number of school districts remaining in our sample after each decision rule was implemented. As part of the baseline filtering process, we excluded "districts" that were actually independent charter schools. Some states assign a unique National Center for Education Statistics

Table 3.1   Identifying Districts for Analysis

Rule	No. of Districts Remaining[a]
Baseline (no rules implemented)	16,416
Rule 1. Local school district that is not part of a supervisory union[b]	12,827
Rule 2. Principally serves the central city of a CBSA[c]	735
Rule 3. There are at least 40 schools in the district	137
Rule 4. School district must receive at least 75% of its students from the major city that it serves	125
Rule 5. City must send at least 75% of its students to the same school district	104
Final size of purposeful sample	*104 districts*

[a] This is the number of noncharter-school-only districts. Because some states treat charter schools as independent school districts, there are 1,345 charter schools included in the 2002–3 Common Core of Data district-level file. These were excluded as a preliminary matter for sample selection.
[b] Supervisory unions typically provide services for groups of small districts. Vermont is the state that chiefly uses supervisory unions, which are run by superintendents and extend over several nearby towns.
[c] CBSA = Metropolitan Core Based Statistical Area.

district classification to their charter schools. Because we excluded these charter districts, and because charter school achievement data were missing from some of the state-level data files, we excluded charter school achievement from all achievement analysis. The CCD district-level data set includes a variable named "TYPE," which designates whether a school district is a "local school district that is not a component of a supervisory union." Filtering on the TYPE variable left us with 12,827 districts.[4] The CCD file also includes a variable named "MSC," which is the NCES [National Center for Education Statistics] classification of "the agency's service area relative to a Metropolitan Statistical Area [MSA]." When we limited our sample to those school districts that "primarily serve a central city of an MSA," our sample size narrowed down to 735.[5]

We crafted Rule 3 in an effort to focus our attention on the largest school districts in the nation. Though mayoral involvement may also be beneficial in smaller districts, the first wave of mayor-appointed school boards has emerged most frequently in the context of large urban districts. We limited our sample to districts with at least 40 schools, as recorded in the CCD database for 2002–3. This reduced the sample to 139.

To operationalize Rules 4 and 5, we first had to take some preliminary steps, requiring use of an additional CCD database: the Public Elementary/ Secondary School Universe Survey Data. We started with a data set of every school in the 137 districts remaining after Rule 3 was implemented. Using these school-level data, we noted the city where the school was located, and we compared that with the district to which the school was assigned. Aggregating up from these school-level data for each district, and then for each city, we were able to construct two measures.[6]

First, we generated the percentage of the school district's students who come from the central city, for example, the percentage of Richmond County students from the City of Augusta. Second, we calculated the percentage of the city's students who attend the major district, for example, the percentage of Phoenix students in the Paradise Valley Unified School District. In the vast majority of cases, these two measures were identical. Every public school student in a school in the city of Chicago, for instance, is assigned to the Chicago Public Schools. But in some cases, as we noted in the first two chapters, there is a disconnect between city and district. Two problems arise: (1) Either the city is served by more than one district or (2) the district serves more than one city. We have discussed why, in these situations, the model of mayor-appointed school boards does not seem as applicable. In setting up our sample of comparison districts, we dropped school districts and cities that exhibited significant types of one of these two problems.[7]

With regard to districts taking in more than just the students from the major city, we stipulated that districts must have at least 75 percent of their students coming from the major city. The rationale here is that the percentage of students from the major city must be large enough to make the mayor's voice in that district a powerful one. If the mayor's city accounts for only 50 percent of the district's students, he or she is less likely to be able to push through reforms. With regard to cities sending their students to more than one district, the districts that we excluded were situated in areas where school districts cut across cities. This type of arrangement does not readily facilitate mayor-appointed school boards.

When we implemented these final two rules, we cut 22 districts, leaving us with a final sample size of 104 school districts.[8] When we talk of our "sample districts," we are referring to these districts. For those readers interested in the demographic data for each individual district, the data are available for download from the online supplement to the book. The sample is nationally representative, covering forty states and the District of Columbia. In the online supplement, we also include details of the distribution, by state, of the districts in our analytic sample.

MEASURING OUTCOMES

Once a sample has been chosen, an equally important and challenging question arises: What outcomes are we concerned about, and how can we measure them? Mayor-led integrated governance is designed to bring about change along many dimensions. We can think of these as broadly falling into four categories:

1. productivity (for example, student achievement)
2. management and governance (for example, financial and organization operations)
3. human capital (for example, characteristics of teachers and leadership)
4. building public confidence (for example, public opinion and awareness about the school district)

Because of its primacy, we will devote the rest of this chapter to discussing only the first category: student achievement outcomes. We will discuss management, governance, and human capital outcomes in chapter seven. We will discuss public confidence outcomes in chapter eight.

Measuring Student Achievement

As Diane Ravitch (2005) has observed, there are "50 states, 50 standards, 50 tests" across the country. Without a uniform testing system, the fifty-state, fifty-test reality leaves us with three distinct methodological challenges: (1) It is easiest to look only at a single district, but what generalized conclusions can we draw from single-district studies? (2) If we want to examine districts in multiple states, how can we collect such a diverse set of student achievement measures? (3) How can comparisons be made across different measures to isolate the effects of mayor-led integrated governance?

Tracking Achievement in a Single District

The most straightforward and most widely used method for evaluating a school district's student achievement is simply asking: How is the district doing year to year? When readers see a headline such as "District Improves Reading Performance" or "District Lagging in Math Achievement," most local newspaper articles will be looking at how this year's district student achievement scores compare with last year's. This approach of looking at achievement in a single district is readily accessible and appropriate in many situations. Some of our earliest studies employed such an approach (Wong and Shen 2001).

But as integrated governance becomes a major urban reform strategy at the national level, more rigorous evaluation of mayoral control is called for. The argument for moving beyond district achievement trend lines goes back to our discussion of inference and scientific method. Our goal here is to evaluate the effects of mayoral control, *relative to the governance structure that would have been in place otherwise.* To make this evaluation, we must have variation on the independent variable of interest, "urban education governance." Choosing only one district, or selecting only districts that have undergone mayoral control, is selecting on the independent variable and makes it difficult to draw inferences about the effects of the policy instrument.

We therefore move now to the national sample we have constructed. In presenting these findings, we aggregate up from our school-level data to arrive at district means. This aggregation process involves two steps, with the two-step process run independently for reading and mathematics. First, for each school in the database, we look to see if more than one grade was tested. If so, we average across all grades in the school to arrive at a "school average" for reading (and separately for math). Because some grades have more students than others, we weight the school average by grade enrollment. If twenty sixth graders and eighty fourth graders are tested in a school, the school's average will be weighted 80 percent to the fourth grade achievement score, and 20 percent to sixth grade. Once we obtain school averages, we then calculate district averages by averaging across schools. To account for the fact that some schools have larger enrollments than others, we weight our averages by school enrollment.

The achievement data support the observation that the majority of our nation's large, urban school districts are underperforming (often severely) relative to state averages. We make available for download in our online supplement the mathematics and reading achievement scores for all our sample districts, for 1999 to 2003. Because year-to-year fluctuations in test scores may be the result of measurement error, we cannot know for sure which trends over time are spurious without more detailed analysis (Kane, Staiger, and Geppert 2002). Raw scores on state achievement tests cannot be compared across districts residing in different states. Because cross-district comparison is needed to compare mayor-appointed school boards with similar districts that are using a traditional governance scheme, we have to develop an analytical approach that will move beyond flat district averages.

Collecting Achievement Data across Many States

Collecting achievement data for even one state over a five-year period can be a daunting task. Recognizing the importance and difficulty of collecting these data, the U.S. Department of Education funded the construction of the National Longitudinal School-Level State Assessment Score Database (NLSLSASD). The NLSLSASD is maintained by the American Institutes for Research, and during the period of our study, it included school-level data for the fifty states, roughly from 1999 to 2003. Some states did not have achievement data available in particular years, but even given some missing data, the database is the single most complete record of school-level student achievement during this period.[9]

In this study, we make extensive use of the NLSLSASD data, supplemented by data provided by state departments of education when the NLSLSASD data were missing. Data from the NLSLSASD are provided state by state. The online supplement includes the details of these achievement data, as used in the analysis.

Standardizing Achievement Data across School Districts

At the center of our analysis are a series of statistical models that attempt to isolate the marginal effect of mayor-led integrated governance on district student achievement. To carry out this analysis, we had to construct a dependent achievement outcome variable that is comparable across districts. As discussed by Robert Yin and his colleagues, this is difficult when trying to compare districts that employ different standardized tests (Yin, Schmidt, and Besag 2006). Because the tests are not uniform, it is not appropriate to simply compare across states. We cannot, for instance, say that a Boston school with 75 percent of its student proficient on the Massachusetts Comprehensive Assessment System (MCAS) is performing at the same level as a Saint Louis school with 75 percent of its student proficient on the Missouri

Assessment Program. Comparisons become even more difficult when states choose to report different measures (e.g., percentile ranks, percent passing).

The problem is analogous to finding a common language to allow people of different countries to speak with one another. Our "universal language" solution in this case is the statistical language of "standard deviations." The process of translating each state's test into standard deviations is called standardization, a statistical method used to compare two (or more) scores that have been measured using different scales. The resulting standardized measures allow us to see how many "standard deviations" each district in the country is above or below its own state mean. This measure of standard deviations is called a "Z-score." We can compare any two (or more) districts with each other by comparing their Z-scores. Statistically, we calculate a standardized "Z-score" that is defined as:

$$Z = \frac{X - \mu}{\sigma} \qquad\qquad (3.1)$$

where X is the district's average performance, μ is the mean state performance, and σ is the standard deviation within the population of all districts in the state. The resulting Z-scores have a mean of 0 and a standard deviation of 1, and they are measured in "standard deviations." A Z-score of positive 1.5 for a district means that the district is achieving at 1.5 standard deviations above the state mean. A Z-score of –0.6 for a district means that the district is achieving at .6 standard deviations below the state mean.

The standardization approach has been used in a number of other situations involving education data being compared across different measures. A Brookings Institution study, for instance, utilized Z-scores when comparing the performance of charter schools across different states. Z-scores have also been used to adjust for different scales on spelling and reading tests. An Idaho study used the approach when it was felt that the student database they were working with was not comparable as raw scores (Loveless 2003; Allinder et al. 1992; Ravitz, Mergendoller, and Rush 2002).

One concern about using Z-scores pertains to the shape of the underlying distribution of achievement scores. Z-scores are only useful statistics when the underlying distribution is roughly normal, that is, the distribution is a bell-shaped curve. Our investigation of the data suggests to us that indeed the distribution is roughly normal. This conforms to our common sense, that there are some exceptional districts, some doing very poorly, and most in the middle.

An acknowledged problem of using the standardized measure is that the results are not as easily understood (Campbell 1994). To use an example that may help to make Z-scores more concrete, consider a family that is going to move to either Milwaukee or Peoria, Illinois. The family's members want to compare the average performance of the two school districts in 2003, but when they gather information, they are not sure how to make the comparison. They see that Peoria is reporting that 58.85 percent of its students are proficient or above scores on the Illinois Standards Achievement Test, while Milwaukee is reporting that 60.69 percent of its students are proficient or above on the Wisconsin Knowledge and Concepts Examinations. How could we help this family compare the two districts?

If we know the 2003 state mean and standard deviation for Illinois and Wisconsin, we can perform the following two calculations. First, for Illinois, we find out that the state mean is 66.6, with standard deviation 16.3. Then, for Wisconsin, we find out that the state mean is 83.06, with standard deviation 9.57. Taking these numbers, we can calculate two Z-scores for the family:

$$\text{Z-score}_{PEORIA} = (58.85 - 66.58) / 16.30 = -.473 \qquad (3.2)$$

$$\text{Z-score}_{MILWAUKEE} = (60.69 - 83.06) / 9.57 = -2.337 \qquad (3.3)$$

With these two Z-scores, the family is now in a much stronger position to make an informed decision. Z-score_{PEORIA} tells the family that Peoria is performing about −.5 standard deviations below the Illinois mean of 66.6 percent. $\text{Z-score}_{MILWAUKEE}$ tells them that Milwaukee is performing about 2.4 standard deviations below the Wisconsin mean of 83.1 percent.

Our process of standardization can best be understood as two, related sets of comparisons that are being made. First, we compare each of our sample districts with other districts in the same state. Utilizing the mean and standard deviation within the state, we are able to calculate Z-scores that represent "the number of standard deviations District A is above/below the mean in State 1." It is important to recognize that in this first round, comparisons are only being made on the *same scores* on the *same achievement test*. We are comparing Boston's percent proficient on the MCAS with other Massachusetts districts' percent proficient on the MCAS. We are comparing Detroit's percent proficient on the Michigan Educational Assessment Program (MEAP) with other Michigan districts' percent proficient on the MEAP. We never compare MEAP with MCAS or with any other state's test. This method, which requires in-state comparisons, forced us to drop three districts from the analysis of standardized achievement. In Washington, Z-scores cannot be calculated because there is only one school district serving the entire District of Columbia. Thus, Washington was dropped from the analysis. Lincoln was dropped because the evaluations used in Nebraska are not meant to be compared across districts. Finally, Des Moines was dropped due to a lack of available data.

An additional concern about Z-scores and comparing across states arises, however, when we recognize that even when using the same test, there are variations in state averages and standard deviations. To illustrate this problem, consider the 2002 reading Z-score calculation for three cities: Huntsville, Salt Lake City, and Sioux Falls. In each of these city's states, our achievement measure was the district's average Scholastic Aptitude Test (SAT) percentile. In Alabama, the average was taken of grades three through eight; in South Dakota, for grades four and eight; and in Utah, for grades three, five, and eight. There is variation in the mean SAT percentile across the three states. Alabama's mean is 51.8, South Dakota's is 65.3, and Salt Lake City's is 51.9. This means, in essence, that the districts in each of these states are being held to a different standard. Sioux Falls, for example, is being held to the South Dakota average of the 65th percentile, while Salt Lake City is being held to the Utah average of 51.9. The calculations are carried out in this way:

$$\text{Z-score}_{\text{HUNTSVILLE}} = (57.26 - 51.75) / 9.73 = .566 \qquad (3.4)$$

$$\text{Z-score}_{\text{SIOUXFALLS}} = (64.52 - 65.27) / 8.15 = -.092 \qquad (3.5)$$

$$\text{Z-score}_{\text{SALTLAKECITY}} = (40.38 - 51.93) / 6.64 = -1.74 \qquad (3.6)$$

When we make this comparison, we see how a difference in state means affects the Z-score. Even though Sioux Falls had a higher SAT percentile than Huntsville, Alabama in 2002 elementary reading, the Z-score for Sioux Falls is lower than Huntsville's. Despite this challenge, there are two justifications for our Z-score approach. The first, which we have emphasized already, is that of necessity. Until and unless national testing programs become more firmly established, it is not possible to find a common metric to measure achievement across states. The second justification is that in practice, achievement in districts is often measured relative to other districts in the state. On state report cards, for instance, comparisons are typically made to state, not national, averages.

After this first round of statistical analysis produces standardized Z-scores, those Z-scores become our dependent variable in a series of regression models. In this second round of comparisons, we are comparing one district's Z-score with another district's Z-score. Because everything is measured in standard deviations, we now have the common metric we need. Although not perfect, we believe it is the best available measure for cross-district comparison.

QUANTIFYING MAYORAL CONTROL

Quantifying mayoral control is essential for conducting the type of cross-district regression analysis we carry out in this study. The ideal measure for our study would be an accurate measure of the actual amount of power and influence the mayor has on the city school system. Such a measure, however, cannot be readily constructed. The "power literature" in political science and sociology, which has since faded from view, struggled with a similar dilemma. To solve the problem, we use "formal, legal authority" as a proxy for "actual" or "real" power/authority. The online supplement includes references to all the legal statutes we used to code these formal powers.

We know that there may be some slippage between formal versus actual power. Just because a mayor is given the institutional mechanisms to take a greater role in governing the schools, it does not necessarily follow that he or she will in fact become a new-style education mayor. In examining the case of Baltimore, James Cibulka calls attention to differences among mayoral aspiration, ambition, attention priority, and style. Mayor Martin O'Malley of Baltimore was less interested in education and gave higher priority to financial solvency. This is in contrast to Chicago's Mayor Richard M. Daley, who integrates education with his overall focus on quality of life.[10]

It should also be acknowledged that our measures of mayoral control focus only on the education domain. We do not have additional measures of power or influence in other policy domains, nor do we have a measure of general control over city budget and finance decisions. We believe that these limitations in measuring influence and power actually make our case more difficult to prove. If it is the case that mayors, even without formal school board appointive power, can exert control over their school system through budgetary or informal mechanisms, then we should not expect to see as much impact associated with formal appointive powers.

Recognizing these limitations, looking at formal powers has several benefits. First, it is a measure that is available for each district. Printed in black-and-white statutes, institutional governance can be readily coded. Second, state legislatures and city residents can directly change formal powers (via charter amendments). From a policy perspective, these are the legal tools available. Third and finally, focusing on formal powers avoids the methodological issues that arise in survey-based measures of influence or power. These issues have been discussed at length within the context of the aforementioned power literature.[11]

Three Dimensions of Mayoral Control of Schools

We have identified three key dimensions in which mayoral control can be institutionalized: the presence of a new-style mayor, formal authority for that mayor to appoint a majority of the school board, and whether the appointive power is legally restricted in any way. Because we are not sure which aspect of mayoral control may be most salient, we consider each aspect independently before summing them up into an index. On the basis of these three dimensions, we create three dichotomous variables. Each variable measures a unique aspect of mayoral control. We use this method—a series of yes/no questions about mayors' formal powers—because it avoids the almost impossible task of somehow specifying a mayor's precise "level of control." For instance, it is not possible to accurately assess whether a mayor has "a lot" or "a little" power. Instead, we try to get at this by thinking about factors that are likely to be highly correlated with mayoral power in the education realm. We consider three factors:

1. *NEW_STYLE*: A dichotomous variable, coded as 1 if the mayor has *adopted a new style of governance*, integrating electoral accountability and school performance. The variable is coded 0 if the school system remains governed within an old-style regime.
2. *MAJORITY*: A dichotomous variable, coded as 1 if the mayor has the power to *appoint a majority* of the school board. The variable is coded 0 if the mayor can appoint zero or any submajority of the board.
3. *FULL*: A dichotomous variable, coded as 1 if the mayor has *full appointment power* for the school board, with no requirement of council, aldermen, or other approval. The variable is coded 0 otherwise.

Because the effectiveness of mayoral control may also depend on the cumulative effect of these powers, we add an additional index variable that sums over the three dimensions above. This index variable, labeled *MAYOR_INDEX*, has a low value of 0 and a high value of 3. We run two sets of models. In Model A, we include the three measures of mayoral control independently. This allows us to test their relative contribution to student achievement and other outcomes. We then run Model B, in which we replace the three individual measures with the composite mayor control index.

Our data set allows us to look over many districts and across multiple years. This means that our unit of observation is not simply the district (as it would be if we had only data from one year), but the "district-year." The values of the mayoral control variables change, over time, within the same district. In New York, for example, the value of the *MAJORITY* variable is 0 for 1999 to 2001, and 1 for 2002 and 2003. Similar changes are seen when a governance shift is made.

An alternative to these measurements would be to measure the percentage of school board seats appointed by the mayor. In an earlier study, we used this measure of mayoral control. We use a different measure here, however, because the previous measure took into account only one dimension of mayoral control. It did not consider, for instance, if there were additional checks on the mayoral appointment power. We now include this dimension with our *FULL* appointment power variable. Further, it is not clear that the phenomenon we want to capture is the percentage of seats appointed. What we want to get at is the mayor's ability to direct policy, and unless the mayor has a majority of the board, adding an additional appointed seat should not be expected to significantly change policy outcomes.[12]

Institutions, Timing, and Lag Effects

Policy and political variation across the group of school districts that we have labeled "new style" serves as a reminder that institutional change may not necessarily be tied to change in mayors' personal priorities or governing styles. Along the gradation of partial to complete mayoral control, we cannot be entirely sure how the formal role of the appointed school board matches up to its actual role. At issue is the question of institutional checks and balances. Is the appointed board simply rubber stamping the mayor's requests, or (even if appointed) does it voice opposition? Do formal measures, such as requiring approval of the budget by the City Council, really provide a check against mayoral power? From a different angle, does giving the mayor formal powers such as hiring the school district chief executive officer actually empower the mayor relative to other interests in the city? These are all important questions, but also questions that we cannot readily introduce into an empirical model. We cannot quantify factors such as "informal influence" or "policy priority" with available data sets. What we can do is address these questions at greater length after conducting our achievement analysis. We pick up this topic again in chapter eight, where we discuss the relationship between changes in institutional governance and building public confidence.

A related question concerns the duration of mayoral control, timing, and possible lag effects. It could be the case that mayors are not able to effectuate changes in the school system until they have been able to establish a new management regime. To the extent that this is true, we would expect to see the effects of mayoral control not in the same year as the reform is implemented but in later years. Although our data constraints affect the extent to which we can evaluate lag effects, we run separate models where we look at one-year and two-year lagged effects. In these models, we are looking at the effect of governance structure in year t on student performance in year $t + 1$

and year $t + 2$. We describe these model specifications in the next two chapters. With more years of data going forward, we may be in a better position to evaluate the long-term effects of mayoral control, beyond a one- or two-year window. Given that our achievement data in this study span only the period 1999–2003, we are not yet able to perform that analysis. In the analysis of finance outcomes, where our data are available for a much longer period, we are able to look at longer lag effects.

A variable that we are not able to measure across all districts is the extent to which the mayoral reform has actually taken root. For instance, have management practices really changed after one year of mayoral involvement? Or how long will it take for mayors to affect teaching and learning in their city's schools? This is related to, but not the same as, the simple duration of the reform. Though a reform is likely to take deeper root the more years it has been in practice, it is not clear that just because a reform has been in place for multiple years it will necessarily have been implemented widely. For instance, a mayor may be in power for three years, but if that mayor makes few systematic changes, the "duration" of the takeover will not accurately represent the low level of systemic implementation of the reform.[13]

ALTERNATIVE EXPLANATIONS

In addition to mayoral control, other district-level factors are likely to have an impact on student achievement. To address each of the following alternative explanations, we develop a quantifiable measure that we enter into our regression equation as a control variable. We present a summary of these measures in table 3.2, and we can think of these alternative explanations as falling into three broad categories: (1) school district characteristics, (2) student background, and (3) governance.

School District Characteristics

Larger districts may have more difficulty in turning around student performance for at least two reasons. First, they simply have more students to teach, and it may take longer for transformative change to ripple through the system. Second, larger districts may be prone to have a larger central office bureaucracy, creating even greater delays in improved teaching and learning. To account for the size of districts, we use the CCD to obtain the enrollment for each district in our sample.

Urban public schools are in competition with the private schools that may attract some of the city's most intelligent students. We therefore construct a

Table 3.2 Measurement of Contributing Factors to Student Achievement in Big-City School Districts

Factor to Be Considered	How We Measured It in Our Analysis
Governance	
Mayoral involvement in education	Three variables (coded as 0 or 1) that measure whether the mayor has (a) adopted a new style of education governance, (b) formal powers to appoint a majority of the school board, and (c) full discretion to appoint. We also combine these three individual factors into an index (0–3) measuring overall mayoral involvement.
Mayor–council form of government	Variable (coded as 0 or 1) noting if the city government has a mayor–council form of government
School board politics	Percent of school board members who are elected in a single-member fashion
School district characteristics	
Size of school district	Student enrollment in school district[a]
Strength of private school market	Percentage of the city's children, age 3–18, who are attending private schools[b]
Financial ties to state	Percentage of school district's education revenue that comes from the state[c]
	Dollars per student spent on instruction, adjusted for inflation and geography
Student background	
Minority representation in student body	Percentage of district students who are Hispanic; percentage who are African American[b]
Special needs population	Percentage of district students who are special education students[b]
Student poverty	Percentage of children living within the school district's boundaries who are identified as living beneath the poverty line[b]

[a]Variable constructed using data from the U.S. Department of Education's Common Core of Data.
[b]Variable constructed using data from the 2000 U.S. Census.
[c]Variable constructed using data from the Annual Survey of Government Finances conducted by the U.S. Bureau of the Census.

measure of the strength of the private school market. Using data from the 2000 Census, we calculate the percentage of the city's children, age three to eighteen years, who are attending private schools.

Local districts often rely heavily on state aid for turning around low-performing schools. To capture this revenue dynamic, we include a measure of the percentage of the district's education revenue that comes from the state. On the expenditure side, we include a measure of per-pupil expenditure on instruction. These revenue and expenditure measures are constructed using data from the Annual Survey of Government Finances conducted by the U.S. Bureau of the Census. This survey gathers data on revenues, expenditures, and debt from more than 15,000 school districts (Census Bureau 2005).

Student Background

In addition to the size of the district, the makeup of the district's student body is likely connected to student performance. Districts serving larger percentages of African American and Hispanic students may see lower overall achievement as they address the racial disparity that continues to exist in American public education (Jencks and Phillips 1998). We use the CCD to calculate the percentage of African American and Hispanic students in each district. Another important control is for the percentage of special education students in the district. The CCD reports, for each district, the number of students in the district who have individualized education plans. Using these data, we created a measure of the percentage of district students who receive special education services.

Since the Coleman Report in 1966 (Coleman et al. 1966), a consistent finding in social science literatures on education has been the strong relationship between family background and student success. Although we do not have information on the background of the actual students tested in our sample, we can use a measure of child poverty as a proxy. In this study, we utilize a measurement of child poverty using data from the 2000 Census School District Demographics System. We measure the percentage of children living within the school district's boundaries who are identified as living beneath the poverty line. This specifically measures child poverty in the school district, not just general poverty in the city. We do not use the related percentage of district students eligible for a reduced-priced or free lunch because the measure was not found to be reliable across time and districts. In its report on the 100 largest school districts, the National Center for Education Statistics itself had difficulty accurately assessing this figure.[14]

Governance

We also look to the fundamental governance arrangement of the city as potentially a contributing factor to education success. The two major governance arrangements in American cities are mayor–council and council–manager. Arguments in favor of council–manager governments are that they allow for professional management of the city, with corruption and patronage politics less likely to emerge. On the other side, it can be argued that without the political power made possible by a mayor–council arrangement, it will be difficult to produce effective citywide reform.

There remains much debate over the relative effectiveness of council–manager versus mayor–council forms of local governance. As related to our study, the relative effectiveness of the form of government is not our primary concern. Instead, the distinction between the council–manager and mayor–council forms is important because mayor–council governments can more readily facilitate mayoral control of schools. Under a council–manager form, a mayor who was given power to appoint the school board would still be subject to council and manager control on the rest of city governmental functions.[15]

Looking at cities with a population of 100,000 or more during the period 1974–85, Wolman, Strate, and Melchoir (1996) find that per capita operating expenditures change when new mayors are elected in mayor–council cities but not in council–manager cities. Baqir (1999) found that a strong mayor system, which gives the mayor some veto power over budgetary decisions, can lead to a curtailment of overspending. Another study by Thompson and Brodsky (1997) took advantage of a natural experiment, in which a city's mayor served first in a government run by a commission voted at large, and then transitioned to a strong mayor–council form of government. Although the mayor's leadership style did not change, perceptions of the mayor did. Though limited to a single city, this adds to the evidence that institutions matter in shaping the behavior and perception of mayors (Wheeland 2002; Baker 2001).

Svara (1987, 1990, 2003) argues that even in council–manager cities, mayors can play an important leadership role. In council–manager cities, Svara (2003, 157) argues that "the mayor leads by empowering others—in particular, the council and the manager—rather than seeking power for himself or herself, and the mayor accomplishes objectives through enhancing the performance of others." In this model, rather than seeking to wrest power away from the council, the mayor must cooperate and work with the council. Although there are ways for mayors to be active in council–manager governments, we believe that theory and the balance of research suggest that council–manager governments are likely to constrain the mayor's ability to enact policy change.

COMPLEXITIES OF URBAN GOVERNANCE

In the field of public administration, a growing body of research suggests that thinking of city governments as either "council–manager" or "mayor–council" may be too simplistic. DeSantis and Renner (2002), utilizing survey data gathered by the International City/County Management Association, find that there are many distinct governance subcategories. Within the council–manager group, they find four subcategories: classic council–manager, council–manager with an at-large mayor, council–manager with an empowered mayor, and unclassified council–manager. Similarly, within the umbrella of mayor–council, they identify four subgroups: "strong" mayor with chief administrative officer (CAO), "strong" mayor without CAO, "weak" mayor with CAO, and weak mayor without CAO.[16]

With so many cross-cutting dimensions identified, DeSantis and Renner (2002, 102) conclude that "contemporary city governments are more complicated than the traditional categories suggest." This is consistent with a growing body of research finding that, over time, mayor–council cities begin to adopt features of council–manager governments, and vice versa (Frederickson and Johnson 2001; Svara 2001).

This insight into the complexities of urban governance has two implications for our analysis of mayor-appointed school boards. First, it serves as a caution that structural dynamics outside our models may be interacting with our independent variables. Although we introduce measures to capture the basic council–manager versus mayor–council distinction, we do not have more nuanced measures that would respond to the more complicated categories laid out by DeSantis and Renner. Second, the move toward "adapted cities" paints a picture of dynamic cities whose governance arrangements are malleable. If cities are already changing governance along other dimensions, reconfiguring governance of the school district may be more readily accepted.

Indeed, the experience of Dallas in 2004 and 2005 shows that these governance discussions are being related to educational outcomes. In 2004, the *Dallas Morning News*, working with analysts from Booz Allen, produced a report titled "Dallas at the Tipping Point: A Road Map for Renewal." The report chastised the Dallas city government for not having closer ties to the school district:

> Few indicators better predict a city's vitality than the performance of its public schools. Student achievement today creates a skilled workforce tomorrow. It attracts business, nurtures wealth and ensures a city's prosperity. So where does that leave Dallas? Not in the game. Even as many big cities move aggressively to bolster public education, City Hall's relationship with Dallas' largest school district remains informal at best.

That arm's-length distance can't continue if Dallas hopes to remain vibrant.[17]

In May 2005, Dallas voters decided against giving their city a strong-mayor form of government. Ennis (2005) opined that this was a great missed opportunity, which could lead to an "incipient municipal meltdown." Whether or not Ennis is correct in his evaluation, the important point here is that governance arrangements are up for public debate, and city schools are a big part of that debate.

To capture these additional governance dimensions, we create a dichotomous variable to measure whether or not a city is under the mayor–council form of government. On the basis of our discussion in chapter 2, we include a measure of the percentage of school board members who are elected from single-member districts. Single-member elections are those where school board members are elected by a subsection of the city, not the city as a whole. This measure is meant to capture the extent to which individual board members may view the success of their own subdistrict as more important than overall district improvement.

METHODOLOGICAL CHALLENGES

Our approach, with its emphasis on cross-district quantitative analysis, is distinct in the field. We believe this quantitative analysis is complementary to the existing scholarship we discussed in the first two chapters. We recognize, however, that our approach has limitations. In this section, we discuss those limitations and our strategies for addressing them.

Distinction from Qualitative Case Studies

Those who prefer detailed case study methodology may find our approach oversimplified. Although we do include case study evidence in chapter six to help explain our analysis in chapters four and five, the bulk of our analysis is quantitative and statistical. Unlike the intensive case study approach, which emphasizes myriad contextual factors, our model is more streamlined: How is the input of mayor-appointed school boards related to the outputs of student achievement, district finances, and human capital reorganization? This does not mean that we believe urban education politics is this "clean." We have acknowledged elsewhere how multilayered and complex it can be. But in the quantitative analysis in this book, we are not trying to *describe* what urban education looks like. We are trying to *predict*, based on the data we have available, what would happen if a school district moved from an elected to an appointed school board.

Also differentiating our study from most others is our longitudinal dimension. It is not just that we are looking at the population of all large, urban, coterminous districts—we are looking at those districts over time. Unless repeat interviews are conducted regularly, the evidence used in case studies remains fixed in time. Our framework, in contrast, is capable of taking on new data, and it is flexible enough to allow these new data to adjust or refine findings. Indeed, we hope to revisit this analysis as new rounds of data become available.

Overreliance on Standardized Test Scores

A challenge can be made to our reliance on only one set of standardized test scores. We do not have available multiple assessment tools from each district, and this is a cause of concern for some. Drawing on the recommendations of a report for the National Association of Secondary School Principals, we agree that "we must rely on more than one source of data to substantiate that student performance, in the overall sense, is improving" (Dusseau, Hurst, and Bitter 2003).

Others have suggested alternative analytic strategies. Clarence Stone, for instance, proposes that we use a measure of "educational effort." Stone and his colleagues (2001, 124–28) were concerned that standardized test scores tended to be "one-dimensional indicators" and that "casual links are loose and unmapped between what schools do and what children know." Educational effort was determined by asking survey respondents to rate the effort of their cities as "(1) doing everything that can be done, (2) doing fairly well, (3) falling short of what we could be doing, or (4) not doing well at all." Responses were then compared across cities.[18]

We do not believe that simply asking the same question to respondents in different cities necessarily produces results that are more comparable than the standardized test scores that we use. Since City A and City B have different histories, a respondent in City A may think the current regime is "doing fairly well" because they've only seen poor effort in the past, while a respondent in City B may be used to a high bar and would respond that results are "falling short." These are the necessary limitations of survey work, and we do not call into question the survey methods. We simply point out that our approach of using standardized test scores is not necessarily less consistent than this approach.

Beyond methodology, however, there is a more fundamental difference in approaches. In defense of the case study approach, Stone and his colleagues (2001, 257) write that "if the focus of the study is the *conjunction* of factors, . . . then the analysis can never produce a neat formula of explanation to employ universally." Precisely because multiple factors are likely to affect school district performance, we want to specify an empirical model that will allow us to consider multiple factors at once. We want to know about the relative magnitude of factors. This allows us to address questions such as: If mayoral control matters, how much? How much more or less do other factors matter for particular outcomes? Our empirical models allow us to answer these types of questions in ways that case studies cannot.

This does not mean that our data could not be improved. Cuban and Usdan (2003) point to a type of data to which we, too, would like to have access: data from each district that track individual students (e.g., as is done in systems like those in Texas).[19] Our data do not allow us to calculate individual student gains. We have repeat observations of a single grade at a school (e.g., third grade reading), but we cannot track the same cohort of students as they progress through a school.

Not Enough High School Data

The NLSLSASD does not include as much high school data as it does elementary school data. This limits the inferences we can make about mayoral control on the high school level. Further, we are limited in the number of measures we have available for measuring "success" in the upper grades. In the 2005 mayoral race, the challenger to sitting Mayor Michael Bloomberg argued that the most important measure of success was high school graduation, on the premise that it would be most strongly linked to lifetime success. In our study, it might be argued that we do not pay enough attention to this, and other related high school measures such as enrollment in advanced placement classes and high school dropout rates.

Here, our response is that we would like to have those indicators available across all 104 districts, but unfortunately comparable data do not exist. The lack of high school data, in particular high school dropout and graduation rate data, is not unique to this study. In fact, the problem is so prevalent that it is currently a high-priority item for the National Governors' Association. In February 2005, the association hosted the National Education Summit on High Schools. At that summit, Bill Gates identified this goal related to measuring high school improvement:

> Publish the data that measures our progress toward that goal. The focus on measuring success in the past few years has been important—it has helped us realize the extent of the problem. But we need to know more: What percentage of students are dropping out? What percentage are graduating? What percentage are going on to college? And we need this data broken down by race and income. The idea of tracking low-income and minority kids into dead-end courses is so offensive to our sense of

equal opportunity that the only way the practice can survive, is if we hide it. That's why we need to expose it. If we are forced to confront this injustice, I believe we will end it. (Gates 2005)

We echo Gates's call for reliable high school dropout data, comparable across districts and states. The U.S. Department of Education has studied this data problem as well, and it has developed *A Recommended Approach to Providing High School Dropout and Completion Rates at the State Level.*[20] Until these and other recommendations are implemented, we are not able to include it in our analysis in this study.

NORMATIVE IMPLICATIONS OF AN EMPIRICAL APPROACH

Scholars have noted that an empirical analysis of education policy can carry with it normative implications.[21] Related to the accountability imperative we described in chapter 1, our normative approach is one that gives center stage to the practical decisions that city leaders will have to make regarding their school systems. As researchers, we believe it is our role to facilitate that decision-making process by providing tangible policy recommendations, grounded in empirical evidence. Throughout the book, we make attempts to clarify and nuance our analyses. We are clear, for instance, that mayor-appointed school boards will not completely turn around a school district. But clarifying limitations about a policy reform does not necessarily mean that the "evidence remains out." Although there is much evidence still to be gathered, we believe that enough evidence is in to draw conclusions about mayor-appointed school boards.

We believe that student achievement on standardized test scores, though not the only measure of school district performance, is an important and effective measure of school performance. Still, we acknowledge the statistical uncertainty that accompanies our estimates and we do not blindly follow test scores as the only means of assessment.

We recognize that education and psychology professionals have argued that students should be evaluated on more than just their test scores. Others have raised concerns that focusing solely on test scores can create perverse incentives for schools and teachers. In this analysis, we use standardized test scores as a proxy for school district performance. This does not mean, however, that if other measures were developed and made available across all districts that they should not be taken into account in the future (American Educational Research Association, American Psychological Association, and National Council on Measurement in Education 1999; Koretz 2002).

In chapter six, we respond to concerns that there is teaching to the test, and that test scores are poor predictors of future performance. We complement our quantitative analysis with a multilevel analysis of how the integrated governance approach affects teaching and learning in low-performing schools. We address macro–micro linkages between city and district governance arrangements and changes in classroom practice by focusing on how principals and teachers respond to the accountability agenda initiated after the mayoral takeover.

CHAPTER FOUR

Integrated Governance as a Strategy to Improve School Performance

IN TODAY'S CLIMATE OF OUTCOME-BASED PERFORMANCE accountability, one question stands out above the rest: Does mayoral control improve student performance? Student achievement is the first thing people think of when they consider education reform. And when standardized test scores are reported each year, they draw citywide interest. In the summer of 2005, for example, upon release of recent New York City test scores, the City Council questioned whether the test score gains claimed by the mayor's office were in fact the result of the governance change. As the chairwoman of the City Council's Education Committee put it, "It's very important that before we celebrate, we understand exactly what kind of phenomena we're talking about" (Saulny 2005). We are in agreement that before integrated governance is widely adopted, we must have a better understanding of the relationship between mayoral control and student performance. In this chapter, we address the issue head-on.

We argue in this chapter that when mayoral control is examined from a cross-district and multiyear perspective, we see that mayors can make a significant, positive difference in raising the achievement levels of students in their cities. We find that an education mayor can bring about positive change of about a 0.1 standard deviation in elementary reading and math. We also find that giving the mayor the power to appoint a majority of the school board is associated with a 0.2 standard deviation increase in high school reading and mathematics. Though other demographic factors continue to play a large role in determining student success, governance arrangements clearly matter.

President Bill Clinton once said that "politics is not about miracles; it's about direction" (Meyer 1999, 54). Similarly, our analysis in this chapter suggests that mayoral control is not about miracles but about positive, significant movement amid a barrage of forces that for many years have prevented urban school districts from prospering. Though mayor-controlled districts still rank toward the bottom of their states in achievement levels, mayors may be laying the groundwork for a long-run push back to the top.

On what evidence do we base these hopes? We said in the previous chapter that it is not enough to simply look at district performance from one year to the next and make conclusions about whether mayors are effective educational leaders. More complex statistical procedures are needed to account for the many other factors that may be influencing the change in student achievement levels. We spend the first part of this chapter introducing the complexities of the statistical procedures we use. With the methods introduced, we spend the remainder of the chapter presenting the evidence for our case. By examining the statistical relationship between elementary reading and mathematics achievement, as well as high school performance, we find support for our contention that mayors can indeed improve student performance.

STATISTICAL METHODS

In this section, we present the details of our analytical approach. We discuss how our theories about mayors and their likely paths of influence can be evaluated using statistical procedures. (For readers interested in the more technical details of the analysis, we have provided a technical appendix at the end of the book.)

How Does Mayoral Control Affect Achievement?

The first step in setting up a proper evaluation of mayors and educational outcomes is to ask exactly how mayors are likely to affect student performance. It might be helpful here to think about what mayors are *not* doing. Mayors are not jumping into the classroom, choosing the books for students to read, or poring over school budgets to see if more money should be spent on supplies. Mayors are operating at a *systemwide* level. In what we describe elsewhere as a politics of partnership, mayors are providing a political shield for the school district central office to operate with less partisanship influencing decisions. Because they operate at districtwide levels, we need to think about outcomes at the district level. We also need to recognize that mayoral influence may not be immediate. Unlike a new superstar teacher who may walk into a classroom and raise student achievement in a month, mayor-led reforms are designed to be long term and systemic. Because of this long-term vision, our analysis must be longitudinal as well as carried out at the district level.

Using statistical language, we can say that our unit of observation in this analysis is the "district-year" and that we have "panel data." This means that we look year to year at districtwide performance. We analyze student achievement over the period 1999–2003 in each of the 101 districts for which we have achievement data from the National Longitudinal School-Level State Assessment Score Database (NLSLSASD). We study reading and mathematics outcomes separately. In some districts for some years, especially the early years 1999 and 2000, some states did not have achievement data in the NLSLSASD. We discuss the data set in more detail in the online supplement to this book. Accounting for these data constraints, for elementary achievement analysis we have 451 district-year observations for reading achievement and 449 observations for math achievement. These observations include the districts we discussed in chapter two: Chicago, Boston, Baltimore, Cleveland, Detroit, Oakland, New Haven, Jackson, New York, and Providence. Washington, D.C., is not included because it is not possible to standardize its performance against other districts in the "state"; that is, Washington is a single-district "state". It does not include the small and midsized districts Harrisburg, Hartford, and Trenton. For high school analysis, where there are less data available, we have 264 observations for reading and 268 observations for math. The smaller number of observations limits the inferences we can make about high school achievement.

The use of panel data allows us to look at two types of changes in governances. First, we have differences across districts; some districts have mayoral control in a given year, while others do not. Second, we observe changes within a district over the period 1999–2003. In Oakland, for instance, elements of mayoral control were not put in place until 2000. In Philadelphia, governance changes occurred in 2001.

District-Level Production Function

In keeping with the economics literature on the relationship between educational inputs and outputs, we use a district-level production function (Hanushek 1979, 1986). Recalling the discussion from chapter three, our output measure is standardized district achievement, relative to other districts in the same state. Standardized achievement is measured as the Z-score of the district, for a given year. We include a series of input variables, with greatest interest in the effect of governance arrangements on district output. In the appendix at the end of the book, we discuss this methodological approach in more detail.

Examining Value Added

Measuring the value added by particular policy reforms is a standard that social scientists hope to use when evaluating reform productivity. In the literature that examines the effects of school funding on achievement, value added is typically modeled either by generating a dependent variable that measures "change in performance from year $t-1$ to year t" or by using performance in year $t-1$ as a control variable on the right-hand side of the equation (Burtless 1996).

We conduct analysis using both models. In this chapter, however, we report and focus on the level scores (with previous year achievement as a control) because it is not clear that in all cases the change in standardized achievement is capturing true achievement gains. The reason for this uncertainty is that during the period 1999–2003 some states were adjusting their assessment tools, changing either the grades tested or the test administered. When changes like this occur, measuring the "change" from one year to the next is not appropriate. Our standardization process corrects for some of the possible biases. For instance, because we are looking at the change in Z-scores, we are not comparing raw proficiency percentages from one year to the next. This means that if a state suddenly rescaled its test in year t, we would not report artificial gains (from the rescaling) from year $t-1$ to year t.

What even standardization cannot correct for, however, is whether the new state test is more favorable to lower- or higher-performing districts. If this is the case, then subtracting last year's Z-score from this year's Z-score would pick up artificial gains (or losses) unassociated with actual change in student ability. Though we report these models in the appendix, we focus on the models where we do not construct a year-to-year change measure.

It is important to note that including the lagged achievement variable is still a very powerful control, regardless of whether the testing instrument changed from one year to the next. The lagged achievement variable is still substantively capturing the "district's performance in the previous year relative to other districts." The only difference is that in the previous year, all the districts compared themselves using a different examination. The end result is the same: standardized achievement distribution with mean of 0 and standard deviation of 1.

Introducing this notion of value added through the use of a lagged achievement control variable enables us to better isolate the effects of governance changes, distinct from influences such as unobserved family background influences, for example, parental involvement. If the assumption holds that parental involvement is roughly the same year to year (e.g., active parents in year $t-1$ are still active in year t and vice versa), then those parental involvement factors will be captured by the lagged achievement variable. To the extent that new factors, which did not determine the previous year's achievement, enter into the present year's achievement production, our model has omitted variables.

Introducing Additional Control Variables

Using the NLSLSASD achievement time series (1999–2003) and cross-sectional ($N = 101$) data, we use equation 4.1 and employ the following base ordinary least squares (OLS) regression model:[1]

$$
\begin{aligned}
ACHIEVE_{it} = {} & \beta_0 + \beta_1 ACHIEVE_{it-1} + \beta_2 MAYORAL\_CONTROL_{it} \\
& + \beta_3 MAYOR\_COUNCIL_{it} \\
& + \beta_4 PCT\_SINGLE\_MEMBER_{it} + \beta_5 PCT\_PRIVATE_{it} \\
& + \beta_6 PCT\_STATE\_REV_{it} + \beta_7 PPE\_INSTRUCT_{it} \\
& + \beta_8 ENROLL_{it} + \beta_9 PCT\_HISPANIC_{it} \\
& + \beta_{10} PCT\_AFR\text{-}AMERICAN_{it} \\
& + \beta_{11} PCT\_KIDS\_POVERTY_{it} + \beta_{12} PCT\_SPECIAL\_ED_{it} \\
& + \delta_s + \gamma_t + \varepsilon_{it} \qquad\qquad\qquad\qquad\qquad (4.1)
\end{aligned}
$$

where $ACHIEVE_{it}$ is the standardized (Z-score) achievement for school district i in year t; $ACHIEVE_{t-1,i}$ is the district's previous year's standardized (Z-score) achievement; $MAYORAL\_CONTROL_{it}$ is either the composite $MAYOR\_INDEX$ or the individual three measures: $NEW\,STYLE$, $MAJORITY$, and $FULL$; $MAYOR\_COUNCIL_{it}$ is a dichotomous variable indicating whether or not the city uses a mayor–council form of government; $PCT\_SINGLE\_MEMBER_{it}$ is the percentage of city school board seats that are voted on in a single-member fashion; $PCT\_PRIVATE_{it}$ is the percentage of kindergarten through twelfth grade students in the city enrolled in private schools; $PCT\_STATE\_REV_{it}$ is the percentage of school district revenue from state sources; $PPE\_INSTRUCT_{it}$ is the district's per-pupil expenditure on instruction, adjusted for inflation and regional cost differences; $ENROLL_{it}$ is the district student enrollment; $PCT\_HISPANIC_{it}$ is the percentage of Hispanic students in the district; $PCT\_AFR\text{-}AMERICAN_{it}$ is the percentage of African American students in the district; $PCT\_KIDS\_POVERTY_{it}$ is the percentage of city residents, age three through eighteen years, who were living below the poverty level in 2000; $PCT\_SPECIAL\_ED_{it}$ is the percentage of district students who have an individualized education plan; δ_s captures state fixed effects; γ_t captures year fixed effects; and ε_{it} is an error term.[2]

Table 4.1 summarizes our set of independent variables, presenting means and standard deviations. The mean in this table is the average for each variable over the 101 districts included in our achievement analysis. For the dummy (1–0) variables, the average can be interpreted as the percentage of the 104 districts that have a mayor–council form of government (in 2001). In our sample, just slightly over half the districts have a mayor–council ("strong mayor") form of government. There is a great range in both instructional expenditures on education and the percentage of revenue derived from the state. There is a similarly large range and variance in the student body demographics, with some districts heavily minority and others not.

Our data are clustered around school districts; for example, we have five observations (1999, 2000, 2001, 2002, 2003) for a single school district

Table 4.1   Summary of Control Variables Used in Achievement Regressions (average values over 1999–2003 reported)

Measure	Mean	Standard Deviation	Minimum	Maximum
Mayoral control measures				
New-style mayor	0.09	0.26	0	1
Majority appointment power	0.08	0.25	0	1
Full appointment power	0.04	0.18	0	1
Mayor control index	0.20	0.62	0	3
Governance measures				
Mayor–council	0.54	0.50	0	1
Percent single-member-elected school board members	32.3	43.7	0	100
Percent in private school	12.1	4.8	3.7	23.8
Finance measures				
Percent revenue from state	51.4	13.9	7.3	76.6
Per-pupil expenditure on instruction, in 2003 dollars[a]	7,344	2,468	4,594	15,264
Student demographics				
Enrollment	69,035	128,413	15,826	1,068,413
Percent Hispanic	18.0	21.0	0.2	97.4
Percent African American	39.0	27.5	0.1	96.0
Percent children living in poverty	21.0	7.6	4.4	40.8
Percent in special education	13.0	3.2	7.0	22.1

Note: The first column presents unweighted means for the 101 districts with achievement data. The second column, standard deviation, is a measure of variance around this mean. This measures how much variation there is between districts. The third and fourth columns present the minimum and maximum values for each variable. This shows the range of values that our control variables have in the sample.

[a]Summary statistics based on a five-year average of the data over the years 1999–2003. Per-pupil expenditure figures are adjusted for inflation and geographical cost differentials, as discussed in the text.

(Chicago). Our clusters (the districts) are independent, but the individual observations are not. To account for this feature of the data, in our OLS regressions, we cluster around the district to obtain robust standard error estimates that adjust for the within-cluster correlation.[3]

In addition to our base model, we consider two models that investigate the possibility of lagged effects from mayoral control. In these alternative models, we make one adjustment to the model presented in equation 4.1. Instead of including *MAYORAL_CONTROL* for year t, we include the measure for year $t - 1$. This is our "Lag 1" Model. We then run a series of models using *MAYORAL_CONTROL* for year $t - 2$. This is our "Lag 2" Model. The results from these models with lagged mayoral control variables are presented alongside the results from the baseline achievement model.

ACHIEVEMENT RESULTS

In this section, we present the results of our statistical analysis. We first discuss the effects of mayoral control on elementary achievement. We then turn our attention to the high school level.

Integrated Governance Raises Elementary School Performance

With the details of the statistical methods now laid out, we turn to the central question of our study: Does mayoral control help to raise student achievement? The answer, simply put, is *yes*. The answer, expressed with more nuance, is that majority appointment power of school board members and the presence of a new-style education mayor are effective tools for raising achievement but that a lack of oversight on the mayor's choices may actually work against this progress. Furthermore, mayors are turnaround artists, not saviors. Our analysis suggests that mayors can steer the ship in the right direction but that there is still a long way to go before their districts achieve acceptable levels of student achievement.

Let us turn now to the specific evidence for our conclusions. All the results for elementary achievement are presented in table 4.2 (reading) and table 4.3 (mathematics). Recalling our model specification discussion from chapter 3, we consider two different models. In the first, labeled "Model A," we include all three measures of mayoral control: whether there is a new-style mayor emphasizing mayoral involvement in education, whether the mayor has formal power to appoint a majority of the school board, and whether the mayor has the power to select school board members without any oversight.

In the second, labeled "Model B," we replace the individual components with the composite mayoral control index.

How is mayoral control related to standardized elementary reading achievement? Looking first at tables 4.2 and 4.3, we see that giving the mayor power to appoint a majority of the city's school board is associated with an increase of 0.15 in standardized elementary reading achievement (table 4.2) and an increase of 0.14 in standardized elementary mathematics (table 4.3). New-style mayors are associated with a similar .11 increase in both reading and math (tables 4.2 and 4.3). These relationships are similar in both the one- and two-year lagged models, where we consider the relationship between present-year achievement and governance arrangements in previous years. Driven by these two aspects of mayoral control, the composite mayoral control index is significantly and positively related to standardized reading achievement in both the baseline and two-year lagged models (table 4.2), and to standardized math achievement in the two-year lagged model (table 4.3). At the same time, however, allowing the mayor full power to appoint school board members, without oversight from a nominating committee, is inversely related to elementary reading and math achievement (tables 4.2 and 4.3).

Putting the evidence from elementary reading and mathematical analyses together, it is clear that mayoral leadership has made a difference in the early grades. Districtwide achievement levels, relative to other districts in the state, are positively associated with new-style education mayors and giving the mayor the power to appoint a majority of the local school board. At the same time, not putting any restrictions on who the mayor appoints to the school board seems to dampen achievement levels. In light of these findings, several policy implications are immediately evident. First, optimal systems should design mayor-controlled systems to include nominating committees that provide the mayor with a slate of candidates from which to choose school board members. Second, evaluation of mayoral control should recognize that improvements resulting from mayoral control may take at least two years to become evident in aggregate statistics.

To fully explain these mayoral control results, we must examine the rest of the contextual variables included in the model. The most important relationship to discuss is the incredibly strong predictive power of previous school district achievement on current district achievement. This is true in both reading and mathematics (tables 4.2 and 4.3), and it suggests that it is difficult to change the absolute position of a district's achievement. If a mayor inherits a district that is performing near the bottom of the pack, no amount of skill from that mayor is likely to make the district leapfrog to the top. Instead, the more realistic goal should be for the mayor to improve the trajectory of

Text continues on p. 88.

Table 4.2 Results from Linear Regression Models for Standardized Elementary Reading Achievement, 1999–2003 (with year and state fixed effects; coefficient and robust standard errors reported)

Variable	No Lag		One-Year Lag		Two-Year Lag	
	A	B	A	B	A	B
New-style mayor	0.11**		0.15***		0.15***	
	(0.05)		(0.06)		(0.05)	
Majority appointment power	0.15***		0.07		0.10**	
	(0.05)		(0.05)		(0.05)	
Full appointment power	−0.15**		−0.19**		−0.10	
	(0.07)		(0.09)		(0.06)	
Mayor control index		0.05*		0.03		0.07***
		(0.03)		(0.03)		(0.02)
Previous achievement	0.85***	0.86***	0.86***	0.86***	0.86***	0.86***
	(0.03)	(0.03)	(0.03)	(0.03)	(0.03)	(0.03)
Mayor–council	−0.03		−0.02		−0.03	
	(0.03)		(0.03)		(0.03)	
Percent single-member-elected school board members	0.009	0.005	0.002	0.002	0.004	0.006
	(0.035)	(0.035)	(0.035)	(0.035)	(0.035)	(0.035)
Percent in private school	−0.52*	−0.49*	−0.54*	−0.49*	−0.51*	−0.49*
	(0.30)	(0.29)	(0.30)	(0.28)	(0.31)	(0.29)

Percent revenue from state	0.28**	0.22*	0.27**	0.23*	0.27**	0.25**
	(0.13)	(0.12)	(0.13)	(0.12)	(0.12)	(0.12)
Per-pupil expenditure, current instruction	0.02	0.01	0.02	0.01	0.02	0.02
	(0.02)	(0.01)	(0.02)	(0.01)	(0.02)	(0.01)
Enrollment (million)	0.01	0.01	0.06	0.04	0.04	0.03
	(0.10)	(0.10)	(0.10)	(0.10)	(0.10)	(0.10)
Percent Hispanic	−0.49***	−0.45**	−0.46***	−0.43**	−0.48***	−0.46***
	(0.18)	(0.17)	(0.17)	(0.17)	(0.17)	(0.17)
Percent African American	−0.50***	−0.50***	−0.46***	−0.46***	−0.50***	−0.51***
	(0.12)	(0.12)	(0.12)	(0.11)	(0.12)	(0.12)
Percent children living in poverty	−0.54*	−0.51*	−0.57*	−0.52*	−0.52*	−0.5*
	(0.29)	(0.28)	(0.30)	(0.29)	(0.29)	(0.28)
Percent special education	0.25	0.50	0.20	0.42	0.24	0.43
	(0.69)	(0.70)	(0.70)	(0.71)	(0.69)	(0.69)
Constant	0.07	0.08	0.07	0.07	0.06	0.05
	(0.14)	(0.14)	(0.14)	(0.14)	(0.14)	(0.14)
Observations	451	451	451	451	451	451
R^2	0.95	0.95	0.95	0.95	0.95	0.95

Note: Two-tailed significance denoted as *p < .1, **p < .05, ***p < .01. All models employ state and year fixed effects. Robust standard errors are produced by clustering on school districts. Enrollment is measured in millions.

Table 4.3 Results from Linear Regression Models for Standardized Elementary Mathematics Achievement, 1999–2003 (with year and state fixed effects; coefficient and robust standard errors reported)

Variable	No Lag		One-Year Lag		Two-Year Lag	
	A	B	A	B	A	B
New-style mayor	0.11***		0.13***		0.13***	
	(0.04)		(0.03)		(0.05)	
Majority appointment power	0.14***		0.10***		0.10**	
	(0.049)		(0.035)		(0.047)	
Full appointment power	−0.19***		−0.19***		−0.16***	
	(0.05)		(0.05)		(0.05)	
Mayor control index		0.03		0.03		0.05*
		(0.02)		(0.02)		(0.02)
Previous achievement	0.86***	0.87***	0.86***	0.87***	0.87***	0.87***
	(0.031)	(0.03)	(0.03)	(0.03)	(0.03)	(0.03)
Mayor–council	−0.03		−0.03		−0.03	
	(0.03)		(0.03)		(0.03)	
Percent single-member-elected school board members	0.06*	0.06*	0.06*	0.06*	0.06*	0.06*
	(0.03)	(0.03)	(0.03)	(0.03)	(0.03)	(0.03)
Percent in private school	−0.65**	−0.62**	−0.66**	−0.62**	−0.65**	−0.63**
	(0.30)	(0.28)	(0.30)	(0.28)	(0.30)	(0.28)

	(1)	(2)	(3)	(4)	(5)	(6)
Percent revenue from state	0.08	0.01	0.07	0.02	0.07	0.03
	(0.13)	(0.12)	(0.12)	(0.12)	(0.12)	(0.12)
Per-pupil expenditure, current instruction	0.010	0.003	0.010	0.004	0.010	0.006
	(0.018)	(0.016)	(0.017)	(0.016)	(0.018)	(0.017)
Enrollment (million)	-0.03	-0.03	-0.01	-0.02	-0.01	-0.02
	(0.09)	(0.09)	(0.09)	(0.09)	(0.09)	(0.09)
Percent Hispanic	-0.39**	-0.34**	-0.38**	-0.34**	-0.38**	-0.35**
	(0.18)	(0.17)	(0.18)	(0.17)	(0.18)	(0.17)
Percent African American	-0.41***	-0.39***	-0.40***	-0.38***	-0.40***	-0.40***
	(0.13)	(0.13)	(0.13)	(0.12)	(0.13)	(0.12)
Percent children living in poverty	-0.49	-0.46	-0.50	-0.46	-0.49	-0.46
	(0.31)	(0.29)	(0.30)	(0.29)	(0.30)	(0.29)
Percent special education	0.47	0.75	0.46	0.71	0.47	0.70
	(0.71)	(0.73)	(0.71)	(0.73)	(0.72)	(0.73)
Constant	0.15	0.16	0.15	0.16	0.15	0.14
	(0.16)	(0.15)	(0.16)	(0.15)	(0.16)	(0.15)
Observations	449	449	449	449	449	449
R^2	0.94	0.94	0.94	0.94	0.94	0.94

Note: Two-tailed significance denoted as $*p < .1$, $**p < .05$, $***p < .01$. All models employ state and year fixed effects. Robust standard errors are produced by clustering on school districts.

the district's performance. Our results are consistent with this policy of tangible, but not miraculous, gains. As table 4.4 shows, all the cities with mayoral control are substantially worse than the other school districts in the state. An increase of 0.15 standard deviations will not move any of the mayor-led districts above the mean in their state. It does, however, put them one small step closer to that goal.

A consistent finding across both elementary achievement models is a significant, inverse relationship between standardized achievement and the percentage of city youth attending private schools (tables 4.2 and 4.3). This may be an indicator of "brain drain," with some of the city's best students opting out of the public school system and into private options. Not surprisingly, the percentage of children in poverty in a district is inversely related to achievement (tables 4.2 and 4.3). This is consistent with the long-standing finding that students with a lower socioeconomic background perform less well in school (Coleman et al. 1966).

In the analysis of elementary reading outcomes, there is a positive relationship between standardized achievement and the percentage of revenue derived from state sources (table 4.2). States may be able to target districts with specialized resources related to literacy. In the analysis of elementary mathematics, there is a positive and significant relationship between achievement and the percentage of school board members elected in a single-member fashion, which means that instead of serving the entire city, the school board member serves a single section of the city. The fact that systems with greater single-member representation are associated with higher achievement levels challenges our hypothesis that more single-member representation would be

Table 4.4   Z-Scores in 1999 for Mayor-Controlled Districts

District	Elementary Reading	Elementary Mathematics
Baltimore	−2.00	−1.96
Boston	−1.13	−0.95
Chicago	−1.40	−1.31
Cleveland	−1.42	−1.13
Detroit	−1.28	−1.34
New Haven	−1.96	−1.82
New York	−0.70	−0.73
Oakland	−0.87	−0.91
Philadelphia	−2.07	−1.88
Providence	−1.47	−1.41

Note: A negative Z-scores indicate performance under the state mean. See chapter three for additional discussion of Z-scores.

unproductive due to fragmented politics. From a broader perspective, how-ever, single-member districts tend to facilitate a closer link between the elected official and the constituencies. The higher achievement levels may suggest a greater degree of accountability under this governing arrangement. Whereas a single-member district may facilitate school improvement for the specific community, mayoral control is designed to elevate accountability to the citywide level.

Both elementary achievement models find significant, inverse relationships between achievement and the percentage of Hispanic and African American students (tables 4.2 and 4.3). The magnitude of these effects is large, approxi-mately three times as large as the effects of mayoral control. As discussed above, because our data are aggregated up from the school to the district level, we need to be wary of ecological inference issues. Nevertheless, in light of scholar-ship that has identified a persistent racial gap in American public education, these results may suggest that though institutional governance changes can raise overall district performance, there is still much to do to lift the achieve-ment of all city students.[4]

Mayoral Control Shows Positive Results in High School Performance

Before discussing the high school results, it is worth emphasizing that the NLSLSASD does not contain as much high school data as it does elemen-tary data. Part of this is due to states' having less high school data readily avail-able for analysis. But whatever the reasons, the consequence for our analysis is that we are left with a much smaller sample when we examine high school reading and mathematics. Specifically, the NLSLSASD does not contain high school data from these states (for which we did have elementary school data): Alaska, Arkansas, Colorado, Connecticut, Louisiana, Maryland, Minnesota, Mississippi, New York, North Carolina, Oklahoma, South Carolina, and Ten-nessee. As a result of these dropped observations, we are left with no districts like New York City, where a mayor appoints a majority, but not all, of the board. We therefore drop the "majority" category from the tables when we present the results.

As we discuss in this chapter and in our conclusion, a high priority for future research in this area remains better data collection and analysis at the high school level. This data collection could cover both achievement scores and other indi-cators such as attendance, dropout, and graduation rates. We will continue to work in this area, and we hope that others will as well. In light of this need for more data, we proceed cautiously in interpreting the high school results that we present in table 4.5 (reading) and table 4.6 (mathematics).

Text continues on p. 94.

Table 4.5 Results from Linear Regression Models for Standardized High School Reading Achievement, 1999–2003 (with year and state fixed effects; coefficient and robust standard errors reported)

Variable	No Lag		One-Year Lag		Two-Year Lag	
	A	B	A	B	A	B
New-style mayor	0.14		0.07		0.13	
	(0.10)		(0.07)		(0.09)	
Majority appointment power	0.19		0.27***		0.21**	
	(0.13)		(0.08)		(0.09)	
Full appointment power	−0.40***		−0.36***		−0.42***	
	(0.13)		(0.12)		(0.15)	
Mayor control index		0.045		0.053		0.063
		(0.07)		(0.07)		(0.07)
Previous achievement	0.67***	0.68***	0.67***	0.68***	0.67***	0.68***
	(0.08)	(0.08)	(0.08)	(0.08)	(0.08)	(0.08)
Mayor–council	0.03		0.03		0.03	
	(0.06)		(0.06)		(0.06)	
Percent single-member-elected school board members	0.03	−0.05	−0.02	−0.05	−0.03	−0.04
	(0.07)	(0.07)	(0.07)	(0.07)	(0.07)	(0.07)
Percent in private school	−0.27	−0.08	−0.26	−0.076	−0.27	−0.08
	(0.94)	(0.88)	(0.94)	(0.88)	(0.93)	(0.88)

	(1)	(2)	(3)	(4)	(5)	(6)
Percent revenue from state	0.54*	0.40	0.54*	0.40	0.53*	0.41
	(0.29)	(0.32)	(0.29)	(0.31)	(0.30)	(0.31)
Per-pupil expenditure, current instruction	0.09*	0.07	0.09*	0.07	0.09*	0.07*
	(0.05)	(0.05)	(0.05)	(0.05)	(0.05)	(0.05)
Enrollment (million)	-0.16	-0.087	-0.17	-0.10	-0.14	-0.11
	(0.11)	(0.15)	(0.11)	(0.15)	(0.11)	(0.16)
Percent Hispanic	-1.1**	-0.99**	-1.1**	-1.0**	-1.1**	-1**
	(0.45)	(0.44)	(0.45)	(0.44)	(0.44)	(0.44)
Percent African American	-1.3***	-1.2***	-1.3***	-1.2***	-1.3***	-1.2***
	(0.24)	(0.26)	(0.24)	(0.26)	(0.25)	(0.26)
Percent children living in poverty	-0.63	-0.59	-0.65	-0.58	-0.65	-0.59
	(0.66)	(0.66)	(0.66)	(0.66)	(0.66)	(0.66)
Percent special education	-0.35	0.15	-0.27	0.15	-0.29	0.16
	(1.0)	(1.1)	(1.0)	(1.1)	(1.1)	(1.1)
Constant	-0.16	-0.11	-0.17	-0.11	-0.14	-0.12
	(0.45)	(0.43)	(0.45)	(0.43)	(0.45)	(0.43)
Observations	264	264	264	264	264	264
R^2	0.86	0.86	0.86	0.86	0.86	0.86

Note: Two-tailed significance denoted as *$p < .1$, **$p < .05$, ***$p < .01$. All models employ state and year fixed effects. Robust standard errors are produced by clustering on school districts.

Table 4.6 Results from Linear Regression Models for Standardized High School Mathematics Achievement, 1999–2003 (with year and state fixed effects; coefficient and robust standard errors reported)

Variable	No Lag		One-Year Lag		Two-Year Lag	
	A	B	A	B	A	B
New-style mayor	0.04		-0.02		-0.01	
	(0.06)		(0.04)		(0.07)	
Majority appointment power	0.17**		0.22***		0.21***	
	(0.07)		(0.05)		(0.07)	
Full appointment power	-0.18**		-0.14*		-0.17*	
	(0.08)		(0.08)		(0.09)	
Mayor control index		0.03		0.04		0.05
		(0.04)		(0.04)		(0.04)
Previous achievement	0.82***	0.82***	0.82***	0.82***	0.82***	0.82***
	(0.06)	(0.06)	(0.06)	(0.06)	(0.06)	(0.06)
Mayor-council	0.02		0.02		0.02	
	(0.05)		(0.05)		(0.05)	
Percent single-member-elected school board members	-0.06	-0.07	-0.05	-0.07	-0.05	-0.07
	(0.06)	(0.06)	(0.06)	(0.06)	(0.06)	(0.06)
Percent in private school	0.77	0.84	0.76	0.85	0.72	0.84
	(0.69)	(0.65)	(0.69)	(0.65)	(0.69)	(0.65)

	(1)	(2)	(3)	(4)	(5)	(6)
Percent revenue from state	0.34	0.26	0.34	0.26	0.33	0.27
	(0.23)	(0.23)	(0.23)	(0.23)	(0.23)	(0.23)
Per-pupil expenditure, current instruction	0.07**	0.07**	0.08**	0.07**	0.08**	0.07**
	(0.03)	(0.03)	(0.03)	(0.03)	(0.03)	(0.03)
Enrollment (millions)	−0.19*	−0.13	−0.19*	−0.14	−0.19*	−0.14
	(0.10)	(0.12)	(0.10)	(0.12)	(0.11)	(0.12)
Percent Hispanic	−0.45	−0.37	−0.45	−0.38	−0.44	−0.38
	(0.31)	(0.29)	(0.31)	(0.29)	(0.3)	(0.29)
Percent African American	−0.75***	−0.71***	−0.75***	−0.71***	−0.76***	−0.72***
	(0.23)	(0.23)	(0.23)	(0.23)	(0.23)	(0.23)
Percent children living in poverty	−0.36	−0.34	−0.36	−0.33	−0.36	−0.33
	(0.46)	(0.46)	(0.47)	(0.46)	(0.47)	(0.46)
Percent special education	−0.29	−0.002	−0.21	0.004	−0.18	−0.001
	(0.63)	(0.66)	(0.63)	(0.66)	(0.65)	(0.65)
Constant	−0.39	−0.36	−0.39	−0.36	−0.40	−0.36
	(0.31)	(0.29)	(0.31)	(0.29)	(0.31)	(0.29)
Observations	268	268	268	268	268	268
R^2	0.89	0.89	0.89	0.89	0.89	0.89

Note: Two-tailed significance denoted as $*p < .1$, $**p < .05$, $***p < .01$. All models employ state and year fixed effects. Robust standard errors are produced by clustering on school districts.

With all the caveats aside, the high school results mirror the elementary results in that majority school board power is significantly, positively associated with higher reading and mathematics achievement, whereas full appointment power without oversight is inversely related to achievement in both subjects (tables 4.5 and 4.6). That the high school results mirror the elementary results gives us reason to think that they are credible. The same processes that lead to improvements in elementary achievement may be operating for high school achievement. Many reforms, such as reducing central office bureaucracy, can be thought to be grade-level neutral. Less red tape in the central office will benefit all schools, regardless of the grades they serve.

The control variables in the high school statistical regressions are generally related to standardized achievement in the same way they were in the regression models on elementary achievement. Once again, we see a significant inverse relationship between standardized achievement and the percentage of Hispanic and African American students in the district. This relationship remains statistically significant in the high school models as well. The magnitude of these effects at the high school level, however, are even more striking. In high school reading, a one-unit increase in the percentage of African American students has more than five times the impact on achievement than a governance switch to a majority mayor-appointed board. Although the conclusion remains that mayors can produce significant, positive change at the high school level, it is evident that deeper challenges remain for a school system to overcome underperformance.

GOVERNANCE MATTERS FOR STUDENT ACHIEVEMENT

Some skeptics believe that the United States' large, urban school districts face too many external obstacles to ever be effective. James Traub (2000), for instance, argues that we are placing too much faith in school systems, which may be incapable of making up for serious socioeconomic deficits. He believes that schools can do something, but not much, and he asks rhetorically, "How powerful can this one institution be in the face of the kind of disadvantages that so many ghetto children bring with them to the schoolhouse door, and return to at home?" (p. 52).

Our empirical analysis in this chapter has asked a similar question, but not rhetorically and with a different answer. We wanted to assess the marginal effects that a change in institutional governance can have on student outcomes, even controlling for all of the socioeconomic deficiencies to which Traub and others point.

The results of our analysis suggest that a governance change that gives the mayor the power to appoint a majority of the school board will lead to a Z-score improvement of approximately 0.1 standard deviation in elementary reading and mathematics. To give these gains some context, we can consider again the starting points of the mayor-controlled districts, measured as their Z-score in 1999 (table 4.4). A first glance at the table shows that every district has a negative Z-score, and most are Z-scores less than –1, meaning that every district in 1999 was performing below the state mean. Most districts were worse than one standard deviation below the mean. If we were to go through the list of other districts in the sample, many would have similar Z-scores.

Our analysis predicts that two years after the introduction of a mayor-appointed school board, achievement will rise approximately 0.1 standard deviation. This is a significant improvement, even if it does not bring the district all the way back to the state average. The limited time span of our data prevents us from predicting long-term changes, but our look at two-year lagged effects, where the relationship between mayoral control and achievement becomes even stronger, leads us to believe that the long-term effects could be at least a 0.1 increase, and perhaps more (tables 4.2 and 4.3).

In the context of high school achievement, it also appears that mayors can have an impact. Because of our smaller sample and more limited data, we can not make as general inferences as we can for elementary achievement. The indications are positive, however, that mayors may be able to have a similar, positive impact on high school reading and math achievement (tables 4.5 and 4.6).

What is encouraging about the elementary achievement results is that they are the *marginal effects of mayoral control*, holding all else constant. In other words, even if poverty levels remain the same, funding levels do not improve, and private school competition holds constant, our model predicts that a governance change will lead to significant, positive improvements in overall district achievement. If mayors can work simultaneously to reduce poverty and increase funding, the overall effect of mayoral control may be even larger in the longer run.

FULFILLING THE PROMISE OF INTEGRATED GOVERNANCE

As we have argued through the first three chapters, mayor-led integrated governance promises to improve student performance by introducing streamlined governance, an alignment of political incentives, a politics of partnership, and a reallocation of resources to their most efficient use. The results of the analysis in this chapter suggest that mayor-led integrated governance, despite its challenges in some districts such as Detroit, is fulfilling its promise to raise student achievement.

A secondary question, which we begin to explore here and more in depth in chapter six, is *how* mayoral control is able to bring about these improvements. To preview that chapter, outcome-based accountability policies under mayoral control can redirect the allocation of resources across the multiple levels of school organization to produce a certain degree of change in curriculum and instruction. Schools and teachers, however, respond to a narrow focus on standardized test scores by targeting resources in ways that fragment the curriculum and undermine improvements in teaching. Teachers' routine curricular and instructional practices remain largely unchanged. Although outcome-based accountability policies may expose the failure of these routines, they may have limited potential to address these failures unless there is a sustained effort to improve the quality of daily instruction.

In addition to these linkages to classroom practice, integrated governance may be successful because it replaces a system of decentralization that could not be properly coordinated for systemwide goals. Chicago provides a good example because it moved in 1995 from a system of extensive decentralization to mayoral control. The contrast in governance styles is stark. Under the old regime, local school councils were the primary conduit for school system governance. The track record of these councils was mixed.[5]

If local school councils are not working, one reason may be that the system of decentralization never really allowed for a full transfer of power (Lewis and Nakagawa 1995). Two options present themselves: Either promote radical decentralization, in the form of parental choice and vouchers; or take another path and consolidate power in the hands of the mayor. Our empirical evaluation of the latter supports the contention that mayors can effectively govern large-city school systems. Fears that city government will simply add an additional layer of bureaucracy onto the school system seem to be unfounded. In short, our analysis provides strong empirical evidence for the contention that mayor-led integrated governance can improve student performance.

CHALLENGES FOR INTEGRATED GOVERNANCE

In this section, we consider several important challenges that mayoral leadership must overcome if it is to be successful in the future. We discuss the challenges posed by the racial dimension of urban politics and the structural constraints of widespread urban poverty.

Addressing Racial Disparities

Although mayoral control can lead to significant improvements in student achievement, it is not a silver bullet. Many challenges remain to be addressed.

Chief among these is the issue of racial disparities and race politics. In light of the concerns of the African American community, our findings that see an inverse relationship between achievement and districts with greater percentages of minorities raise important questions about the ability of mayor-led integrated governance to serve the city's minority population.

Some evidence from Chicago further heightens concern about racial politics. On the basis of a comparison of interviews from before and after the change to mayoral control in Chicago, Chambers (2002, 664) finds that "post-1995 school board evaluations are much lower than those for the school boards created after the 1988 legislation." Chambers's concern is that the city's minority community has little say in the progression of educational reform. Focusing on Chicago, she argues that "although the school system continues to receive praise in the local and national media for improved student performance, the sentiment at the community level does not correspond with these reports, nor is there clear evidence that student performance is on the rise" (p. 664).

Although we believe our study does provide clear evidence that overall student performance is on the rise, our data do not allow us to properly evaluate the claim that minority students' achievement is significantly raised by mayor-led integrated governance. We hope that future research in this field will tackle this important issue. Until those data are analyzed, however, we must be sensitive to the cities' minority populations when they voice concerns about changes in institutional governance.

Poverty as a Structural Constraint

In addition to race politics, underlying structural factors such as child poverty remain a barrier to improving student achievement. A 1-percentage-point reduction in child poverty improves test scores by 0.5 standard deviations. In comparison with the governance changes just discussed, this is nearly three times greater in magnitude. The relative magnitude of urban poverty to governance change suggests that education reform must continue to be coupled with overall improvement in the quality of city residents' lives. This, we believe, is not a reason to look away from mayoral control (on the grounds that reducing poverty is more important) but rather a reason to see the two issues as interwoven. A mayor who sees how reducing poverty will improve student achievement, which will in turn bolster the mayor's electoral support, is a mayor who may be more likely to aggressively seek funds to help reduce local poverty rates. Indeed, some of the findings we present in chapter seven suggest that new-style mayors are doing just that—looking for outside help to address the needs of their most disadvantaged students.

FUTURE RESEARCH DIRECTIONS

This study is the most ambitious empirical study of mayoral control to date, because it is the first to use achievement data from more than 100 districts, spanning forty states. This study is also the first to use fixed-effect regression techniques on such data to isolate the effect of institutional governance changes. We believe that these innovations make our study unique and its findings of note. At the same time, however, we want to be the first to acknowledge the limitations of our data set. Primary limitations to the data are that the study spans only 1999 to 2003; it is lacking in high school achievement data and other indicators; and it does not have achievement broken out by racial group for every district.

We hope that future research will be able to take advantage of growing state- and district-level data sources. One of the benefits of an empirical approach such as ours is that once the analytic framework has been established, data from additional years and districts can be included without the startup costs. The marginal cost of adding an additional year of data to our database is likely to be proportionately less than setting out to perform a case study of a new district. In this way, our study can be extended by us and by others. Existing hypotheses can be tested with new data, new hypotheses can be developed, and in the process, we can learn more about the effects of mayor-led integrated governance.

We identify three promising directions for future research. First, research can explore mayoral control in the context of small and midsized localities. The political and social dynamics in these smaller cities require a slightly different theory than the one we develop in this study to discuss big-city school districts. Second, research can attempt to gather individual-level data from as many states as possible, to look at individual gains within the context of mayor- and nonmayor-led districts. Moving to the level of individual students, if it is possible across a large number of districts and states, will allow for much more detailed analysis of issues such as the racial gap. Third, as mayoral control settles in across the nation, the long-term effects of the reform can begin to be evaluated. With comparable data for a longer period (ten or more years), we can answer questions about sustainability and possible cyclical effects.

CHAPTER FIVE

Considering the Gap between High- and Low-Performing Schools

SINCE THE PASSAGE OF THE NO CHILD LEFT BEHIND ACT, there has been close scrutiny of the achievement gap and the needs of the lowest-performing schools. In this context, mayoral control raises questions of equity. Though in the previous chapter we examined the effects of mayoral control on overall district achievement, we did not look at *where* those gains are coming from. Does mayoral control contribute to, or help to reduce, achievement inequality in school districts? That is the question we explore in this chapter. We examine the nature of the achievement gap between the top- and bottom-performing schools in each school district in our sample, using statistical analysis to compare mayor- and nonmayor-led districts.

In examining these issues, we hope to better explain the redistributive aspects of mayoral control. The likelihood of redistribution within an integrated governance framework is open for theoretical debate. On one hand, integrated governance offers mayors an opportunity to reallocate resources to the schools most in need. In cities that experience a shrinking revenue base, mayors can institute fiscal discipline, prioritize resources in terms of needs, and improve efficiency in service delivery. On the other hand, electoral incentives and competition with other school systems may lead the mayor to invest more heavily in schools that serve high-achieving students. Mayors may see high-achieving schools as a better tool for targeting likely voters or recruiting middle-class families to the city. In our empirical assessment in this chapter, we weigh the evidence in support of both theories, and we find that on balance mayor-controlled systems are simultaneously associated with wider achievement gaps but not with declining performance in the bottom quarter. Put another way, all schools in these districts appear to be gaining, but those at the top of the distribution are gaining at faster rates.

We examine the data in several ways to arrive at this conclusion. First, we examine the performance of schools in the lowest 10th and 25th percentiles from 1999 to 2003. We track school performance in both mayor- and non-mayor-led districts. Second, we examine the ratio of high-performing (top 25 percent) schools to low-performing (bottom 25 percent) schools. We employ fixed-effects regression models to compare across districts and specify the effects of mayoral control on this inequality ratio. Third, we conclude the chapter with a discussion of the implications of these findings in designing urban education policy.

TRACKING THE LOWEST-PERFORMING SCHOOLS AS A COHORT

For more than a decade, both scholarly and popular works have brought to light the continued inequality in America's public schools. Some scholars, such as Mintrop (2004), have argued that to close the achievement gap, inputs must complement outcome-based accountability systems. Mayors in charge of urban school systems have the ability to redirect funds to instructional purposes and potentially develop new funding sources. Such new resources may allow for improved performance in the lowest-performing schools. To see if this is the case, we examine the performance of the cohort of schools that was lowest performing in 1999, the start of our five-year window of achievement data analysis.[1]

For each district in the sample, we examined the distribution of school performance in 1999. We identified the schools that fell in the lowest 10 percent in 1999, and also marked schools in the lowest 25 percent in 1999.[2] We then tracked these cohorts of low-performing schools over the period, through 2003, to see if their performance remained stagnant or if they improved. We examined elementary and middle schools separately. We did not examine high school cohorts because most districts do not have enough high schools to constitute (at the school level) a large enough cohort of low-performing schools.

Performing this cohort analysis allows us to address the questions: Do these schools end up in the same spot where they started? Or do they make genuine progress during this period? But without student-level data, it needs to be noted that this analysis cannot directly address what is happening to the lowest-performing *students*. We do not know, for instance, if students in the lowest-performing schools are staying in those schools or transferring elsewhere. At the end of the chapter, we discuss again the desire for student-level data that will help address persistent questions of the achievement gap.

Progress Seen in the 10 Percent Lowest-Performing Schools

Looking at the data on performance in the lowest 10 percent of schools, we see that schools that were performing worst in 1999 were still struggling in 2003, though with some improvements in selected grades. We present elementary achievement results in table 5.1, and we present additional results from middle school grades in the online supplement to this book. In Chicago, steady improvement is seen because the lowest-performing schools in grade three doubled their reading achievement (from 10 to 23 percent) and mathematics achievement (from 16 to 34 percent) over the observation period. There was similar progress made in grade five in Chicago. In grade eight, however, Chicago's lowest 10 percent of schools seem to have flatlined a bit by 2003. In Cleveland, progress was seen in grade four. Cleveland grade six achievement also improved gradually over this period.

New York saw perhaps the strongest improvement over this period in grade four, rising in reading from 10 percent proficient to over 35 percent proficient, and in mathematics from 20 percent proficient to over 50 percent proficient in 2003. The trend was evident before mayoral control was put into place in 2002, but large improvements were also made in math in 2003. New York saw improvements in grade eight as well.

If we look at the characteristics of these low-performing schools, we see that schools in the lowest 10th percentile have higher percentages of their students eligible for a free or reduced-price lunch. In the online supplement, the details of these school characteristics are available for downloading. In Washington, for instance, the district average is roughly 68 percent free lunches, with the bottom 10 percent schools having 80 percent free lunches. In many districts, there are also higher concentrations of minority students. In Chicago, for instance, the district average is just over 51 percent African American enrollment, but in the lowest 10th percentile of schools, enrollment is between 80 and 85 percent African American. In Cleveland, too, the percentage of African Americans in the lowest 10th percentile of schools is more than 20 percent greater than the district average.

Progress in Performance in the Lowest 25 Percent of the Schools

In addition to looking at the extremes of the distribution, we wanted to get a sense of schools in the lowest quartile. In table 5.2, we track the performance

Table 5.1 Tracking the Lowest 10th Percentile of Elementary Schools, Selected Districts, 1999–2003
(percent of students proficient on annual state examinations reported for each district)

City	Grade	No. of Schools	Reading					Mathematics				
			1999	2000	2001	2002	2003	1999	2000	2001	2002	2003
Baltimore	3	11	3.6	11.8	10.8	10.5	31.2	0.4	4.8	11.6	8.6	31.7
Baltimore	5	10	3.8	9.5	13.4	13.2	46.3	1.3	9.0	18.4	13.9	18.9
Boston	4	20	0.0	3.1	17.6	22.2	22.6	0.7	4.1	4.3	8.1	10.6
Chicago	3	52	10.0	15.9	18.2	17.2	23.3	15.8	18.9	28.7	27.8	34.1
Chicago	5	47	14.6	17.5	18.4	19.8	23.5	7.3	12.8	18.0	19.2	27.7
Cleveland	4	9	14.4	15.7	20.3	20.9	n.a.	9.2	15.8	18.8	27.2	n.a.
Detroit	4	17	n.a.	n.a.	10.6	14.4	36.1	n.a.	n.a.	16.4	21.6	25.3
New Haven	4	4	5.8	8.5	12.0	9.7	15.7	8.0	21.5	24.6	29.5	33.0
New York	4	34	10.0	22.9	25.5	26.6	36.9	19.5	23.4	30.4	33.3	53.9
Oakland	3	9	10.9	15.9	20.8	19.7	15.4	10.7	18.3	29.0	24.2	23.0
Oakland	4	6	9.5	9.5	10.5	13.0	10.0	9.7	19.3	15.0	21.4	19.3
Philadelphia	5	19	1.7	7.2	8.9	9.2	n.a.	0.4	5.2	6.1	10.5	n.a.
Providence	4	3	19.7	22.7	36.2	31.3	24.3	0.0	2.3	10.0	12.3	14.1
Washington	3	12	31.9	40.7	40.2	39.3	n.a.	30.5	43.9	46.6	46.9	n.a.
Washington	4	14	32.9	39.5	38.4	40.1	37.9	31.6	41.5	42.7	43.2	41.8

Note: n.a. = not available. Achievement can be compared year to year within a given district, but without proper statistical controls, figures cannot be directly compared with each other because different tests are being used in each district. When within-district comparisons are not appropriate (e.g., change of test from one year to next), we report a missing value. See the discussion in the chapter text for the methods used to identify the lowest 10th percentile. All achievement measures are percent proficient, with two exceptions. The achievement measure in Detroit is percent satisfactory + above, and the measure in Washington is normal curve equivalent.

of the lowest 25th percentile of elementary schools in mayor-controlled districts for selected grades. We present the same data for middle schools in the online supplement. The virtue of looking at the 25th percentile is that it is likely to be less subject to outliers such as a school that makes one-time exceptional progress in one year. The lowest-10th-percentile measurements will be more sensitive to such shifts.

The first thing we notice about the lowest-25th-percentile schools in mayor-controlled districts is that, similar to the lowest 10th percentile, these schools are struggling immensely to meet state performance goals. In general, the proportion of students meeting state standards is only slightly greater than those in the bottom 10th. This suggests that the problem of low-achieving schools in these districts is not limited to a small set of very poor schools but is a more systemic problem.

In addressing this problem, the progress of the 25th-percentile schools resembles that of the bottom 10th percentile. Looking at Chicago again, the bottom-25th-percentile schools seem to be making gradual, positive gains in both reading and mathematics, across grades three, five, and eight. New York math scores again improved significantly in 2003, after smaller improvements in previous years. In Boston, gains are seen in fourth grade reading, but the same growth is not seen in math.

The demographics of these lowest-25th-percentile schools show that the student bodies are composed of greater proportions of students eligible for free and reduced-price lunches. In many cases, the difference is greater than 10 percent, suggesting that the lower-achieving schools are dealing with more challenging student populations. With the exception of New Haven, Oakland, and Providence, these lowest-performing schools are also educating greater percentages of African American students than the overall district average.

Explaining Inequality Ratios

Although tracking low-performing schools serves as a useful first step in evaluating mayoral control, we need to take additional analytic steps to specify the effects of mayoral control on the achievement gap. Specifically, we need to develop a measure that is comparable across districts. We discussed in chapter three the reasons why we cannot directly compare achievement measures across districts. To get around this problem, we look at the ratio of the top quarter of schools to the bottom quarter of schools. We refer to this as the "75/25 ratio," because it represents the average performance of schools in the 75th percentile and above, divided by the average performance of schools in

Table 5.2 Tracking the Lowest 25th Percentile of Elementary Schools, Selected Districts, 1999–2003 (percent of students proficient on annual state examinations reported for each district)

City	Grade	No. of Schools	Reading					Mathematics				
			1999	2000	2001	2002	2003	1999	2000	2001	2002	2003
Baltimore	3	27	5.6	11.2	11.1	9.5	32.7	1.6	4.8	13.5	8.2	34.9
Baltimore	5	27	5.9	13.9	15.9	13.8	41.8	3.1	10.2	18.1	14.8	26.1
Boston	4	20	0.0	3.1	17.6	22.2	22.6	2.5	8.4	6.6	8.7	7.1
Chicago	3	113	13.7	18.3	20.4	20.2	24.0	20.4	20.6	31.1	29.5	35.3
Chicago	5	112	19.1	19.1	21.9	22.9	26.1	10.4	13.5	18.2	18.9	27.5
Cleveland	4	21	19.6	19.3	22.1	26.6	n.a.	14.8	18.4	22.8	30.5	n.a.
Detroit	4	41	n.a.	n.a.	16.2	19.8	46.5	n.a.	n.a.	23.5	26.6	34.2
New Haven	4	7	6.6	10.9	12.4	10.8	13.7	11.0	19.6	21.6	26.8	31.9
New York	4	84	13.9	24.9	28.0	30.2	37.5	25.4	25.8	33.1	34.8	55.4
Oakland	3	17	14.2	18.6	21.8	23.7	16.5	16.5	22.5	27.6	23.3	24.7
Oakland	4	15	11.9	13.3	13.0	19.5	8.9	11.8	17.9	19.8	22.6	19.7
Philadelphia	5	48	3.8	9.4	9.6	12.2	n.a.	1.6	5.5	6.9	11.0	n.a.
Providence	4	6	27.4	25.1	34.7	32.3	29.2	0.4	2.3	10.4	16.5	14.0
Washington	3	26	34.7	41.5	39.6	40.9	n.a.	35.6	45.8	48.1	47.3	n.a.
Washington	4	29	35.4	41.2	42.6	43.0	39.5	34.4	42.0	43.6	45.3	42.2

Note: n.a. = not available. Achievement can be compared year to year within a given district, but without proper statistical controls, figures cannot be directly compared with each other because different tests are being used in each district. When within-district comparisons are not appropriate (e.g., change of test from one year to next), we report a missing value. See the discussion in the chapter text for the methods used to identify the lowest 10th percentile. All achievement measures are percent proficient, with two exceptions. The achievement measure in Detroit is percent satisfactory + above, and the measure in Washington is normal curve equivalent.

the 25th percentile and below. The 75/25 ratio becomes our dependent variable in our statistical analysis of the achievement gap.[3]

To provide a sense of what these ratios look like, table 5.3 presents the inequality ratios for the mayor-controlled districts for elementary grades. We present the middle school inequality ratios in the online supplement. Most of the ratios hover around the value of 2, implying that schools in the top quarter of the district score twice as well on the state achievement test than do their counterparts in the bottom quartile. Looking over the time span of 1999 to 2003, it is difficult to make generalizations about trends across districts. New York appears to be narrowing the achievement gap in elementary schools, even before the advent of mayoral control, but the New York achievement gap for grade eight does not similarly close. Chicago's achievement gap during this period remains roughly the same for elementary reading and mathematics.

Specifying How Mayoral Control Affects Achievement Inequality Ratios

To better explain these inequality ratios, we turn to multivariate analysis similar to the analysis conducted in chapter four. Here, the unit of analysis is the grade-district-year. For each year 1999 through 2003, we measure the 75/25 ratio as it is available for different grades across different districts. In this part of the analysis, we look at all districts in the sample, not just those with mayoral control. Our data are *school-level* data, which means that as a prerequisite, a school district must have enough schools in a particular grade to consider the inequality spread among them. A district with only four schools, for instance, would be too prone to outliers. To be included in our analysis, our decision rule was that a particular district-grade must have at least ten schools. Because school districts typically have more elementary schools than middle schools, and more middle schools than high schools, we separated out our regressions into separate elementary and middle school categories. The middle school category only had 107 district-grades with at least ten observations, and because of this skewed and reduced sample, we focus solely on the elementary grades.[4]

Some districts have more than one grade worth of data available, and consequently they supply more of the observations in our analysis. Because different grades are involved, we introduce the variable $GRADE_i$ to serve as an additional control. If it is the case that certain grades are associated with lower inequality ratios, this control variable will capture that effect. Aside from this addition, however, we model the relationship between the 75/25

Table 5.3 Inequality Ratios of Mayor-Controlled Districts, Selected Elementary Grades, 1999–2003

(75th percentile / 25th percentile)

City	Grade	Reading					Math				
		1999	2000	2001	2002	2003	1999	2000	2001	2002	2003
Baltimore	3	2.47	2.608	2.427	2.157	1.631	4	4.17	3.827	3.592	1.63
Baltimore	5	2.337	2.461	2.121	2.257	1.429	3.639	3.261	2.752	3.513	1.797
Boston	4	3.667	5.5	1.867	2.538	2.846	3.333	3.667	4.5	4.6	4.333
Chicago	3	2.316	2.368	2.043	2.146	2.15	2.16	2.409	2.032	2.155	1.903
Chicago	5	1.8	2	1.909	2.091	1.929	2.313	2.6	2.389	2.717	2.071
Cleveland	4	1.815	2.146	1.869	2.17	n.a.	1.874	2.349	2.299	2.5	n.a.
Detroit	4	1.369	1.323	1.6	1.498	1.299	1.383	1.264	1.36	1.546	1.563
New Haven	4	3.5	2.8	2.206	2.404	1.857	2.714	2.412	2.516	1.923	1.645
New York	4	2.102	1.944	1.924	1.775	1.668	1.819	1.971	1.765	1.735	1.409
Oakland	3	2.353	2.538	2.571	2.588	2.5	2	2.556	2.333	2.333	1.96
Oakland	4	3	2.5	2.75	2.125	2.875	2.429	2.625	2	1.905	2.056
Philadelphia	5	3.525	2.934	3.375	2.951	n.a.	6	5.12	4.475	3.988	n.a.
Providence	4	1.429	1.69	1.435	1.44	1.306	3.5	4	2.548	1.881	2.099
Washington	3	1.316	1.244	1.256	1.282	n.a.	1.35	1.318	1.267	1.289	n.a.
Washington	4	1.289	1.293	1.268	1.275	1.297	1.289	1.326	1.279	1.267	1.262

Note: n.a. = not available. Ratios can be compared year to year within a given district, but without proper statistical controls, ratios cannot be directly compared with each other because different tests are being used in each district. When within-district comparisons are not appropriate (e.g., change of test from one year to next), we report a missing value. See the discussion in the chapter text for the methods used to calculate the 75/25 percentile ratios. All achievement measures are percent proficient, with two exceptions. The achievement measure in Detroit is percent satisfactory + above, and the measure in Washington is normal curve equivalent.

ratio and inputs using the same production function model as we used for achievement:

$$
\begin{aligned}
\text{75-25\_RATIO}_{it} = {} & \beta_0 + \beta_1 \text{75-25\_RATIO}_{it-1} + \beta_2 \text{MAYORAL\_CONTROL}_{it} \\
& + \beta_3 \text{MAYOR\_COUNCIL}_{it} \\
& + \beta_4 \text{PCT\_SINGLE\_MEMBER}_{it} + \beta_5 \text{PCT\_PRIVATE}_{it} \\
& + \beta_6 \text{PCT\_STATE\_REV}_{it} + \beta_7 \text{PPE\_INSTRUCT}_{it} \\
& + \beta_8 \text{ENROLL}_{it} + \beta_9 \text{PCT\_HISPANIC}_{it} \\
& + \beta_{10} \text{PCT\_AFR-AMERICAN}_{it} \\
& + \beta_{11} \text{PCT\_KIDS\_POVERTY}_{it} \\
& + \beta_{12} \text{PCT\_SPECIAL\_ED}_{it} + \beta_{12} \text{GRADE}_i \\
& + \delta_s + \gamma_t + \varepsilon_{it}
\end{aligned}
\tag{5.1}
$$

where 75-25_RATIO_{it} is the ratio of the highest-performing to the lowest-performing quartile of schools in school district i in year t; $\text{75-25\_RATIO}_{i,t-1}$ is the district's previous year's 75/25 ratio; $\text{MAYORAL\_CONTROL}_{it}$ is one either the MAYOR_INDEX or the set of NEW STYLE, MAJORITY, and FULL; $\text{MAYOR\_COUNCIL}_{it}$ is a dichotomous variable indicating whether or not the city uses a mayor–council form of government; $\text{PCT\_SINGLE\_MEMBER}_{it}$ is the percentage of city school board seats that are voted on in a single-member fashion; PCT_PRIVATE_{it} is the percentage of kindergarten–twelfth grade students in the city enrolled in private schools; $\text{PCT\_STATE\_REV}_{it}$ is the percentage of school district revenue from state sources; PPE_INSTRUCT_{it} is the district's per-pupil expenditure on instruction, adjusted for inflation and regional cost differences;[5] ENROLL_{it} is the district student enrollment; PCT_HISPANIC_{it} is the percentage of Hispanic students in the district; $\text{PCT\_AFR-AMERICAN}_{it}$ is the percentage of African American students in the district; $\text{PCT\_KIDS\_POVERTY}_{it}$ is the percentage of city residents, age three through eighteen, who were living below the poverty level in 2000; $\text{PCT\_SPECIAL\_ED}_{it}$ is the percentage of district students who have an individualized education plan; δ_s captures state fixed effects; γ_t captures year fixed effects, and ε_{it} is an error term.

The inclusion of state fixed effects is important here because the distribution of each state's testing results is not known. We do not know, for instance, if the Illinois state assessment has a more compressed achievement range than does the Massachusetts state assessment. We want to control for the possibility that 75/25 ratios are a result not of the district's productivity but simply the nature of the state examination. Including state fixed effects provides this statistical control.

MAYORS AND THE ACHIEVEMENT GAP

Having set up the analysis, we are ready to answer the question: Does mayoral control increase the achievement gap? The answer, based on our results presented in table 5.4, is *yes*. Although majority appointment power is inversely and significantly related to the reading achievement gap, the overall mayoral control index is positively, significantly related to inequality in both reading and mathematics (table 5.4). There is also a positive relationship between new-style mayors and the achievement gap in elementary reading. These positive relationships, as we further discuss in the next section, may be a result of mayors' interests in maintaining high-performing schools to anchor middle-class communities in the city. We also find that higher percentages of single-member district board members are associated with greater 75/25 ratios in math, suggesting that this governance arrangement as well can lead to more stratification.

What other contextual factors influence the achievement gap? Looking also at the nongovernance control variables, the first result that draws attention is the strong predictive power of previous inequality on existing inequality in both reading and mathematics (table 5.4). This result is not surprising, and it reminds us that reducing entrenched achievement inequality is a difficult task. We see that larger per-pupil expenditure is inversely associated with the 75/25 ratio in math, suggesting that greater resources may be effective in reducing the math achievement gap. The only student background variable that is significantly related to the 75/25 ratio is the percentage of special education students in the district. The magnitude of the effect of special education on the gap is quite large, suggesting that it is an important factor in explaining the achievement gap. Interestingly, the measures of minorities in the student body are not significant in these initial models. This may be explained by the fact that in districts with very high minority populations, both high- and low-performing schools will serve primarily minority students.

Mayors Promote the Competitive Position of their Schools

Our cross-district analysis of 75/25 ratios finds a positive relationship between mayoral control and the ratio in both elementary reading and mathematics. A move from an old-style governance regime to a new-style governance is associated with roughly a 0.38 increase in the 75/25 ratio in elementary reading. The magnitude of this impact will depend on the baseline ratio in a particular city. In a school district that had about the same inequality as Chicago, the baseline would see the best 25 percent of schools outperform

Table 5.4 Results from Linear Regression Models for Elementary Reading and Mathematics Achievement Inequality, 1999–2003 (75th/25th percentile ratio, with year and state fixed effects)

	Reading		Mathematics	
Variable	A	B	A	B
Previous inequality	0.34***	0.37***	0.67***	0.67***
	(0.10)	(0.10)	(0.05)	(0.05)
New-style mayor	0.38***		0.11	
	(0.09)		(0.20)	
Majority appointment power	−0.26***		0.18	
	(0.09)		(0.15)	
Full appointment power	0.08		0.09	
	(0.13)		(0.20)	
Mayor control index		0.11*		0.12**
		(0.05)		(0.06)
Mayor–council	−0.10	−0.08	0.11	0.11
	(0.07)	(0.07)	(0.12)	(0.12)
Percent single-member-elected school board members	0.07	0.12	0.18*	0.17*
	(0.10)	(0.10)	(0.10)	(0.09)
Percent in private school	0.29	0.23	−2.10	−2.09
	(0.62)	(0.71)	(1.99)	(1.97)
Percent revenue from state	−0.66*	−0.49	0.09	0.07
	(0.36)	(0.32)	(0.41)	(0.39)
Per-pupil expenditure, current instruction	−0.09	−0.08	−0.10*	−0.10*
	(0.06)	(0.06)	(0.05)	(0.05)
Enrollment (million)	0.14	−0.01	0.13	0.15
	(0.17)	(0.17)	(0.21)	(0.21)
Percent Hispanic	0.31	0.20	−1.38	−1.39
	(0.56)	(0.54)	(1.33)	(1.33)
Percent African American	0.01	0.08	−0.10	−0.13
	(0.27)	(0.25)	(0.44)	(0.42)
Percent children living in poverty	−0.53	−0.88	−0.52	−0.42
	(0.94)	(0.93)	(1.45)	(1.41)
Percent special education	2.54	2.92	5.66*	5.62*
	(2.00)	(1.96)	(3.02)	(2.85)
Grade	0.02	0.02	−0.00	−0.00
	(0.01)	(0.01)	(0.01)	(0.01)
Constant	1.79***	1.61***	1.08*	1.10*
	(0.56)	(0.57)	(0.58)	(0.56)
R^2	394	394	413	413
N	0.77	0.76	0.88	0.88

Note: Two-tailed significance denoted as *$p < .1$, **$p < .05$, ***$p < .01$. All models employ state and year fixed effects. Robust standard errors are produced by clustering on school districts.

the lowest 25 percent of schools roughly 2 to 1. Our analysis suggests that in this district, the introduction of mayoral control would change that ratio to 2.38 to 1.

One way of interpreting the finding that mayors and achievement stratification are positively linked is that mayors, facing competition from both the suburbs and private schools, may need to invest resources into high-performing schools to stem "brain drain." In metropolitan areas where districts are competing for high-performing schools, it is likely that the city's overall performance might significantly improve if two out of every ten departing brain drain students can be kept. Increasing numbers of mayor-led school boards, for example, have introduced more rigorous curricular programs, such as advanced placement and international baccalaureate classes, as a strategy to attract well-prepared students. Another explanation may be the assessment structure itself—for instance, Chicago's first wave accountability focused on the achievement of the top students as well as what is being called the "bubble" students (those on the cusp), whereas the No Child Left Behind Act focuses on the bottom quartile. The data in our study capture only the first year of the act, when schools were just starting to adapt (Mintrop and Trujillo 2004).

Mayors and the Middle Class

It may also be the case that the mayors see a greater need to initially establish stronger schools for middle-class residents before tackling the greater problem of turning around the school district's worst schools. High-performing schools serve as an anchor for middle-class families. In a 2005 keynote address at the Delivering Sustainable Communities Summit, Chicago mayor Richard M. Daley (2005) evaluated his school reforms using that imagery: "So how does government help build stronger neighborhoods? . . . You start by building what I call community anchors: schools, libraries, parks and police and fire stations. *The most important anchor, by far, is the school.*"

Recognizing this link between citywide economic interest and education is important when considering the relationship between redistribution and development. As Paul Peterson (1981, 43) has argued, "In some cases redistribution may be economically beneficial. . . . [But] in the contemporary United States, . . . it must be recognized that in most cases redistributive programs have negative economic effects" for the city as a whole.[6] In the realm of education, mayors may see a need to respond to corporate and civic interests that are demanding high-performing schools for the city's tax base.

Although we do not go so far as Peterson (1981, 99) in arguing that focusing on equality "comes at the expense of the development of the big-city economy," we recognize that mayors are caught between competing interests. Certainly, turning around low-performing schools can have positive economic effects. Mayors need to be mindful of the development of a new, skilled labor force that draws on all sectors of the city. Redistributive programs can go hand in hand with the citywide interest.

These results may provide some evidence to support the concerns of those who believe that mayoral control will lead to programs that favor business interests (Cuban and Usdan 2003). But it is important to recognize that although mayoral control is associated with higher 75/25 ratios, it does not appear to be the case that the lowest-performing schools are getting worse. Instead, they are not improving as fast as some of the highest-performing schools. In this view, mayoral control is a reform that improves student performance overall but, at least initially, improves student performance at a greater rate in the upper quartile of city schools.

These dual findings raise a question of trade-off and citywide interest that are at the heart of most inequality discussions. Should the city focus on raising the "floor" of student achievement or focus primarily on closing the gap, even if that means dropping the "ceiling"? We believe that at this time in the history of U.S. urban centers, there is a great need for maintaining a strong, middle-class city population core. High-performing schools are necessary to attract and keep those residents in the city. A strong middle-class presence enables the city to build a broader political coalition for intergovernmental lobbying. The middle class also forms a strong "voice" to air concerns on education quality. In addressing the challenges of the lowest-performing schools, cities must also recognize that their mission may be made quite difficult by the levels of poverty and special education needs of students in those schools. In this view, the most efficient use of resources may be to make simultaneous investments in both high-performing and low-performing schools, understanding that the overall 75/25 ratio may expand as a consequence.

FUTURE RESEARCH AGENDA

Although our analysis of inequality using school-level data is revealing, student-level data would be quite helpful in future research. Student-level data would allow us to develop a better understanding of the racial gap in these mayor-controlled districts. In some cases, as Olszewski-Kubilius and Seon-Young (2004) have shown, the racial gap may be addressed by providing advanced programs to minority students. The data we use in this study do not allow us to see, in each district, how schools are addressing racial and achievement gaps or how students are moving between schools. As more districts develop these individual student-level measures, it will become possible to aggregate up from individual students, to school, district, state, and then national levels.

CHAPTER SIX

Accountability and Urban High Schools: The Challenge of Improving Instructional Practices

THE PREVIOUS CHAPTERS OF THIS BOOK HAVE EXAMINED mayoral control as a strategy to improve student achievement in low-performing school districts. These chapters have discussed how mayoral control facilitates an integrated governance arrangement in which authority at the systemwide level is streamlined and political incentives converge to target resources to low-performing schools. In this chapter, we turn to Chicago's experience with mayoral control between 1995 and 2000 with the specific interest of examining how the governance approach affects teaching and learning in low-performing schools.

Past studies on mayoral control have tended to focus on whether the governance approach increases district civic and political capacity. In contrast, we explore macro–micro linkages between city and district governance arrangements and changes in classroom practice by focusing on how principals and teachers in Chicago responded to the accountability agenda initiated in the early years of mayoral takeover (Cuban and Usdan 2003; Henig and Rich 2004; Wong et al. 1999; Wong and Shen 2003). Through our multilevel analysis, we show that mayoral control created political conditions in Chicago that allowed for an alignment of goals and strategies aimed at improving school and student achievement that were particularly conducive to a high-stakes accountability agenda. At the same time, we discuss the limitations of this kind of large-scale reform for substantively altering classroom teaching and learning.

Although prior district-level studies of mayoral control have important implications for school and classroom practice, few have linked district-level authority to empirical analyzes of school and classroom practices. Increasingly, districts are understood to play an important role in providing support for school reform and improving teaching and learning (Hightower et al. 2002; Honig and Hatch 2004; Louis, Febey, and Schroeder 2005; Wong and Rutledge 2006). Districts serve as important mediators between federal and state policy, on the one hand, and schools, on the other. Further, districts often set conditions for instructional improvement and are well poised to address issues of intradistrict equity (Hightower et al. 2002; Honig and Hatch 2004; Marsh 2002). Yet districts can only facilitate policy coherence and organizational collaboration among major actors if they have both the internal support from faculty and staff and the external support from parents and community members. The research on district influence has focused little on the conditions that give districts the capacity to take on large-scale reform. Mayoral control represents an important way that districts can garner support from multiple constituencies for ambitious school- and classroom-level change.

Chicago's experience with mayoral control is particularly instructive of the extent to which the alignment of political actors under mayoral control can facilitate the implementation of an accountability agenda aimed at improving school and student achievement. In 1995, the Illinois State Legislature gave Mayor Richard M. Daley control of the school system. With this new authority, the mayor appointed a School Reform Board of Trustees and chief executive officer (CEO) for the school district. In the first year of mayoral control, the new administration took several important actions to strengthen fiscal and political support for the school system. The following year, the CEO, Paul Vallas, and the School Reform Board of Trustees launched an educational accountability agenda focused on raising standards and improving student performance.

In this chapter we examine how mayoral control provided the context for school and classroom reform in high schools in Chicago. The chapter draws on qualitative case studies we conducted in three Chicago high schools to address the following questions: (1) How did mayoral control facilitate systemwide reform? (2) What form did systemwide reform take? (3) How did principals and teachers implement the district's accountability agenda? (4) How did district policies shape instruction? Though the depth and sustainability of the reforms launched under mayoral control remains an ongoing empirical question, there is little doubt that mayoral control created conditions conducive for large-scale change in Chicago schools. Through this multilevel qualitative analysis, we identify the mechanisms used by the district to implement reforms in Chicago's high schools and consider, in particular, the implications of mayoral control for classroom teaching and learning.

MAYORAL CONTROL AS A DISTRICT REFORM

As discussed earlier in this book, mayoral control reduces competing political actors and strengthens the school district's political capacity to undertake large-scale systemwide reform. Recent studies have identified the important role that school districts serve by setting common expectations for administrators and teachers (Wong et al. 1999; Louis, Febey, and Schroeder 2005), building professional communities (Talbert and McLaughlin 1994), and developing common curricular and instructional strategies (Massell and Goertz 2002; Spillane 1996). Studies have also focused on the organizational characteristics of systemwide reform, highlighting the different mechanisms employed by districts (Firestone 1989) as well as the variation between and among district schools in terms of curricular and instructional capacity (Spillane 1996). Though reform efforts face challenges—including political fragmentation, disparities between districts and schools, unequal external support, lack of systemwide instructional coherence, and teacher turnover and inexperience (Anderson 2003)—as a whole these studies reveal the powerful effect that districts can have in initiating and sustaining meaningful school change.

Studies on resource allocation in schools have also documented how managerial functions performed at the districtwide level define the fiscal, personnel, and curricular resources that have a substantial bearing on school and classroom activities (Barr and Dreeben 1983; Gamoran 1988). Indeed, how a school operates is affected by systemwide decisions such as staff development, choice of curriculum and assessment standards, administrative promotion, interpretation of and compliance with federal and state mandates, and integration of school and other social services in the city. The top of the system, for example, exercises influence over the quality of middle-level administrators in charge of curricular development, program operation, and the application of assessment standards to schools. Similarly, districtwide curriculum frameworks and assessments facilitate and constrain decisions at the school and classroom levels regarding who gets taught, what, by whom, and how.

At the same time, principals and teachers are street-level bureaucrats (Lipsky 1980). They mediate policies created at the district level through their everyday decisions and routines. Implementation studies have long documented how frontline workers, like teachers and principals, effectively set policy as they reinterpret and translate external mandates in ways that often directly contradict policymakers' original intentions (Pressman and Wildvasky 1973; Wong and Anagnostopoulos 1998; Wong 1991). Lipsky argues that the high levels of discretion exerted by street-level bureaucrats stem, in large part, from the endemic uncertainties and complexities of the tasks that these workers perform. In our case, teaching is a highly complex activity. The goals of teaching tend to be diffuse, contested, and difficult to measure objectively and on a large scale. It is thus difficult to align means and ends in any conclusive manner. Further, teachers and principals must rely for results upon students, who are compelled by law to attend school and who frequently have little interest in or motivation to engage the subjects at hand (Anagnostopoulos and Rutledge 2003; Cohen 1989). For teachers in urban schools, the chronic lack of resources and ever-increasing demands for services intensify complexities. Given these endemic uncertainties and complexities, teachers, and to a lesser extent principals, tend to respond to external accountability mandates by focusing resources on obtaining measured objectives—that is, raising test scores—even as they lower expectations for student learning and ration resources and commitment to students who are perceived as having the most chance of succeeding (Lipsky 1980; Anagnostopoulos and Rutledge 2003).

The street-level bureaucrat perspective provides insight into how principals and teachers in low-performing schools are likely to respond to the accountability agendas that have been closely related to mayoral control, especially as it has been enacted in Chicago. Other implementation studies in education highlight the salience of teachers' professional commitments, capacities, and collegial relationships for their implementation of externally derived policy (Ball and Bowe 1994; Coburn 2001, 2004; Jennings 1996; Spillane, Reiser, and Reimer 2002; Hill 2001). In high schools, subject matter and subject departments centrally organize how teachers think about their work, how they identify themselves professionally, their collegial relations, and their classroom practices (Talbert and McLaughlin 1994; Siskin 1994; Grossman and Stodolsky 1998). They are, thus, key policy mediators. Finally, principals' and teachers' responses to policy also manifest efforts by each to defend or extend their authority over key activities and resources. Such strategic responses tend to be particularly important during periods when major shifts in policy, such as those affected by outcome-based accountability mandates, unsettle conventional relationships and practices. These shifts make possible new practices as they make available new sets of resources and relationships; at the same time, they may also result in efforts at retrenchment (Anagnostopoulos and Rutledge 2007).

Taken together, Barr and Dreeben's resource allocation model and implementation literature highlight the important role of school districts in the design and implementation of systemwide reform while also acknowledging the salience of both school-level organizational structures and principals' and teachers' professional discretion for the effects that mayoral control can exert on classroom teaching and learning. Mayoral control has the potential to streamline implementation by creating political conditions that diffuse district-level confusion and conflict. Though conditions of mayoral control vary by urban area, reducing institutional fragmentation can contribute to a coherent approach to academic accountability. At the same time, principals and teachers will undoubtedly shape and reshape this approach. We turn now to examine the case of Chicago to understand how the district's experience with mayoral control contributed to a systemwide refocusing of classroom practice. We pay particular attention to how principals and teachers negotiated instructional authority, allocated and used instructional resources, and targeted their efforts and commitments in response to the district's accountability agenda.

MAYORAL CONTROL IN CHICAGO

In 1995, the Illinois state legislature enacted the Chicago School Reform Amendatory Act, granting Mayor Richard M. Daley control of the Chicago Public Schools (CPS). This law—passed with the support of the mayor, the business community, and the governor of Illinois—strengthened and centralized the CPS administrative structures. It mandated a mayor-appointed School Reform Board of Trustees and the creation and mayoral appointment of a CEO charged with overseeing district and school performance. It also eliminated several commissions, including the School Finance Authority and the School Board Nominating Commission. Through several measures—including the consolidation of a number of funded programs (e.g., kindergarten–sixth grade reading improvement, substance abuse prevention, Hispanic programs, gifted education) and the reallocation of state Chapter 1 funds from the schools to the district—the law also gave administrators greater control over the fiscal infrastructure and revenues of the district (School Code of Illinois 1996).

Once in office, the district's leadership team moved quickly to restore public confidence in the schools. In 1995, the board undertook a number of highly visible initiatives to eliminate waste and corruption within the system. It established the Office of Investigations to identify instances of misconduct by employees and financial improprieties by contractors and vendors. In a number of highly publicized events, the Office of Investigations identified specific incidents of waste—for example, $1 million worth of spoiled food stored in a warehouse and $5 million in wood, tools, and supplies stockpiled in four schools. By disclosing and resolving these incidents, the district sent the message to the community that the new leadership would not tolerate fiscal irresponsibility.

The new administration also downsized the central office. Within one year of implementation, the number of staff positions in the central administration had declined by 21 percent. The majority of these cuts came from

citywide administration and services. The reduction was achieved by award-
ing contracts to private providers for food services, distribution, and facilities. Other reductions were obtained by consolidating the eleven district offices
into six regional offices.

The distribution of appointments within the central office also reflected
the mayor's focus on fiscal conditions and the management of the system.
The mayor drew the majority of initial district appointments from other city
agencies and from the business community. Between 1995 and 1997, 54
percent of appointments to the CPS's central office came from city hall, 21
percent from the private sector, 9 percent from other public institutions,
6 percent from nonprofit organizations, and only 9 percent from within the
school district.

Taken together, these actions significantly improved public confidence in
the ability of the board and central administration to govern the schools and
strengthened the district's reputation. An analysis of public perception of the
district's performance in its first year (1995–96) shows that the board, central office, and the mayor made significant gains over their 1993–95 performance ratings (Wong and Moulton 1996). Though all seven governance actors
included in the analysis made gains in public confidence over this period, only
the performances of the three city actors edged into the "satisfactory" category.[1]
The performance of the other actors remained in the "poor" region, indicating that survey respondents were still not satisfied with the overall performance
of the governor, the Democratic and Republican lawmakers, and the Chicago
Teachers Union.

To further enhance public confidence in the schools, the central office instituted several mechanisms to respond to school-level complaints. The Office of Schools and Regions became responsible for dealing with referrals from
parents, teachers, and principals, and for resolving community and parent
complaints. "The management team—the CEO, chief of staff and deputy, and
the officers of the four units—are very responsive to the general public, almost to the point where I wonder if I am spending my time as well as I could,"
one elementary school principal explained during the 1995–96 school year
(in an interview on April 17, 1996).

To address systemwide accountability concerns, the district established the
Office of Accountability at a time when such offices were rare. "Accountability," as it came to be called, consolidated the oversight and monitoring of
schools in one department. Directed by the chief accountability officer, Accountability provided schools in the system with a number of services, including the coordination of school intervention programs, guidelines on how to
evaluate principals and teachers, and support on balancing budgets. With an
accountability agenda that relied heavily on test scores as the gauge of student achievement and progress, the district employed statisticians to analyze

data and convey scores back to schools. Overall, Accountability served an important function under mayoral control. It institutionalized accountability as a bureaucratic office within the school system and in so doing it conveyed the importance of accountability to both internal actors and the general public.

Mayoral control gave Mayor Daley the opportunity to apply his governance approach across city departments, including the school system. Through a set of highly visible and well-publicized reforms and appointments, he set a new accountability agenda for the school system that was consistent with his governance approach. By investing his political capital, the district became an extension of his business-oriented approach to mayoral governance. By applying managerial, fiscal, and infrastructure reforms from business to the schools, he addressed the district's legitimacy crisis. These reforms resulted in less governance fragmentation and greater coherence at all levels of the school system and set the stage for an ambitious and, at that time, new approach to improving performance.

The Accountability Agenda

By taking advantage of his new powers to set its financial house in order, the mayor and the CEO, Paul Vallas, cleared the way for a full focus on teaching and learning. In the second year of mayoral control, the district launched a highly visible educational accountability agenda focused on improving school and student achievement. From the vantage point of the mayor, the CEO, and other school administrators, the governance arrangements of earlier administrations had not directed enough resources at teaching and learning. In public remarks, district officials sent a consistent message of their perceptions of the school system. For example, Vallas described the CPS before his arrival as having "no focus on academics at all. Did you have cronyism? Did you have corruption? Did you have a lack of standards—lack of accountability? All of those things" (*Attleboro Sun Times* 1997). In May 1997, the mayor painted a similar picture regarding the district's high schools, saying, "We have a long way to go. [High schools] have been lousy in the past, and no one's been fired about it. The high school system was a complete mess. You know it, I know it" (*Chicago Sun-Times* 1997). That same spring, Vallas explained the rationale for the new accountability agenda by saying, "A little pressure never hurt anybody" (*Attleboro Sun Times* 1997). Cozette Buckney, the district's chief education officer from 1995 to 2000, typified the approach when she said, "People have got to know that when there is educational failure there is an end game. Schools can close. Students can be held back. But we also help people succeed."[2] About high schools, she said that "we have to do something drastic" (*Catalyst* 1997).

Policy Tools

The CPS accountability agenda initiated in October 1996 drew on three types of policy tools: regulatory sanctions, including formal sanctions against low performance applied to students and schools; support for low-performing students and schools; and professional discretion for school-level control over the design and implementation of improvement programs.[3] The initiatives differed in the type and degree of district intervention and the level(s) of school organization at which they were aimed. Table 6.1 identifies the different types of policy tools that the district employed in relation to its three major accountability initiatives directed at the high schools: probation, academic promotion, and systemwide curricular standards and assessments. The district employed two main sanctioning policies. The district's probation policy, begun in October 1996, sanctioned schools if 15 percent or less of their students scored below grade level on the nationally normed Iowa Test of Basic Skills (ITBS) or the high school equivalent, the Test of Achievement and Proficiency (TAP). The following year, the district reconstituted seven high schools that had been under probation in 1996, when the schools' scores showed no improvement. Reconstitution required that all employees, from the principal to the support staff, reapply for their jobs or find other employment. In 1997, the district fired five of the seven principals in the reconstituted schools. Because of the union contract, the district had to continue to employ teachers not rehired by the reconstituted schools for a limited period. The district did remove these teachers from the reconstituted schools rather than allowing them to remain teaching. The district removed schools from their sanctioned status once 25 percent or more of their students scored at or above grade level on

Table 6.1 District Policy Tools under Mayoral Control

Type of Policy Tool	Probation/ Reconstitution	Academic Promotion	Chicago Standards and Assessments
Sanctions	Threat of restaffing Public reporting of low performance	Grade retention	CASE exam
Support	External partners Probation managers	Summer remediation program	Chicago Standards and Framework documents
Professional discretion	Principal selection of external partners and probation managers	Promotion waivers Hiring teachers in summer remediation program	Choice of implementation plan

the TAP or ITBS. During the period of this study, the district placed 117 schools on probation. From 1997 to 2000, forty-seven schools were removed from probation and reconstitution.

Under its promotion policy, the district retained students in the third, sixth, eighth, and ninth grades if they failed to meet the district cutoff score for promotion on the ITBS for elementary and middle school students and the TAP for high school students. If students did not meet the district's cutoff point in the spring, students were expected to enroll in a summer remediation program specifically designed to help them meet district standards. If students still failed to meet district requirements for promotions after the summer program, they were retained.

In addition to sanctions, the district also employed support tools. It sponsored a number of initiatives aimed at providing support to both sanctioned and nonsanctioned schools. For sanctioned schools, it assigned probation managers and external partners.[4] Its expectations for these consultants included working with principals and teachers to design meaningful school reform and professional development aimed at improving student achievement.

To complement its use of nationally normed standardized tests, the district began implementing its own standards-based curricular assessments in 1997. That year, it adopted a revised version of the Chicago Academic Standards for all grade levels, produced programs of study for ninth and tenth grade academic courses that specified core content, skills, and processes to be taught each semester, and began piloting the Chicago Academic Standards Exam (CASE) in the high schools. The CASE tested students' knowledge of the skills, content, and (in English) texts identified in the program. It had two parts, a multiple-choice section and a constructed response section that required students to write short essays in response to predetermined prompts or, in mathematics, to explain their solutions to a word problem. The district scored the multiple-choice section, while teachers at each school scored the constructed responses using district rubrics. Students had to earn at least a 50 percent to pass the CASE. Each section was weighted equally. In 1998–99, the year of this study, the district intended to use CASE results as another criterion for placing schools on probation and for determining students' promotion from tenth to eleventh grade.

With the development of the CASE for ninth and tenth graders and the use of the nationally normed TAP to determine school sanctioning status and promotion, the district placed these two assessments at the center of its expectations for high school teachers. Yet, within the district's accountability agenda, the two tests served different purposes. The TAP, used in its high-stakes capacity, set benchmarks for student achievement that the district could use to compare and sanction schools. The district released school TAP scores to the press, thus publicly identifying schools by their average test scores. The

CASE, in contrast, was intended to structure and improve teachers' curricular and instructional decisions by clarifying goals and objectives for each subject matter. The CASE tested students' mastery of the content, skills, and processes delineated by the Chicago Standards and Frameworks. Significantly, the Standards and Frameworks did not mandate specific instructional activities or strategies for teachers; they provided only "suggested" activities and lists of resources (Wong et al. 2001).

Through these multiple policies and initiatives, the district sought to remediate low-performing schools, stop social promotion, set clear curricular and instructional expectations, and improve the performance of its high schools. By using both nationally normed and locally developed criterion-based assessments, the district established measurable achievement standards for schools and students that parents and the general public could understand. Yet despite these interventions, the district still left much of the implementation of its accountability agenda to the professional discretion of principals and teachers. Though principals and teachers were expected to respond to district policies, during the period of our study, the district did not place restrictions on the nature of this response. In this way, principals and teachers retained site-level discretion as to how to meet district expectations. For example, the district set few parameters on the reforms probation schools developed with external partners. In the implementation of both the TAP and the CASE, the district also left much to the discretion of school-level actors. Teachers and principals could determine the curricular and instructional approaches they undertook to prepare students for these tests; the district did not mandate that schools use particular test-preparation or curricular and instructional programs in relation to these tests.

At the same time, the testing policies served as an external pressure directing principals and teachers toward the goal of improving student achievement. To be sure, the high-stakes nature of the TAP policies placed more pressure on school actors than did the constraints from the CASE. Nevertheless, the two policies worked together to constrain principals and teachers' curricular and instructional practices. They represented an effort to narrow the curriculum and restrict the options available to both school administrators and teachers. Within this context, then, principals and teachers had professional discretion to respond to district testing mandates or risk, for principals, job termination and, for teachers, the stigma of working in a school publicly labeled "failing."[5]

The Study

To understand how school actors responded to the district's accountability agenda, we conducted longitudinal, multilevel, qualitative case studies. This approach allowed us to track the implementation of the district's accountability agenda at the district, school, teacher, and classroom levels. Though not generalizable, the depth and duration of our study allowed for both a chronological and thematic analysis of implementation, revealing important similarities and variations in the implementation of district policy across sites (Polkinghorne 1995).

At the district level we interviewed the CEO, the chief education officer, the head of the Accountability Office, and other central office staff responsible for developing and implementing programs in curriculum and instruction, professional development, and high school restructuring, as well as overseeing the implementation of probation and reconstitution. We also collected documentary materials from the board, including board policies, budget information, minutes of the Chicago School Reform Board of Trustees meetings, publications describing programs and the district's curriculum standards, frameworks, and sample assessment questions.

To examine the effects of the district's accountability agenda on CPS high schools and classrooms, we conducted cases studies at three high schools between 1996 and 2000. The studies provided strong longitudinal and comparative analysis both within and between schools. The three high schools in our study—Greene, Reed, and Weston—experienced different degrees of district intervention: Greene was placed on probation but removed after a year, Reed remained on probation for several years, and Weston was reconstituted after a year of probation. Even after reconstitution, Weston remained under probation for the duration of our study. Demographically, all schools had high percentages of racial minorities and low-income students. The student bodies of the schools ranged from roughly 75 to 100 percent racial minority and from 80 to 100 percent low income. Though the schools represented different levels of district intervention, all could be considered "low performing" as indicated by TAP reading scores. From 1995 to 2000, the early years of mayoral control, Greene averaged roughly 23 percent of students scoring at or above national norms on the TAP reading section, Reed averaged 17 percent, and Weston averaged 8 percent. In this way, the case study schools were similar to other high schools in the district. During the same period, on average, 25 percent of students scored at or above national norms on the TAP reading section.

At each school we conducted annual, semistructured interviews with the principal, administrators in charge of instruction, and mathematics and English teachers.[6] Interviews focused on how individuals understood and responded to the district's accountability initiatives, particularly probation/ reconstitution and the curricular standards and assessment policies. We also asked questions about the social organization of the school and faculty responses to school-level efforts to implement district policies. From

1996 to 2000, we conducted approximately two hundred interviews with principals, other school administrators, and mathematics and English teachers.

To understand the effects of high-stakes policies on principals and teachers, we observed ninth, tenth, and eleventh grade English and mathematics classes across the three schools, selecting the high-stakes grades for each year.[7] In this way, we observed two teachers from each discipline and each high-stakes grade in the fall and in the spring for four years. We observed teachers who had primary assignments in the high-stakes grades, observing the same class and section taught by these teachers for two or three consecutive days in both the fall and spring. We conducted observations at two points in the year in order to examine the effects of district policies on teachers' curricular and instructional decisions. Second-semester observations were conducted one to two months before the district's administration of the TAP. By visiting English and math teachers twice a year for a series of classes, we were able to document the range of curricular and instructional strategies that the teachers employed. During the four years of the study, we collected approximately 250 hours of observations in math and English classes.

To understand the effects of the city's CASE on the high schools and classrooms, we observed two tenth grade teachers at each school teach *To Kill a Mockingbird* during the 1998–99 school year. The district mandated that teachers teach this novel for the CASE. We observed one section of English II taught by each teacher. Each class was observed at least eight times over the course of the unit, for a total of 62 hours of observations. For all classroom observations, we took verbatim accounts of classroom instruction over the course of the instructional unit. Audiotapes of classrooms were recorded and transcribed. Finally, we interviewed each teacher to understand in more detail how they used district support, in the form of professional development, external partners, test data and curriculum documents to plan their instruction, their goals and objectives for the unit, and their assessment of the unit's effectiveness with students.

Both principal and teacher interviews were coded using three broad categories. The first category focused on how principals and teachers described the implementation of the district's sanctioning policy of probation and the support policies of curricular and instructional standards and frameworks. Here, we looked at how principals and teachers interpreted the policies and the implementation plan they developed and initiated in response. The second category worked backward, looking at how principals and teachers talked about the two assessments, the TAP and the CASE, specifically looking at the language they used to describe the different assessments and how school actors explained the tests' effects on their curricular and instructional goals. Finally, we examined what school actors said explicitly and implicitly about the district, schools, teachers, and students.

We conducted numerous analyses of classroom observations. To assess how teachers responded to the high-stakes assessments and school-level mandates in response to these assessments, we classified classroom activities into three categories: test taking, reading/test skills development, and other instruction.[8] To understand if there was a difference in instruction when teachers taught to the TAP versus when they taught to the CASE, we coded classroom transcripts according to the length of each instructional activity and the type of activity involved. This enabled us to determine the academic demands of instructional activities. We also looked at the types of questions that teachers asked when preparing students for the TAP and the CASE. These analyses, discussed in more detail in the findings section, gave us the opportunity to compare instruction within and among schools. It also provided a comparison of the schools' implementation of the two assessments, the TAP and the CASE, as well as an analysis of district-level initiatives aimed at improving teaching and learning.

THE CASE STUDIES

In this section we focus on how principals and teachers responded to the district's three main types of leverage: formal sanctions, support for low-performing students and schools, and professional discretion. We discuss the initiatives principals and teachers pursued at each school and then focus on the implementation of the two assessments, the TAP and the CASE. Though each school in our study responded directly to district policies, they pursued different approaches, reflecting both internal priorities as well as different levels of district pressure. By looking at school as well as classroom-level implementation, we track how principals and teachers negotiated implementation and, in turn, how this shaped classroom instruction.

From the perspective of mayoral control, this section on school and classroom implementation has several implications. At one level, it reveals how principals and teachers negotiate and prioritize the multiple policies initiated under an ambitious accountability reform. At another, it shows how, together, the two assessments the district employed and the related Chicago Academic Standards and Frameworks contributed to a systemwide focus on teaching and learning. In what follows, we discuss whether these multiple policies lead to contradictory or complementary school-level initiatives. We also discuss the implications for teaching and learning.

School-Level Responses to Probation and the CASE

Greene High School: Shared Focus on Reading

The principal of Greene High School, Sam Adams, had been principal for six years when the school was put on probation in October 1996. Adams's response to the probation policy and his efforts to raise test scores reflected an instructional approach aimed at motivating all teachers to improve test scores through instructional strategies. In terms of the CASE, however, Adams left the design and implementation to the English teachers. So while the response to the high-stakes TAP represented a whole-school approach, the implementation of the CASE was left to the discretion of the subject matter departments.

In the first year of our study, Adams adapted a collegial training model in response to probation. Building on a writing initiative he had employed the previous year in response to the school being placed on the state's academic watch list for poor performance on the state writing assessment, he convened a committee of school administrators and selected department chairs and teachers and charged them with developing a common instructional focus on reading. Working with reading experts from a local university, members of the committee debated ways to address adolescent literacy and reached a consensus on what constituted effective reading instruction. This committee was then constituted as the school's official Reading Committee. The year the school was placed on probation, the Reading Committee organized mandatory in-services and voluntary Saturday workshops designed to introduce teachers to different strategies for teaching reading. These strategies represented a range of approaches to teaching reading, including constructivist approaches, vocabulary building, identifying the main idea of a reading passage, and plot mapping. In terms of test practice, activities focused directly on the skills emphasized by the TAP, such as making inferences, comparing and contrasting, and sequencing. They also included test-taking strategies and practice test taking.

For the next three years, the school's major response to the district's use of the TAP to measure and monitor school performance continued to be directed by the Reading Committee and centered on its related professional development activities. Faculty "experts" introduced "reading strategies," as they came to be called, at weekly faculty meetings. Time was set aside after these meetings for the faculty to meet again—usually in their departments—to review and discuss their implementation of the week's strategy. The Reading Committee developed a monthly schedule for all faculty members that established the days teachers were to teach certain strategies. In the third year, as the school moved further from sanctioned status, Adams restructured the schedule of weekly workshops, alternating them with department meetings. This reinforced Adams's other efforts to foster curricular standardization among subject matter departments by mandating that teachers co-develop and implement common course midterm exams and finals. In this way, though Adams emphasized the teaching of reading to improve TAP reading scores, in other areas Adams reinforced teachers' departmental efforts and relationships.

In addition to launching the schoolwide reading initiative, over the course of our fieldwork, Adams also took advantage of district funds and opportunities to institute an international baccalaureate program and to increase the number of advanced placement courses for higher-scoring students. Adams called his efforts, as a whole, an "academic" approach to school improvement. He considered the Reading Committee as an integral component of this approach.

While pursuing this academic approach, Adams also increased the monitoring and evaluation of teachers. He asked the Reading Committee to develop a checklist that administrators used in impromptu visits to teachers' classrooms. Despite teachers complaining about the evaluative approach, he felt that the practice was not only an important way of keeping track of faculty compliance with the reading initiative but also sent the message that he was overseeing instruction. The monitoring also manifested the expansion of his instructional authority.

The district removed Greene from probation in the summer of 1997 after student reading scores on the TAP had doubled and mathematics scores had gone up by 95 percent. Even with this success, Adams continued with the programs he had initiated the probationary year. From his perspective, probation had facilitated a focus on academic achievement that he did not want to disrupt. Not only did he see the opportunity to build on the progress already made, but he did not want to leave the school vulnerable again to stigmatization. As he explained, "When probation came along, that created the sense of urgency that I needed to really focus the professional work that the teachers were doing on improving instruction, first of all, reading and writing, those areas. Putting more of a classroom focus on them, in the school, the teachers that did what they did, there was an accountability there, that we were all responsible."

Teachers' responses to the strategies were generally positive, with no group mobilizing opposition to the principal's initiatives. Though there were departmental differences reported between English and mathematics teachers, with math teachers complaining that the reading strategies took time away from their curriculum, both English and math teachers reported following the reading strategies calendar. Compliance among English teachers did taper off significantly during the last two years of our study as student test scores increased and the threat from sanctioning decreased. Math teachers, however, continued to enact the reading strategies, complying in large part to avoid negative sanctions from the school's principal. Significantly, though they stopped implementing the reading strategies, English teachers believed that the reading initiative had helped to create a common culture around instruction. As one English teacher explained at the end of our study, "Every Monday we had the workshops, which we were required to attend. After the first year, they started to get a bit repetitive and boring but he [the principal] did create, I think, a culture of awareness, a culture of fostering teacher ability in the classroom, particularly how they worked, incorporating reading strategies into the classroom."

In contrast, the principal's reaction to the CASE was to leave its implementation to the discretion of the English department. He did not initiate any policies or programs in response to the CASE, nor did he seek to restructure English department organization. Instead, he expected the English department to oversee the teachers' response to the CASE, which they did by restructuring their curriculum around common eight-week course exams structured around the district's curricular and instructional standards. English teachers at the school thus took the implementation of the CASE seriously. Though teachers expressed some frustration with the lack of information from the district regarding the CASE, particularly during its first year of implementation, Greene's English teachers reported that the exam and the curricular frameworks that accompanied it were aligned with their own curricular and instructional practices. The CASE tended to reinforce rather than challenge or redirect the teachers' understanding and practice of the "real" English curriculum. At the same time, the CASE also reinforced Adams's efforts to standardize curriculum within the subject matter departments. It provided a common text around which the teachers co-developed course curriculum and final exams.

Reed: Conflict in Implementation

Juan Quitral became principal of Reed in 1996, the year the district placed the school on probation. Quitral, who had worked at the school as both a teacher and assistant principal for over twenty years and had developed the school's nationally recognized school-to-work program, inherited a highly contentious faculty. The district placed Reed on probation shortly after it removed the school's former principal, whom many faculty members characterized as divisive. Probation, and Quitral's responses to it, thus became intimately tied to the conflict that had emerged within the school around the previous principal's leadership.

The faculty's response to Quitral's efforts to institute a reading strategies program modeled after the one Adams had developed at Greene illustrates how teachers sought to undermine Quitral's efforts to implement an instructional response to probation focused on reading. Within the first year of being placed on probation, Quitral used district funds to hire a reading specialist to design and oversee a schoolwide reading program. The reading specialist initiated several programs, with varying success. In the summer of 1998, the specialist met with a group of teachers appointed by the principal to design a schoolwide reading strategies program and to develop a teacher-as-trainer dissemination model. The teachers who worked with the specialist during the summer were to assist small groups of teachers across the school's faculty to learn and implement the reading strategies throughout the year. By the time the 1998–99 school year began, the reading specialist had produced a large reading strategies manual, designated weekly reading strategies that were identified in the school's daily bulletins, and begun to oversee staff training. She had also begun, along with assistant principals, to visit classrooms to monitor teachers' use of the reading strategies. With a group of newly hired reading teachers, the reading specialist further developed the curriculum for the developmental reading courses targeted at ninth through eleventh graders who had scored below national norms on the TAP reading section.

Within the first semester of the 1998–99 school year, a group of faculty members began openly resisting the reading specialist's initiatives. Teachers complained that the reading specialist lacked the requisite administrative credential to observe them. Further, several teachers rejected the reading manual as too complicated and argued for using different approaches. Quitral responded to these challenges by halting the specialist's observations and by allowing teachers to choose from two other reading programs, in addition to the one the specialist had designed as a whole-school effort. While the specialist continued to identify weekly reading strategies in the school bulletin, teachers did not have to adopt these strategies. According to Quitral, half the teaching faculty refused to implement the reading approach overseen by the reading specialist that year. Though Quitral acquiesced to teachers' complaints about the reading strategies, he continued with the TAP components of the original plan. Even this mandate, however, was diminished. By the second year of our study, only English teachers were required to prepare students for the TAP reading section.

For Quitral, teachers' resistance to the reading strategies program represented the problem of teachers' subject matter identities prevailing over the view that they were all "teachers of reading." Teacher interviews confirmed this perception. Teachers in both departments repeatedly characterized the teaching of reading, as defined in the principal's mandates as a set of discrete skills, as outside their purview. This was particularly pronounced among the school's mathematics teachers, who as a department resisted the principal's reading mandates on the grounds that the mandates would take time away from teaching math. Interestingly, one of the strategies that the staff of the

mathematics department used in their efforts to counter the principal's reading mandates was to launch their own TAP preparation effort. Using the
district's emphasis on TAP scores strategically, the math teachers devoted
roughly one month to reviewing for the TAP math section. When the school's
math scores increased for two consecutive years, while the reading scores decreased or remained stagnant, the math teachers used the scores to justify their
continued resistance to teaching reading. Among the English teachers, resistance to the principal's reading mandates grew over time. At the end of the
study, we found that the English teachers devoted very little class time to either
the reading strategies or the reading test preparation mandates. Instead, they
launched a departmentwide writing effort.

Along with condemning teachers' refusal to teach reading, throughout the
study Quitral repeatedly maintained that inadequate teaching of basic skills
was the cause of the school's low performance and that many teachers on his
staff did not care sufficiently about their students or accept responsibility for
teaching them; to address poor instructional skills, teachers needed to learn
new methods. Yet Quitral felt that he had very little power to influence teachers' behavior in general and teaching in particular. Though he offered before-
school, paid staff development opportunities, he also noted that he could not
mandate teachers' attendance. Given his relationship with the teachers at the
school, he was unable to exert leadership to change teaching practices. He
noted, "This is a school set in its ways."

Like Adams at Greene, Quitral played almost no role in relation to the
CASE. The role he did play reflected his troubled relationship with the teaching faculty. Quitral became embroiled in a struggle with English teachers over
their plan to teach the screenplay version of *To Kill a Mockingbird* rather than
the actual novel. The principal argued that the district's program of study
clearly stated that the objective was for students to read and understand the
structure of a novel. He mandated that the teachers teach the novel and assigned an assistant administrator to monitor their compliance. Though teachers did teach the novel, two of the three primary tenth grade English teachers
had the students read the screenplay rather than completing the last third of
the novel.

Along with their successful efforts to reject Quitral's reading strategies program, the teachers' decision to use the screenplay demonstrates how teachers
at Reed challenged and ultimately undermined the principal's attempts to
assert his instructional authority in association with the district testing policies. Unlike teachers' responses to principal reading mandates at Greene, at
Reed, teachers not only resisted becoming "teachers of reading" but also as-
serted their subject matter identities. The department served as the site of
teachers' coordinated efforts not only to reject the "teaching of reading" but
also to launch counterinitiatives that allowed them to reassert their subject

matter expertise. Though the mathematics teachers launched their own TAP preparation initiative, during the school's third year on probation the English department developed and enacted a departmentwide writing initiative, thus shifting the focus of the curriculum away from the "teaching of reading."

The English teachers' decision to teach the screenplay was also a response to time constraints placed on them by district policy. Because they were the only teachers held responsible for preparing students for the TAP reading section, they actually had little time to teach the novel, which is quite long. Throughout their interviews, teachers consistently referenced the time constraints associated with the district's use of both the TAP and the CASE.

Weston: Whole School versus Test Focus

Jane Lawrence became principal of Weston the year before probation was announced. She had been a science teacher at the school before becoming one of the major leaders of the site-based management movement at the school in the early 1990s. Probation did not surprise Lawrence or the faculty. Like Greene, Weston had been placed on the state's watch list based on its scores on the state assessment. After showing no gains in scores under probation, the school was reconstituted.

Over the four years of the study, Lawrence initiated three strategies aimed at addressing probation and low performance. First, she instituted a new administrative position, the reading coordinator, to organize and oversee schoolwide test practice. Second, she sought to reassign teachers and students in an effort to maximize test scores. Finally, while pursuing this testing focus, the school also began an ambitious restructuring into academies. As will be discussed below, toward the end of our study, English teachers resisted this approach and proposed their own response to low student achievement.

The test-focused approach aimed to "improve reading" through a focus on testing, according to the principal. Though the approach was identified by teachers from the beginning as narrow and criticized for not being literacy based, the teachers implemented the instructional routines embedded in the principal's initiatives. Each week the reading coordinator disseminated cross-curricular, TAP-style readings to all teachers. Teachers administered these practice tests on Tuesdays and reviewed them with students on Thursdays, but only after the reading coordinator had processed the bubble sheets and shared the results with the principal. Every five weeks, the teachers administered a longer reading test. The reading coordinator also designed weekly packets so teachers could focus on specific skills tested on the TAP.

As mentioned, at the end of the second year of this study, teachers began to express dissatisfaction with the principal's approach. Though they continued to comply with her directives, they complained that the approach was too narrowly focused on testing and lacked a broader focus on reading. At the same time, these teachers differed on what constituted an effective reading program. One teacher advocated a mastery-learning approach, while two others argued that English instruction should be literature based. As the end of the school year approached, to diffuse conflict, Lawrence decided to support both initiatives. She gave one teacher, the new English department chair, funds to develop a reading course—to be mandatory for ninth grade students—based on a basic skills model. She gave the other two teachers summer money to align the ninth and tenth grade English curricula with the CASE. By responding to teacher demands, Lawrence reoriented the school's reading instruction away from test taking and toward a literacy- and literature-based model. Though this approach did little to reconcile the pedagogical differences within the English department, it did placate the demands of two powerful factions within the department.

Throughout the study, Lawrence closely monitored student TAP scores. She identified the exact number of students needed to bring the school to the 20 percent mark required for the school to be removed from probation. Not surprisingly, she used TAP scores to place students into formal and informal tracks. Students were assigned to classes with like-scoring peers with the goal of focusing resources on students who would do best on the TAP. The ninth grade class, for example, was tracked based on both status and scores. One-fourth of the ninth grade students were categorized as "demotes" or repeat freshmen. These students were removed from all classes with ninth graders who came to the school directly from the eighth grade. In addition, higher-scoring ninth and tenth grade students were placed in an honors track. Though Lawrence also kept track of those teachers whose students' test scores were improving and those whose students' scores were not improving, she showed no evidence of using this information in any way other than to inform teachers of their scores in individual meetings.

Lawrence's other approach to probation was to initiate a restructuring of the school around small learning academies. This was in line with the school's prior history of efforts to create small learning communities that could provide students with increased social as well as academic support. For this initiative, Lawrence drew closely on the expertise of the school's external partners. In the second year of our study, the school was turned into several different academies, each focused on a different theme, such as mathematics and technology and graphic arts. For Lawrence, this approach provided students with both a clear focus for their high school years and more social and academic support. It also gave the teachers greater decision-making authority with regard to their students and the curriculum.

This reform immediately encountered resistance. From the first meeting in which the academies were discussed, teachers questioned whether the distinct academies would ever be implemented according to the model. In addition, with half of the in-service meetings being spent discussing school reform, teachers felt frustrated with what they perceived as a lack of focus on instruction and academic achievement. The first year of the initiative, most teachers, however, did participate in the organization of their particular academy. When the school opened the following year with a drop in enrollment of nearly 210 students, the viability of the small-schools model was compromised. Teachers' cynicism intensified. Along with voicing concerns, many teachers elected not to attend meetings of their academy. Lawrence soon recognized that enrollment instability and faculty frustration were undermining the program, so she chose to funnel resources into the strongest of the academies and left teachers of the less organized academies the discretion to participate in academy in-service time. Though this practice angered those teachers who were actively participating in the academies initiative, Lawrence chose not to challenge noncompliant teachers.

If Lawrence's response to probation and test score improvement reflected two very different approaches, her approach to the CASE revealed similar tensions between teachers' professional instructional authority and administrative control. As was discussed above, in the third year of the study, several English teachers at Weston mobilized to reorganize the ninth and tenth grade curricula. Over the summer, they developed scripted lesson plans organized around CASE goals and objectives. Though all ninth and tenth grade English teachers were expected to implement the curricula, Lawrence did not enforce this provision, so soon only those teachers who had developed the curricula were implementing them. Like the other principals, Lawrence chose not to spend political capital on the CASE.

Comparison of Instructional Implementation of the TAP and CASE by School

In this subsection we explore the extent to which the various initiatives that the schools implemented in response to the district's accountability agenda influenced teachers' instruction. Given the emphasis at the school level on the TAP and the stakes that the district attached to it, we would expect to see a greater influence on teachers' instruction exerted by those school initiatives associated with the TAP than by those associated with the CASE.[9] We also explore the relationship between the teachers' efforts to prepare students for the two tests, considering both differences between the tests and across the schools, as well.

We compared instruction using two different sets of analyses.[10] First, we were interested in knowing the types of activities teachers employed in their instruction. We were interested, in particular, in identifying the amount of time teachers devoted to preparing students for district assessments. In addition, we wanted to compare the time teachers spent engaging students in *procedural* activities, or activities that required students to follow routines and rules with little academic engagement, versus *substantive* activities that engaged students in developing knowledge of core subject matter content, skills, and processes. Examples of procedural activities were management activities, during which teachers discussed classroom routines or instructions for particular activities; and seatwork, during which students worked independently on completing worksheets. We also categorized recitations and lectures as procedural activities because they typically involved teachers rather than students engaging with content or processes while students either watched passively or provided short responses to questions with predetermined answers. Examples of substantive activities were discussions, during which teachers and students posed open-ended questions and examined multiple perspectives and interpretations of content; and student presentations, in which students presented their work, usually extended writing, to the class. This analysis revealed the breadth of instructional activities employed by teachers as well as the success of the principals to direct instructional practice through their school-level mandates. Classroom transcripts were coded according to the length of each episode or activity and the type of activity involved.

In addition, we were interested in the types of questions teachers asked students in their daily instruction. We wanted to know if there was a difference between the types of questions teachers asked when district assessments were mediated by school-level policies, in the case of the TAP, or if there was not, as generally happened with the CASE. Toward this goal, we analyzed the questions teachers asked students about the novel, classifying them using a taxonomy of reading skills developed by Hillock and Ludlow (1984). We classified questions according to these categories: (1) Literal questions included questions that asked students to identify information and details directly stated in the text. (2) Simple inferential questions required students to bring together two or more pieces of information closely located in the text to draw a conclusion or make a generalization about a relationship in the text. (3) Complex inferential questions required readers to bring together several details and elements from across a literary work to construct interpretations of themes and relationships, and to identify and elaborate upon an author's view of the human condition.

We also identified several other types of questions that occurred frequently in the classrooms we observed. These were (1) literary terms, questions that asked students to define or identify literary terms, such as hyperbole, simile, and the like; (2) general knowledge questions, which asked students to draw on commonly known facts about people, events, or objects; (3) vocabulary questions, which asked students to define specific words from the text; and

(4) personal opinion questions, which asked students to give their own opinion about an event or character in the novel. These questions tended to be lower level as they typically did not require students to make clear connections to the text, or to provide supporting details or elaboration.[11]

Our comparisons did not reveal any qualitatively significant differences in the ways that the teachers taught across the schools. Table 6.2 reports the findings of our activity analysis. As the table indicates, teachers across the three schools overwhelmingly engaged students in procedural activities. Teachers devoted from 75 to 80 percent of the classroom time we observed to activities such as management, recitation, lectures, and reading aloud. In contrast, teachers spent much less time, only from 2 to 19 percent of observed class time, on substantive activities such as discussion, group work, and student presentations. Instruction in all three schools thus looked similar to English instruction in urban secondary schools nationwide (see Applebee 1993; Nystrand 1997).

Not surprisingly, we found that teachers in the sanctioned schools, Reed and Weston, continued to engage in more test practice and test-related activities than they did at Greene. Interestingly, when teaching classes in which they explicitly prepared students for the TAP, teachers engaged in more management activities than when they taught *To Kill a Mockingbird*. Though table 6.2 reports the percentage of observed class time devoted to all procedural activities, our analysis indicated that, when they prepared students for the TAP with school-mandated activities, teachers spent between 21 and 27 percent of their time managing students' activities. This is compared with between 13 and 18 percent of observed class time spent on management during classes aimed at preparing students for the CASE. This difference suggests that when teaching *To Kill a Mockingbird*, teachers engaged in fewer activity transitions and engaged students in more sustained instructional

Table 6.2 Activity Analysis by School (percent)[a]

School	Assessment	Procedural	Substantive	Testing	Diversion
Greene	TAP	88	7	0	5
	CASE	83	2	14	1
Reed	TAP	76.5	13	10.5	0
	CASE	75	13	11	1
Weston	TAP	77	19	3	1
	CASE	85	4	8	3

Note: TAP = Test of Achievement and Proficiency. CASE = Chicago Academic Standards Exam.
[a]Percent of classroom time observed in English classes in the case study schools.

activities than when they prepared students for the TAP. Further, teachers in Greene and Weston also tended to engage students in more substantive activities when they focused on preparing teachers for the TAP than the CASE. This difference was particularly clear at Weston, where teachers devoted 10 percent of observed class time to having students work together in groups on test preparation materials. Overall, our analysis of classroom activities documents an emphasis on procedural activity, suggesting that the district's policies had little impact on improving the quality of teaching and learning in the high schools we studied.

The question analysis reveals a similar emphasis on low-level academic activities in both the TAP- and the CASE-oriented classes. Table 6.3 reports the findings of our classroom question analysis. Teachers engaged students roughly the same amount of time in complex inferential questions in the CASE and TAP classes. When they taught *To Kill a Mockingbird*, however, they asked more literal and simple inferential questions than they did when they taught TAP activities. During the latter, teachers asked more questions that we categorized as "other," which included questions that focused on vocabulary, student opinion, or general knowledge. These questions tend to place lower-level intellectual demands on students.

Taken together, our analyses of classroom activities and questions suggest that despite very different school-level programs, there did not seem to be major differences in the kinds of activities and the nature of the questions teachers asked at the different schools. At the same time, there were differences between the TAP and CASE classes. Our question analysis, along with the interview data, suggest that teachers focused on content and engaged students in more literary-based questions when they taught the novel in preparation for the district's CASE. In TAP classes, in contrast, teachers engaged students in a number of different activities, moving from recitations about literary texts to test practice to talk about current events. Further, we found that the instructional activities aimed at improving TAP scores tended to be discrete activities; they were not integrated into the broader curriculum.

CONCLUSION

Chicago's experience with mayoral control illuminates its potential and limits for improving instruction in city schools. Under mayoral control, district leadership reorganized central administration in ways that reduced fragmentation and improved public confidence in the schools. These changes helped to restore the district's political capital, enabling its leaders to develop and implement an ambitious educational agenda. Indeed, one of the main accomplishments of mayoral control in Chicago was that it focused the entire district

Table 6.3 Question Analysis by Assessment and School

School	Assessment	Literal Questions	Simple Inferential Questions	Complex Inferential Questions	Other	Total
Greene	TAP (n)	74	37	26	142	279
	%	27	13	9	51	100
	CASE (n)	109	20	8	9	146
	%	75	14	5	6	100
Reed	TAP (n)	177	74	8	444	703
	%	25	11	1	63	100
	CASE (n)	60	22	8	14	104
	%	58	21	8	13	100
Weston	TAP (n)	92	35	3	78	208
	%	44	17	1	38	100
	CASE (n)	97	37	2	10	146
	%	66.5	25.5	1	7	100

Note: TAP = Test of Achievement and Proficiency. CASE = Chicago Academic Standards Exam.

on academic achievement. Mayoral control provided a common structure for systemwide change in the country's third-largest school system.

On the one hand, as our case studies suggest, the focus on improving student achievement, particularly through an emphasis on test-based accountability, prompted significant changes at both the school and classroom levels. Principals and teachers in the Chicago high schools we studied targeted instructional resources toward improving student performance on standardized tests of reading and mathematics and on district curricular assessments. Though this included devoting instructional time and activities directly to test preparation, principals and teachers also initiated changes aimed at enriching teaching and the learning opportunities they provided to their students. For example, the Weston principal worked with the school's external partners, a resource the district provided low-performing schools placed on probation, to reorganize the school into small learning communities to provide students with more academic and social support. At Greene, the principal reorganized the school schedule to give teachers time to develop, together, both their instructional repertoires and common curricula in their respective subject matters. Even at Reed, where the district's accountability agenda contributed to considerable conflict between the principal and teachers, probation prompted teachers' curricular collaboration. In part, in efforts to resist the principal's mandates regarding reading instruction, Reed's English teachers developed and initiated a new writing curriculum that coordinated writing instruction across courses and grade levels. Thus, whereas the principals and teachers, both across and within the high schools we studied, instituted a variety of school and classroom changes in response to the district's accountability agenda, the systemwide focus on issues of instruction and achievement prompted them to reexamine their practices and to coordinate their work around efforts to improve student achievement.

Conversely, the depth and sustainability of these efforts were not clear. Though principals and teachers directed time and resources to preparing students for the assessments that the district used to measure and monitor student and school performance, instruction overwhelmingly focused on lower-level academic tasks in the classrooms we observed. Teachers seldom engaged students with classroom texts beyond the level of identifying basic information or making simple inferences. Further, more than two-thirds of classroom activities engaged students in procedures and routines instead of substantive learning. Rather than prompting an improvement in the learning opportunities that the schools and teachers provided to their students, the high schools we studied tended to reinforce conventional instructional practices when adapting district assessments. Further, the district's emphasis on standardized reading tests prompted a type of curricular fragmentation that countered the efforts at coherence that we noted above; teachers taught discrete reading skills that were disconnected from the broader subject matter curriculum. The "teaching of reading" remained at odds with the teaching of the high school curriculum.

In short, our research in Chicago high schools documents how mayoral control can focus the efforts and resources of city school systems on improving student achievement at the same time it reveals the deep challenges that such systems face in fundamentally improving curriculum and instruction. Under mayoral control, raising student achievement became the driving concern for both principals and teachers in Chicago's high schools. The reforms instituted during the early years of mayoral control in Chicago focused on high-stakes accountability for students. These reforms did prompt a change in priorities and routines in schools and classrooms. This common focus prompted, in turn, efforts to establish more curricular and instructional consistency and coherence. Yet such efforts did not result in a clear improvement in the quality of the learning opportunities the schools provided to their students. Deep improvements in curriculum and instruction remained to be seen by the end of our study.

Still, mayoral control in Chicago provided a common structure for system-wide change in the country's third-largest school system. It facilitated movement toward curricular and instructional coherence. It provided equal support to high-poverty, low-performing schools and sought to address disparities between schools by holding all to common standards of student achievement. At all levels, the governance approach focused district and school actors on a common goal: improving student achievement. As the city's school system and others like it move forward, building the capacity of administrators, principals, and teachers as well as sustaining the public's will and support to deepen and sustain this focus will be critical.

CHAPTER SEVEN

Toward Strategic Deployment of Resources

MAYOR-LED INTEGRATED GOVERNANCE AS A REFORM policy is distinguished by its broad reach. Mayors are in a position not only to improve teaching and learning but also to fundamentally alter the financial and management conditions in which teaching and learning occur. At the same time, however, they are operating in an environment that is often hostile to change. Whether or not mayors can make good on their promise to improve fiscal efficiency remains an open question. In this chapter, we address this question by examining a wide range of fiscal management and staffing indicators. We are able to examine these data going back over ten years, and the results of our statistical analysis suggest that mayors are attempting to adopt a new fiscal strategy that emphasizes fiscal discipline, performing more efficiently, and efforts to redirect resources toward instruction and away from general administration.[1]

We conduct our investigation of fiscal performance in four parts. We first set the stage by laying out theoretical expectations of integrated governance in the areas of management and human capital. We then describe the data we use to measure financial and staffing outcomes. These data allow us to carry out fixed-effects models over an eleven-year span, and they cover our entire sample of 104 districts. In the final two sections of the chapter, we evaluate the results of this analysis and discuss the implications of these results for mayor-led integrated governance.

INTEGRATED GOVERNANCE AND FISCAL MANAGEMENT

Integrated governance is designed to give the mayor enough power to overcome local inertia and increase the school district's institutional capacity in the areas of management efficiency, human capital, fiscal prudence, and a broadened pool of diverse expertise. At the same time, however, there is the possibility that mayors may *not* be able to overcome existing barriers to reform. Entrenched interest groups such as teachers' unions, established district leadership that is used to operating without city hall interference, and citizen groups opposed to centralized management may all serve as checks against an aggressive mayoral reform strategy. To the extent that these multiple veto points serve to keep the school district insulated from mayoral encroachment, the promise of mayoral takeover may not be realized.

To begin with, the issue of mayoral financial discretion raises a broader question about the mayor's fiscal powers. Typically, an elected school board enjoys fiscal autonomy from city hall. The board approves its own budget and, within state-specified parameters, raises bond revenues for capital improvement projects. Teacher and principal salaries, which account for approximately 80 percent of current operating spending, are guided by the board's agreements with unions. This substantial budgetary independence is unique in municipal services because the mayor has authority over spending in all major service areas. When a mayor is granted the power to govern a city's schools, city hall plays an instrumental role in making allocation decisions and in making sure that the system is financially solvent.

Management

The increase of mayoral involvement in schools is closely related to the politics and functions that public schools serve at the local level. From a fiscal perspective, public schools constitute one of the largest local employers. The Chicago Public Schools, for example, ranks as the second largest public employer in the state. Further, education dominates the local budget. Though not a part of most cities' budgets in a technical sense, education expenses range anywhere from 25 to 35 percent of total city expenses. Schools' heavy reliance on local property taxes has a great impact on a city's taxing and spending capacity. Thus, when mayors take charge of schools, management and budgetary issues become a top priority. The business community in each mayor-led district has played an instrumental role in the transformation to appointed school boards (Cuban and Usdan 2003).

If business leaders see mayoral control as analogous to a corporate restructuring, it must also be acknowledged that restructuring an underperforming firm does not necessarily produce a turnaround. If the "fundamentals" remain unchanged, mayors may not be able to generate the change they promise. In the context of the school district and "education marketplace," if the tax base, student population, and parents/consumers are relatively fixed, it may be difficult to bring about systemic change. Whether or not mayors are able to overcome such challenges, however, is for the analysis to answer.

In our study we consider revenues per pupil; capital outlays per student; the distribution of revenue streams between federal, state, and local sources; and the overall fiscal health of the district (measured as "total revenues − total expenditures" ÷ total expenditures). We also track the overall level of expenditures per student.[2] All the financial indicators discussed in this chapter are drawn from data collected by the Annual Survey of State and Local Government.

Integrated governance theory provides a mix of expectations about mayors' performance in the fiscal realm. One clear expectation of integrated governance is that fiscal health under mayoral leadership should improve. Improving the school district's bottom line is likely to raise public confidence in the system and help the mayor's electoral standing. Beyond fiscal health, however, the ex ante predictions of integrated governance are more nuanced. Integrated governance recognizes that from a financial perspective, mayors may be pursuing potentially cross-cutting objectives. On one hand, mayors have an interest in fiscal discipline and in reallocating those funds to the most productive sectors of the school system. Mayors may also be interested in cost cutting to improve efficiency. On the other hand, however, mayors want to deliver their constituents expanded and higher-quality services that may require additional funds. Mayors may also see investments in the school system, both short and long term, as both productive and a show of confidence.

As we have stressed throughout this book, integrated governance is a flexible form of urban governance that allows local conditions to determine which strategies the mayor will adopt. Nevertheless, if local conditions are similar across municipalities, and if mayors tend to adopt similar strategies, then we will see a generalizable pattern emerge in the data. The question in this chapter is whether such a pattern exists between mayoral leadership in education and fiscal decision making. Given that mayors have competing options that may both appear attractive, which path will they take?

Human Capital

In addition to improving fiscal stability, integrated governance allows the central decision-making authorities more flexibility in resource allocation. In

particular, mayors may be able to reduce school district central office inefficiencies, thereby allowing for greater investments in teaching, learning, and
student service provision. In terms of upgrading human capital, mayors are
likely to desire a greater investment in those employees with the most direct
contact with students, matched with a smaller investment in noninstruction
personnel. Like changes in the budget, successful changes in staffing allocations must also overcome significant inertia.[3]

In particular, because mayoral control involves an external authority trying to permeate an existing district power structure, it may be difficult to move
beyond changes at the top—for example, in central office management.
Washington provides an illustration of this inertia effect. As part of then-
superintendent Paul Vance's central office transformation plan, in the summer of 2002 all central office employees were asked to interview for rehiring.
Though the district was able to bring in a new leadership team with diverse
experience, it ended up rehiring a majority of the same lower-level employees.
Anecdotal evidence suggests that a number of these employees believed they
would outlast this newest wave of reform. Whether or not mayors are able to
surprise these employees and bring about substantial change in the aggregate
is once again a question for the analysis to address.

In this study we look for evidence of shifts in human capital investments
in two ways. First, in terms of expenditures, if mayoral takeovers are successful in changing budgeting practices, we should see a higher per-pupil expenditure on instruction, student support services, and school administration
services. These are the funding areas that most directly affect teaching and
learning. Conversely, we would expect to see an inverse relationship with expenditures on central office and general administration services. If the budget is too unwieldy or existing powerbrokers in the district cannot be overcome
or persuaded, such positive effects may not arise. Second, we look at staffing
distributions defined by the actual number of employees in particular positions. Here, we expect to find that successful mayoral control is positively
associated with the district's percentage of teachers, aides, and student support. Again, these are the areas most directly affecting teaching and learning.
We expect to see an inverse relationship between mayoral control and the
percentage of administration and supervisors. The absence of such effects
would lend credence to the alternative theory that district inertia is too much
to overcome, even for mayor-appointed regimes.[4]

Considering Factors Other Than Mayoral Control

In examining management and human capital outcomes it is important to
consider a host of confounding factors that may explain the variation. It may
not simply be the change to a mayor-appointed board, but also the length

of time that the appointed board has been in place that produce improvements. Especially when implementing longer-term programs, the results of mayoral control may be tied up with the number of years the takeover has been in effect. We consider the lagged effects of mayoral control by running separate models that connect outcomes in year t to governance arrangements in year $t-5$. In contrast to our achievement analysis, where the data limited us to looking only at a maximum of two-year intervals, in our financial analysis we are able to look at longer, five-year intervals.

We control for the same set of additional variables considered in the empirical analysis of chapters four and five. Considering financial outcomes, these student and district characteristics are likely to be significant factors. Larger districts are likely to enjoy economies of scale that smaller districts cannot. We would thus expect higher revenues. Larger districts, however, also face unique challenges and may require assistance beyond their local tax base. We would thus expect more revenues to flow from state and federal sources. Due to more complexity in service delivery, a larger district may also require that a greater percentage of its resources be allocated toward central office and administrative personnel. Turning to our measure of child poverty, school districts serving larger populations of at-risk students or operating in worse economic conditions should receive a greater percentage of their revenue from federal funds, which are frequently earmarked for redistributive purposes. Worse-off districts may also need to allocate more resources to student services and may have a more difficult time maintaining fiscal stability.

Including the additional governance measures—mayor–council and the percentage of school board members elected by a single member—will help to specify the relationship between local political arrangements and fiscal outcomes. As we discussed in chapter 3, there is debate within the public administration field as to the effects of these governance structures on fiscal outcomes.

USING A PANEL DATA APPROACH

To consider the relationship between mayor-appointed school boards and measures of effective management and improvements in human capital, we employ a panel data approach. The districts included in this sample are all 104 districts identified by the decision rules introduced in chapter three. Unlike the achievement analysis, when we were limited by data considerations, we have financial and staffing data for all these districts, and for the entirety of our eleven-year period of observation, 1993–2003.

Measuring Financial and Staffing Outcomes

The financial outcome data used for cross-sectional analysis in this chapter come from the Annual Survey of Government Finances conducted by the U.S. Bureau of the Census. The Annual Survey gathers data on revenues, expenditures, and debt from more than 15,000 school districts. In addition to this financial data, we use the National Center for Education Statistics' Common Core of Data (CCD) as a source for our demographic control variables, as well as data on district staffing patterns. Both data sources provide data that are comparable across time and across districts.

In analyzing the financial data, we construct two general types of variables from the raw Annual Survey of Government data. The first type is a measure of *allocation*, examining financial subcategories as a percentage of the whole. The second type is a measure of *magnitude*, exploring the amount (dollars per student) being spent in various subcategories. All our allocation measures are reported as percentages, and all our magnitude measures take into account enrollment and are therefore reported as dollars per student. For each revenue and expenditure measure, we consider both allocation and magnitude.

On the revenue side, we analyze the breakout by federal, state, and local revenue sources. On the expenditure side, we again look at every category and subcategory reported on Form F-33, which is the shorthand name for the School District Financial Survey administered to school districts to collect their financial information. Readers interested in summaries of all the variables we include in the model can find further details of the construction of our revenue and expenditure measures in the online supplement to the book. We also consider several measures of debt (measured as dollars per student). Finally, we draw the revenue and expenditure sides together to look at the overall fiscal health of the school district. We compute fiscal health as "total revenues minus total expenditures divided by total expenditures."

Developing Measures on Staffing

Our measures of management are staffing measures derived from the CCD. We examine the percentage of employees in various district positions. The CCD reports, for each district, the number of full-time equivalent employees in a number of positions: teachers, aides, instructional coordinators and supervisors, guidance counselors, librarians/media support staff, local education agency administration, and school administration.[5] On the basis of these figures, we construct a series of measures that can each be read as "percentage of all school district employees who are teachers, aides, administration, supervisors, student support, and guidance staff."[6]

Adjusting for Inflation and Cost of Living

Using these outcome measures, we are able to construct a data set containing data from the 104 largest urban school districts that are coterminous with a major city. Data are available from 1993 through 2003. The timing of the first mayoral takeover (Boston in 1992) coincides well with the starting points for the two national data sets. We make adjustments for inflation to make all dollar figures constant in 2003 dollars. To make these adjustments, we use the Bureau of Labor Statistics' Constant Dollar Employment Cost Index. Because the majority of school district expenditures are used on salaries and wages, we use the index for State and Local Governments' Educational Services.[7] To adjust for geographic cost differentials, we use the geographic cost of education index (GCEI) developed by Chambers (1998). This index appears to be the most applicable adjustment measure currently available. The index is currently only available for three years: 1987, 1990, and 1993. On one hand, this presents a problem because our financial data are from later years. On the other hand, if the relative costs between geographies remain relatively constant over time, we should not seriously bias our findings by incorporating this index. Luckily for our analysis, one of the conclusions from Chambers's analysis is that "the patterns of geographic variations in cost do not change substantially over time and that the GCEI estimated for any given year provides a reasonable estimate of the GCEI for adjacent years" (p. x). Given this consistency across years, we do not believe that adjusting our figures with the 1993 index will seriously jeopardize the validity of our results. Put another way, by relying on this index, we work under the assumption that cities that were more expensive in 1993 remained, by and large, just as expensive in the late 1990s (Chambers 1998; Fowler and Monk 2001).

Specifying the Effects of Mayoral Control

Using our time series (1993–2003) and cross-sectional data (104 districts), we employ a fixed-effects regression model similar to the model in chapters four and five. Because we are now analyzing financial outcomes, we do not use the financial control variables that we used in the earlier models. The base model for our finance and staffing regressions takes the form of

$$
\begin{aligned}
OUTCOME_{it} = {} & \beta_0 + \beta_1 MAYORAL\_CONTROL_{it} + \beta_2 MAYOR\_COUNCIL_i \\
& + \beta_3 PCT\_SINGLE\_MEMBER_{it} + \beta_4 PCT\_PRIVATE_{it} \\
& + \beta_5 ENROLL_{it} + \beta_6 PCT\_HISPANIC_{it} \\
& + \beta_7 PCT\_AFR\text{-}AMERICAN_{it} + \beta_8 PCT\_KIDS\_POVERTY_{it} \\
& + \beta_9 PCT\_SPECIAL\_ED_{it} + \delta_s + \gamma_t + \varepsilon_{it} \qquad (7.1)
\end{aligned}
$$

where $OUTCOME_{it}$ is the financial or staffing outcome measure for school district i in year t; $MAYORAL\_CONTROL_{it}$ is either the $MAYOR\_INDEX$ or the set of $NEW STYLE$, $MAJORITY$, and $FULL$; $MAYOR\_COUNCIL_{it}$ is a dichotomous variable indicating whether or not the city uses a mayor–council form of government; $PCT\_SINGLE\_MEMBER_{it}$ is the percentage of city school board seats that are voted on in a single-member fashion; $PCT\_PRIVATE_{it}$ is the percentage of kindergarten–twelfth grade students in the city enrolled in private schools; $ENROLL_{it}$ is the district student enrollment; $PCT\_HISPANIC_{it}$ is the percentage of Hispanic students in the district; $PCT\_AFR\text{-}AMERICAN_{it}$ is the percentage of African American students in the district; $PCT\_KIDS\_POVERTY_{it}$ is the percentage of city residents, ages three through eighteen years, who were living below the poverty level in 2000; $PCT\_SPECIAL\_ED_{it}$ is the percentage of district students who have an individualized education plan; δ_s captures state fixed effects; γ_t captures year fixed effects, and ε_{it} is an error term. In addition to this baseline model, we consider models with five-year lagged governance. We cluster on the school district to provide for robust standard errors.

MAYORAL EFFECTS ON RESOURCE ALLOCATION

We now turn to the results of our analysis of the relationship between mayoral control and the financial management of the school district. We consider the effects that mayors have on fiscal discipline, district spending patterns, and staffing allocation decisions. We also discuss the mechanisms by which these changes in management practice may be occurring.

Mayoral Control and Fiscal Discipline

Does mayoral control lead to greater per-pupil revenues? Our results, presented in table 7.1, suggest that they do not. The power to appoint a majority of school board members is significantly and negatively related to per-pupil revenues (table 7.1, no-lag model). After five years, allowing the mayor full appointive power of board members is significantly and negatively associated with revenues as well (table 7.1, five-year lagged model). The presence of a new-style mayor is not related in a statistically significant way with per-pupil revenues.[8] Returning to the general question of whether a mayor can overcome institutional inertia and broader economic trends, the negative relationship between mayoral control and per-pupil revenues suggests that factors beyond the mayor's control may determine revenue levels. Faced with limited options for raising new funds themselves, and dealing with urban districts that already rely heavily on state and federal compensatory funding, mayors may have to reframe their financial aims. Rather than infuse the school district with new money, they may be forced to work more efficiently with the same or even fewer resources.

Looking at the additional statistical results for the entire sample of 104 districts confirms that there is a positive, significant relationship between per-pupil revenue and the size of the school district. Similarly, there is a positive, significant relationship between per-pupil revenues and districts that serve greater percentages of special education, African American, and Hispanic students (table 7.1). Greater per-pupil revenue is also positively and significantly associated in these models with the percentage of students in private schools.

Mayoral Spending Decisions

To streamline the presentation of results, we focus now on the most prominent of the mayoral control reform options: giving the mayor formal power to appoint a majority of the school board. In table 7.2, we present the marginal effects of majority appointive power, controlling for the presence of a new-style mayor and whether or not the mayor's school board appointments are subject to other restrictions.

Our analysis finds that at the baseline, mayoral control is inversely associated with the level of per-pupil spending on instruction and support; but given five years, the *percentage* spent on instruction and support increases (table 7.2). The distinction between percentage allocation and overall expenditure levels is an important one. Mayor-led districts are not spending more, but they are spending differently. Mayor-led districts are reallocating resources to instruction and instructional support.

In the five-year lagged models, mayoral control is significantly and negatively related to year-end outstanding debt (table 7.2). That a similar significant relationship is not seen in the baseline model may suggest a long-term spending strategy. Initially, mayors may need some cushion to fund new programs or get the district's finances in order. As a consequence, debt remains at the end of the year. Once mayoral control is established, however, mayors may be able to reduce the district's debt.

Mayoral control and general administration expenditures are significantly and negatively related. Both the level of per-pupil expenditure on general administration (table 7.3) and the percentage of expenditures allocated to general administration (table 7.4) are inversely related to mayoral control.

A positive and significant relationship exists between general administration expenditures and districts with stronger private school climates, higher percentages of special education students, and a higher percentage of African American students (tables 7.3 and 7.4). These positive and significant relationships may reflect spending designed to address particular student needs beyond the scope of regular administration spending.

Table 7.1. Results from Linear Regression Models for Total Revenue per Pupil, 1993–2003 (with year and state fixed effects; baseline and five-year lagged models)

Variable	No Lag		Five-Year Lag	
	A	B	A	B
New-style mayor	0.77		1.51	
	(0.55)		(1.39)	
Majority appointment power	−0.88**		−0.07	
	(0.36)		(1.04)	
Full appointment power	−0.42		−3.05***	
	(0.37)		(1.11)	
Mayor control index		−0.20		−0.51
		(0.19)		(0.54)
Mayor–council	0.62**	0.65**	0.52*	0.63**
	(0.28)	(0.28)	(0.27)	(0.27)
Percent single-member-elected school board members	−0.05	−0.04	−0.19	−0.07
	(0.33)	(0.33)	(0.27)	(0.30)
Percent in private school	7.73***	7.73***	8.09***	7.92***
	(2.25)	(2.28)	(2.14)	(2.23)
Enrollment (million)	−0.00**	−0.00**	−0.00**	−0.00**
	(0.00)	(0.00)	(0.00)	(0.00)
Percent Hispanic	2.05**	1.97**	2.09**	2.05**
	(0.91)	(0.91)	(0.91)	(0.91)
Percent African American	4.34***	4.33***	4.27***	4.31***
	(0.95)	(0.95)	(0.92)	(0.92)
Percent children living in poverty	−3.42*	−3.33	−3.10	−3.36
	(2.06)	(2.06)	(2.02)	(2.07)
Percent special education	6.60**	6.83**	5.97**	6.65**
	(2.86)	(2.86)	(2.75)	(2.79)
Constant	5.29***	5.23***	5.37***	5.27***
	(0.63)	(0.63)	(0.61)	(0.62)
N	1143	1143	1143	1143
R^2	0.86	0.86	0.87	0.86

Note: Two-tailed significance denoted as $*p < .1$, $**p < .05$, $***p < .01$. All models employ state and year fixed effects. Robust standard errors are produced by clustering on school districts. Financial data measured in thousands of dollars, inflation adjusted to 2003 dollars.

Mayors' New Strategic Priorities

Synthesizing the findings of our analysis of mayors and school finances, we believe that the big picture story is one in which new-style mayors are becoming more strategic in prioritizing their resource allocation and management. Central to this strategy is the notion of fiscal discipline in constraining

Text continues on p. 153.

Table 7.2 Marginal Effect of Mayoral Power to Appoint a Majority of the School Board on Financial and Staffing Outcomes

Measure	Per-Pupil Amount		Allocation (Percent)	
	Baseline	Five-Year Lag	Baseline	Five-Year Lag
Total revenue	-0.876**	-0.068	-0.004	-0.010
From federal sources	-0.102	-0.191*	-0.008	-0.002
From state sources	-0.580	-1.255**	0.032	-0.037
General formula assistance	0.183	-0.833*	-0.012**	0.017
Special education programs	-0.181***	0.093	-0.002	0.004
Transportation programs	-0.036	0.034	-0.003	-0.002
Staff improvement programs	-0.047**	-0.048	-0.031***	-0.000
Compensatory and basic skills programs	-0.362***	-0.056	-0.004*	-0.001
Vocational education programs	-0.037*	-0.020	-0.004	-0.009*
Capital outlay and debt service programs	-0.071	-0.097**	-0.000	0.001
School lunch programs	0.002	0.002	0.004	-0.032
From local sources	-0.154	1.351	-0.007	-0.034
Property taxes	-0.217	-0.779	0.002	-0.001
General sales	0.025	-0.015	0.000	-0.000
Public utility taxes	0.002	-0.004	-0.009	-0.016
Individual and corporate income taxes	-0.136	-0.233	0.003	-0.000
All other taxes	0.010	-0.020	0.017	0.122*
Parent government contributions	0.073	2.504*	0.012	-0.002
Revenue from cities and counties	0.084	-0.054	-0.003	-0.000
Revenue from other school systems	-0.037	-0.011	-0.001	-0.001***
Tuition fees from pupils and parents	-0.005	-0.017**	-0.000	-0.000

Total expenditures	−0.139	−0.143	0.009	−0.012
Total current spending for instruction	−0.428***	0.172	0.001	0.009**
Total current spending for support services	−0.356**	0.324	−0.002	0.014**
Pupil support	−0.145**	0.039	−0.009***	−0.010
Instructional staff support	−0.055	0.202	0.009***	−0.000
General administration	−0.087***	−0.106	0.000	0.007
School administration	0.025	−0.021	0.003	0.009
Operation and maintenance of plant	−0.087**	0.045	0.002	−0.000
Student transportation	0.004	0.152	−0.003	−0.007**
Total current spending for non–elementary and secondary programs	−0.096	0.024	−0.004	−0.001
Community services	−0.066	0.030	0.002*	−0.000
Adult education	−0.049	−0.012	−0.000	−0.000
Other	0.019	0.007	−0.024*	−0.054***
Capital outlay expenditures				
Construction	−0.466***	−0.663**	0.004	0.001
Instructional equipment	0.008	0.001	0.002	0.002
Other equipment	0.025	0.036	−0.001	0.014
Nonspecified equipment	0.016	0.021*	0.001	0.014**
Land and existing structures	−0.018	0.218	0.004	−0.002
Salaries and wages				
Total salaries and wages	−0.311	0.241	−0.004	0.004*
Instruction	−0.057	0.004	−0.002	0.007*
Pupil support	−0.071	0.031	−0.003***	−0.002
Instructional staff support	−0.041	0.112	0.006***	−0.001
General administration	−0.032***	−0.015	−0.001	0.010*

(*continued*)

Table 7.2 (Continued)

Measure	Per-Pupil Amount		Allocation (Percent)	
	Baseline	Five-Year Lag	Baseline	Five-Year Lag
Debt				
Outstanding at beginning of fiscal year	0.147	−2.168		
Issued during the fiscal year	−0.423	−0.363		
Retired during the fiscal year	0.237	0.202		
Outstanding at end of fiscal year	−0.514	−2.736*		
Outstanding at beginning of fiscal year	−0.053	0.069		
Outstanding at end of fiscal year	−0.047	0.093		
Fiscal health	0.033**	0.010		
Staffing (percent)				
Teachers	0.019	−0.078		
Aides	0.003	0.011		
Supervisory staff	−0.000	0.009*		
Guidance	0.002	−0.004		
Student support	−0.005	0.006		
Administration	−0.010	0.003		

Note: Two-tailed significance denoted as *$p < .1$, **$p < .05$, ***$p < .01$. Marginal effects calculated based on fixed-effect regression analysis as described in text. These are the marginal effects for our measure, MAJORITY, a dummy variable indicating whether or not the mayor has the formal authority to appoint a majority of the city's school board members. We control in the regressions for the other two aspects of mayoral control, full appointive power and presence of a new-style mayor. Financial data are measured in thousands of dollars, inflation adjusted to 2003 dollars.

labor costs. We see this in the inverse relationship between mayoral control and expenditures (table 7.2). Education mayors, while continuing to partner with labor unions, seemed able to leverage cooperation (or concessions) from the school employees' unions. In Chicago, to be sure, the 1995 act precluded a teachers' strike during the first eighteen months of mayoral control.

Table 7.3   Results from Linear Regression Models for Per-Pupil Expenditures on General Administration, 1993–2003 (with year and state fixed effects; baseline and five-year lagged models)

Variable	No Lag		Five-Year Lag	
	A	B	A	B
New-style mayor	0.05***		0.09	
	(0.02)		(0.07)	
Majority appointment power	–0.09***		–0.11	
	(0.02)		(0.08)	
Full appointment power	–0.04*		–0.13	
	(0.02)		(0.10)	
Mayor control index		–0.03**		–0.06**
		(0.01)		(0.03)
Mayor–council	0.01	0.02	0.01	0.01
	(0.01)	(0.01)	(0.01)	(0.01)
Percent single-member-elected school board members	–0.01	–0.01	–0.02*	–0.01
	(0.01)	(0.01)	(0.01)	(0.01)
Percent in private school	0.37**	0.37**	0.41***	0.40***
	(0.15)	(0.15)	(0.14)	(0.14)
Enrollment (million)	0.00	0.00	0.00	0.00
	(0.00)	(0.00)	(0.00)	(0.00)
Percent Hispanic	–0.01	–0.02	–0.01	–0.01
	(0.04)	(0.04)	(0.04)	(0.04)
Percent African American	0.11**	0.11**	0.10**	0.11**
	(0.04)	(0.04)	(0.04)	(0.04)
Percent of children living in poverty	0.02	0.03	0.05	0.03
	(0.08)	(0.08)	(0.07)	(0.08)
Percent special education	0.29*	0.31*	0.25*	0.28*
	(0.16)	(0.16)	(0.15)	(0.15)
Constant	–0.01	–0.01	–0.00	–0.01
	(0.03)	(0.03)	(0.03)	(0.03)
N	1143	1143	1143	1143
R^2	0.52	0.51	0.54	0.52

Note: Two-tailed significance denoted as *$p < .1$, **$p < .05$, ***$p < .01$. All models employ state and year fixed effects. Robust standard errors are produced by clustering on school districts. Financial data are measured in thousands of dollars, inflation adjusted to 2003 dollars.

Another aspect of mayors' strategic priorities seems to be improving bureaucratic efficiency by reducing expenditures on general administrative purposes. Mayoral control lowered the level of spending on general administration (table 7.3) and also reduced the percentage of expenditures on general administration (table 7.4). By reducing general administrative costs, mayors free up

Table 7.4 Results from Linear Regression Models for Percent of District Expenditures on General Administration, 1993–2003 (with year and state fixed effects; baseline and five-year-lagged models)

Variable	No Lag		Five-Year Lag	
	A	B	A	B
New-style mayor	0.48**		0.69	
	(0.20)		(0.59)	
Majority appointment power	−0.87***		−0.98	
	(0.22)		(0.67)	
Full appointment power	−0.39		−0.81	
	(0.24)		(0.87)	
Mayor control index		−0.27**		−0.50**
		(0.11)		(0.24)
Mayor–council	0.06	0.08	0.01	0.04
	(0.14)	(0.14)	(0.14)	(0.14)
Percent single-member-elected school board members	−0.20	−0.19	−0.24*	−0.20
	(0.14)	(0.14)	(0.13)	(0.13)
Percent in private school	3.48**	3.48**	3.84**	3.71**
	(1.52)	(1.55)	(1.51)	(1.52)
Enrollment (million)	0.00	0.00	0.00	0.00
	(0.00)	(0.00)	(0.00)	(0.00)
Percent Hispanic	−0.46	−0.52	−0.47	−0.47
	(0.38)	(0.40)	(0.38)	(0.38)
Percent African American	0.77	0.76	0.63	0.65
	(0.51)	(0.51)	(0.52)	(0.52)
Percent of children living in poverty	0.94	1.01	1.19	1.09
	(0.87)	(0.88)	(0.87)	(0.87)
Percent special education	1.57	1.72	1.27	1.47
	(1.68)	(1.69)	(1.63)	(1.65)
Constant	0.44	0.39	0.47	0.45
	(0.28)	(0.28)	(0.28)	(0.28)
N	1143	1143	1143	1143
R^2	0.41	0.39	0.41	0.40

Note: Two-tailed significance denoted as $*p < .1$, $**p < .05$, $***p < .01$. All models employ state and year fixed effects. Robust standard errors are produced by clustering on school districts. Financial data are measured in thousands of dollars, inflation adjusted to 2003 dollars.

more money for instructional purposes and may improve public confidence that wasteful spending is not occurring in the district. The trend of mayors spending more on instructional purposes is also seen in their decision to prioritize this type of spending over noninstructional services such as support services, transportation, and some operations costs.

A third aspect of mayoral control emerging from our analysis is the need for leadership to do "more with less," presumably by improving district efficiency. Though we do not have a direct measure of efficiency, we find some circumstantial evidence to suggest new spending priorities under mayor-controlled systems. Given five years to implement their strategies, mayor-led systems allocate more salaries and wages to instruction (table 7.2), thus prioritizing the resources that most directly affect the quality of teaching. Another indicator we see are allocations for "other" non–elementary and secondary programs declining at both the baseline and five years (table 7.2).

How can mayors support their new strategic agenda, with its stronger focus on the instructional core, investment in long-range improvement, and labor cost containment? Our data analysis suggests that it is *not* supported by bringing more money into the system (table 7.1). In particular, mayors are managing school systems with reduced per-pupil revenue from local sources such as property taxes and tuition fees from city families.

Mechanisms for Change

If mayors are indeed making a difference in how much and in what ways city dollars are spent on education, how are they doing it? Answering this question requires consideration of mayoral fiscal leadership generally. Mayors can apply fiscal discipline and accountability to the school system in both formal and informal ways (Daigneau 2006). During the late 1970s and the 1980s, as well as the early 2000s, when cities faced severe fiscal stress, mayors began to adopt a new governing culture, often characterized as the New Political Culture (NPC) (Clark and Hoffman-Martinot 1998; Wong, Jain, and Clark 1997). The NPC-oriented mayors tend to focus on management efficiency and emphasize quality-of-life issues. Growingly responsive to concerns of the taxpayers, NPC mayors move away from policies defined by traditional party labels and organized groups like political party machinery, service providers' unions, and ethnic group coalitions. In NPC regimes, the left–right continuum has become less relevant as the relation between social and fiscal issues has weakened. Fiscal responsibility is no longer strongly linked with social conservatism and vice versa (Clark and Hoffmann-Martinot 1998). In reforming the management of agencies, NPC mayors accelerate contracting out (Miranda 1994), guarantee a holding down of taxes, focus on efficient management, and introduce outcome measures for periodic evaluation. These changes tend to overlap with the policy vision of civic-spirited business leaders and the taxpaying electorate (see Schumaker 1991). The quality-of-life issues are often defined in terms of the city's physical environment, parks and recreation, and public education.

In mayor-led school systems, consistent with the NPC milieu, improvement in financial management seems likely to occur during the first couple of years. An analysis of documentary sources on mayor-appointed boards suggests that there is improvement in financial and administrative management. These districts seem able to show financial solvency, often turning a deficit into a balanced budget. The school boards in mayor-controlled systems may also be able to raise the bond rating, maintain labor peace, improve client satisfaction, and improve efficiency at the central office. In Chicago, for example, in response to labor peace and balanced budgets, Standard & Poor's raised the school district's bond rating from BBB– to BBB in March 1996, then to A– in 1997. This favorable bond rating enabled the appointed board to raise billions of dollars to finance the first citywide capital improvement project in decades.

Even when mayors do not have appointive power over school boards, they can play an instrumental role in fiscal policy. In Nashville, for example, the school budget has to be approved by the mayor and the City Council. The Nashville school board asked for a budgetary increase from $510.5 million in 2004–5 to $570 million in 2005–6. Mayor Bill Purcell balked at the request, saying that the board's proposal included "some things we need to do this year, some things that can wait until next year and some things that we do not need to do at all" (*Tennessean* 2005). Subsequently, the mayor and the City Council decided to meet the school board in the middle, approving a new budget of $540.7 million. The additional funds would have come from a combination of higher local property taxes and a state sales tax. Under a compromise brokered by the mayor, 80 percent of the additional sales tax would have supported schools, while 20 percent would have paid for a senior citizen tax relief program. However, an overwhelming majority of the voters did not approve the tax increase. To some observers, Purcell's actions offer an example of how mayors can exercise fiscal checks and balances when educational spending is under increasing public scrutiny.

In well-managed cities, mayors also can institute a broader climate of fiscal accountability across local government agencies, including school districts. By sharing financial, management, and auditing expertise with the school system, city hall can improve capital projects, balance the budget, and even support union–management negotiations. A key effort is to contain escalating labor costs, which are in part driven by medical costs as well as collective bargaining agreements. Mayors have cautiously taken steps to leverage incremental accommodations from the school employees' unions. Many cities are contracting out services to competitive bidders that in turn must show results. The lessons municipal agencies have learned by outsourcing various services are transferable to many services that school districts provide in house, such as transportation, food service, information technologies, human resource management, and safety services.

Modest Influence on Staffing Patterns

Although mayors may be able to institute changes in school district financial management, it appears that district employees may be insulated from sweeping changes brought in by mayoral control regimes. Mayoral control measures are not statistically significantly related to increases in the percentage of district staff who are teachers, administration, or student support (table 7.2). In the five-year lagged models, there is a positive, significant relationship between majority appointment and the number of supervisory staff per student. That this is the only significant relationship suggests that although many of these new-style districts hope to adopt a corporate model of school governance and "transform" the central office, the mayor may have diminishing direct effects on human capital as we move down the organizational structure and out of the district's central leadership offices. These organizational constraints are not a surprise, because large urban school systems are complex, multilayered institutions with existing cultures and practices. The duration of the takeover reform is likely important in changing these long-held practices.

These null findings on human capital impact are in contrast to the expectations generated by a true integrated governance regime. From the mayor's office, which takes into consideration the interest of the city as a whole, failing schools are constrained by the broad community and institutional context, such as gangs, crimes, and health. To turn around failing schools, the expectation is for mayor-appointed school boards to be more likely to allocate more supportive staff to combat social problems in the immediate school environment. For example, mayor-appointed school boards have instituted vision tests in inner-city schools when they found that many elementary students failed the tests in part because they could not follow the materials presented on the blackboard. That such anecdotes do not correspond to shifts in aggregate staffing numbers may again suggest that, to borrow the description by Frederick Hess (2002), mayors may find themselves swinging a pickaxe rather than driving a bulldozer.

The Timing of Mayoral Impact

One of the great benefits of a longer observation period, here covering more than a decade, is that we can look for longer-term effects of mayoral control. In a number of the results we have presented, we have identified differences between the baseline and the five-year lagged models. Some effects of mayoral control are not seen immediately, but only five years down the road. It is not hard to imagine why such a delay might exist.

To get spending priorities in place, the mayor must rely on a new management team that shares the priorities of city hall. It takes time to get such a team in place. Although top management may be integrated, the lower strata of district operations may remain insulated from city hall and the changes the mayor wishes to bring about. Keeping in mind that mayor-appointed boards have generally been introduced to districts that are at or near "bankruptcy," it may be unrealistic to expect to see sizable changes in the aggregate figures so quickly. The lagged effects also speak to the importance of political stability in the system. The stability ushered in by mayor-appointed boards may offer the greatest promise for reallocation of funds and improved management.

Mayors face significant barriers as they attempt to introduce integrated governance to their city school districts. Although district management (put in place by the mayor) may speak with much enthusiasm about their work, and although there are certainly anecdotal examples of positive change, our analysis suggests that when aggregated districtwide, mayors may be able to bring about change only if they have enough time. As Paul Vallas commented when he was running the Chicago schools, "In order to change the system, you really needed to not only change department heads, but you needed to go three, four deep" (Shipps 2003b, 22).[9] Time allows them to create the broad-based support required for sustained reform efforts.

IMPLICATIONS FOR FUTURE RESEARCH

The analysis in this chapter represents a significant step forward in our understanding of the relationship between mayor-led integrated governance and school district financial outcomes. There remain a number of important future directions, however, for researchers to address. First, an emerging body of literature has begun to look at fiscal disparities between schools in the same district (Hill and Roza 2004). These intradistrict studies reveal much about otherwise unseen inequalities. If such measures could be developed across a large number of urban school districts, we could compare mayoral-control to non-mayoral-control cities to see if and how funding between schools is affected by integrated governance.

Second, even if mayoral control is understood to be a positive factor in explaining variations in these financial outcomes, it is not clear whether it is integrated governance per se or a particular policy that was instituted by a takeover regime. The question to consider is whether the successful policy could have been implemented just as well by an elected school board. Alternatively, it may be that the changes come not from integrated governance specifically but simply from the fact that this is a new policy. To the extent that "just shaking up the system" would produce the same outcomes, the effects attributed to mayoral control would again be overstated.

Third, an aspect of mayoral control that likely bears on the outcomes we measure, but that we cannot adequately quantify, are the management styles of the chief executive officers (CEOs) that mayors place in charge of their districts. Many have anecdotally observed that big cities have turned to "outsiders" to run their school systems. But in Chicago, former CEO Vallas was successful in part because he was a political *insider*. To the extent that our findings suggest that district staffing and expenditure inertia may initially prevent mayors and their appointed managers from introducing sweeping changes, political bargaining may be an important prerequisite for success. For cross-district empirical analysis, "leadership" indexes could be developed to operationalize the professional backgrounds of school district leaders (Hurwitz 2001; Russo 2003).

MAYORS IN THE TWENTY-FIRST CENTURY

The start of the twenty-first century has ushered in a new paradigm of urban school governance. Instead of introducing corrupt patronage, mayors are now emerging as possible catalysts for more efficient and productive city schools. But many skeptics still question whether mayors can do it. Can increased mayoral involvement in running city school districts improve fiscal health, streamline management, and ultimately improve student achievement?

Unlike a century ago, when reformers could only rely on the persuasiveness of their theories, today we have access to more concrete data than ever before. In chapters four and five, we presented data supporting the contention that mayors can indeed improve school performance. In chapter six, we discussed at least one way that these improvements are enacted through changes in classroom practice. In this chapter, we have added another layer to the story. Mayors, when given sufficient time, can succeed in their attempts to push for more efficient, strategic school district spending priorities. Recognizing fiscal constraints and operating without raising the level of per-pupil expenditure, mayor-led regimes are making improved choices about how to better allocate district funds.

CHAPTER EIGHT

The Political Dynamics of Building Public Support for Education

IN ADDITION TO THE PRODUCTIVITY AND MANAGEMENT improvements that we have discussed over the course of the last four chapters, education mayors have the potential to build public confidence in their cities' school systems by raising public awareness about reform efforts and improving public opinion about city schools. Achieving this goal of increased public confidence requires a mix of institutional reform and personal leadership from the mayor. In this chapter, we explore both of these dimensions.

There are theoretical arguments on both sides of the mayoral leadership debate. On one hand, the integrated governance perspective posits that mayoral leadership will emerge due to the electoral benefits now tied to strong school district performance. On the other hand, it has been argued that, theoretically, mayors do not need to produce actual school improvement but need only to "spin the schools" to make it appear as if the schools are improving. Such a position is consistent with the work of Kent Weaver (1986), who finds that politicians seek blame avoidance (e.g., "The school district's problems are the result of the entrenched interests") and credit claiming (e.g., "I am the one who is responsible for rising test scores"). When politically motivated leaders enter the realm of school leadership in this way, questions can be raised about the democratic nature of integrated governance. Should we expect city residents to have more or less voice in a mayoral led school system? In discussing these competing views, we draw on theories of leadership in promoting a citywide interest (Shen 2003).

To evaluate both these theories, we explore public opinion data about mayoral control. Although we do not have comparable data across districts, our synthesis of existing public opinion data suggests that the public may be split on its support for mayoral control. We also see a significant split along racial lines as to the desirability of the reform. Drawing on Jeffrey Henig's analysis (2004), we suggest that these splits reflect concerns from the African American professional community about ceding control of a system in which they have exercised considerable leadership.

We examine how city governments relate formally to their city school districts. We study our sample of 104 cities and identify formal linkages that exist. We also examine the websites of each city to see how, if at all, they link themselves to the city school district. We find that the traditional separation of city services from school district services remains the norm in the vast majority of cities. Finally, we analyze the public stance that mayors take regarding their cities' school districts. Using the most recently available State of the City speech for the sample districts, we perform qualitative content analysis. To guide this analysis, we develop a coding scheme to track the ways in which the schools are mentioned in the speeches.

THEORIES OF MAYORAL LEADERSHIP AND DEMOCRATIC PROCESS

We begin the chapter by examining the role of the mayor in American cities. We consider the institutional constraints and political incentives facing the mayor. This general discussion of the mayor's political roles is important because it is the backdrop against which the mayor's educational leadership occurs.

The Office of the Mayor

In the United States, the duties attached to the mayor's office vary significantly. In smaller towns and cities, the mayor's office may be more ceremonial than substantive. In a small town in Michigan, for example, a high school senior won the mayor's post in 2005. When cities are governed by city managers, mayors may also have less responsibility. But even in city manager districts, mayors can play a role in developing policy. In the context of large, urban, mayor–council cities, mayors play their greatest role. They lead the city in developing economic and social policy (Associated Press 2005; Svara 1987; Morgan and Watson 1992; and Wikstrom 1979).

There is a scholarly debate over the impact that mayors can have. Political scientist Paul Peterson introduced the theory that "city limits" prevent local governments from acting as if they were an independent nation-state in addressing redistributive needs. In the Peterson framework, economic determinants are the dominant factors influencing the formation of city policy. Peterson's theory was modified by Wong (1990), placing renewed focus on the *political* elements of local choice. In an extensive study of Baltimore and Milwaukee, Wong showed that although economics may constrain choices, political factors are still significant in determining final policy outcomes.

Empirically, there remains debate about the extent to which mayors can influence policy. On one hand, some scholars have found that mayors' active support for community programs affected the likelihood of program adoption. On the other hand, Edmond Keller (1978), in a study of the impact of African American mayors on policy, found that external constraints limited the ability of mayors to push through new programs. Our own empirical analysis in this book suggests that mayors may be more effective in some areas (e.g., raising overall district achievement) and more severely constrained in other areas (e.g., changing staffing distributions amid much district inertia). The interest in mayoral involvement in education happens in a context of emerging interest in mayors as potential leaders of progressive politics. But it also occurs in some cities at the same time that mayoral power is being fundamentally challenged (Kuo 1973; Keller 1978; Nichols 2005; McDonald 2003).

Considering Mayoral Stability and Turnover

One prominent concern about mayor-appointed school boards is that the reform is tied too closely to individual mayors. Portz, Stein, and Jones (1999, 160) raise the issue of mayoral continuity: "Mayoral turnover can undermine the support structure for the schools. . . . A new mayor might relegate the schools to a lower rank on the priority list, thereby weakening a key link between the schools, city hall, and the larger community. Alternatively, a new mayor might move to replace school reforms with a new set of strategies." An existing mayor might also see her or his fortune change. In San Diego, for instance, a 2005 scandal ruined the fortunes of Mayor Dick Murphy. If Murphy had been running the school system as well, a leadership void would have immediately been created. One solution for cities that expect leadership turnover is to contract out services. In this logic, instead of integration, the city would want to "contract out" its education services to the school district (Dotinga 2005; Clingermayer and Feiock 1997).

In our view, institutionalizing control in the mayor's office can provide stability. Usdan and Cuban (2003, 50) observe that in Boston, the mayor-appointed school board has "succeeded in establishing the necessary political stability upon which large-scale improvements in student achievement must be predicated." But the authors and others wonder: What will happen when Mayor Menino or Mayor Daley leaves? The issue of high leadership turnover in urban education has been well documented. When turnover occurs in local government, service provision can be adversely affected.[1]

We believe, however, that the trend is toward holding big-city mayors accountable for city schools. In the 2004 Milwaukee mayoral election, both candidates voiced the same sentiment on the campaign trail. In an interview with the local newspaper, the incumbent Mayor Marvin Pratt said, "I don't want to sound trite, since everyone says they want to be the education president or the education mayor, but I think you have to have a primary focus on that issue." His challenger, Tom Barrett, observed, "If you were in this office 30 years ago talking to someone running for mayor, they would probably have read a chapter on staying away from the schools, since it's quicksand. But I think public education is just so important to the future of the city" (Carr 2004). In this view, it is as if the mayor has no choice but to get involved in education. To the extent that this sentiment is indeed grounded in the office of the mayor, we would expect to see stability in an integrated governance framework.

Mayors and Political Incentives

If we examine the "political logic" at work in mayoral control, the central question is whether or not the mayor's political incentives (e.g., reelection or legacy) will lead him or her to improve the schools. When a mayor steps in and takes control of the city's school district, accountability is placed squarely in his or her hands. According to the integrated governance theory, mayors are then held accountable by the voting public. If voters see that the schools are not improving, they can vote the mayor out of office. If voters find that the schools are improving, the mayor will gain more constituents. Understood in this way, the great promise of mayoral control is that the mayor's desire for reelection and a broader constituent base will motivate him or her to put great effort into improving the school system.

It can be observed, however, that regardless of whether or not improving the schools leads to more votes, to increase their chances for reelection, mayors do not necessarily need to improve city schools—they only need to *make it look as if* the schools are improving. This subtle distinction between the appearance of improvement and actual improvement has important implications for sustained school improvement. As Frederick Hess has argued, political incentives shape urban school reform in ways that emphasize visible, short-term improvement at the expense of more effective, long-term improvement strategies. Focusing so much on short-term goals results in what Hess (1998, 52) calls "policy churn," a lot of reforms but little improvement over time. The same logic may be applicable to mayoral control.

Mayors who have a political stake in school district performance may be more likely to place a positive spin on the city schools than mayors who are not responsible for school districts. Anecdotal examples from New York before mayoral control and Chicago illustrate this claim. In New York, when a majority of the school board was not appointed by the mayor, there was consistent criticism from the mayor. As noted in an opinion piece by Arthur Levine (2000), the New York system was one that allowed "the mayor to remain a critic who attacks the quality of the schools and their leaders." If mayors are in charge, however, they may sing a different tune. Chicago provides an example of this phenomenon. When disappointing test scores were announced in 2000, the *Chicago Tribune* reported that "just days after reporting disappointing results from one set of student exams, Chicago Public Schools officials on Monday released new scores from a different test that show small but steady improvements at elementary and high schools" (Martinez 2000).

Similar issues have been raised in other cities. James Cofield of the Black Political Task Force in Boston argues that "[Mayor] Menino claims accountability when [the schools] look good, and backs away when things do not look good. He really hides behind the school committee until something good comes out" (Van Lier 2001, 1). In Cleveland in 2003, the school district saw great improvement in test score performance. Although the district was not able to maintain this high level in subsequent years, in 2003 it went on a campaign to announce its successes. A public service advertisement in the *Cleveland Plain Dealer* announced, "Wow. Something to celebrate. Cleveland Municipal School District was the most improved in Ohio and one of the most improved in the entire nation."

In this chapter, where we examine the public face of mayoral leadership, it is important to keep in mind these competing expectations. Looking at how the public reacts to mayoral leadership, through our analysis of public opinion, will provide us with a better understanding of how the political incentives shape mayors' actions.

The Saliency of Education

When mayors take over the schools, the schools become one of many issues that they must consider. Henig (2004, 211–12) observes that these competing interests can divert mayors' attention: "Mayors face constituencies that may pull them irrevocably to devote time and resources to competing priorities such as economic development, crime, and tax cuts." In contrast, Henig argues that "elected school boards do not need to consider these competing priorities to nearly the same extent, and can serve as a more focused advocate for investment in the local schools."

A parallel point can be made about the decisions that city voters must make in the two regimes. When dealing with a directly elected school board, city voters can evaluate their school board candidates based solely on school district performance. When evaluating a mayor, however, voters will take into consideration not only the schools but also public safety, the economy, and the overall quality of life. Henig's argument, and the argument about school board voting, is valuable in pointing out the trade-off that mayor-appointed school boards bring about: Mayors have more on their plates, but they also have more power to do something. These trade-offs in mayoral roles are summarized in table 8.1.

How should these trade-offs be resolved? We have both a theoretical and an empirical answer. Theoretically, we start with the premise that education is one of a bundle of services. When voting for the mayor, a resident is voting on the overall quality of life. A mayor has to stand before the voters and has to show that he or she has the evidence and track record to improve the quality of life for the city as a whole. In this view, the policy areas (e.g., education, crime, economy) are not being viewed by voters or the mayor as discrete compartments. Rather, the mayor is seen as creating general enabling conditions for success in all these areas. In addition, holding mayors accountable only for education would only insulate and isolate the schools from these other services. This sort of political insulation does not square with the reality of increasingly integrated municipal services. As services become more integrated, education is seen as connected to housing, crime, and poverty. The bundle of services offered by the mayor to the city represents the mayor's choices about relative investments in each area, and it is on this overall package that citizens hold the mayor accountable.

Empirically, we can examine some existing survey data about the saliency of education in voters' minds. One piece of data comes from an exit poll taken at the March 2005 Los Angeles mayoral primary election. Exiting voters were

Table 8.1 Potential Trade-Offs Given Mayoral Control and the Saliency of Education for City Voters

Degree of Mayoral Control	Low Saliency	High Saliency	Issues that Voters Must Consider
More	Power to stabilize policy	Power to expand policy	All policy domains
Less	Status quo maintained by school board	Mayor uses indirect influence on school board	Only education

asked, "Which of the general issues—if any—were most important to you in deciding how you would vote for mayor today?" In response, 48 percent of voters named education, far outpacing the second-most-named issue of crime at 31 percent (Loyola Marymount University 2005).

Similar sentiments were expressed on the opposite coast. New York voters were asked in 2005 about how important education would be in the next mayoral election. These survey questions were developed and administered by the Quinnipiac University Polling Institute, which we describe in detail in the next section. The question was asked to voters twice, in 2002 (three years before the election) and in September 2005 (just a couple of months before the election). In 2002, 51 percent of all voters said that Mayor Bloomberg's handling of the schools would be "very important," and another 32 percent said that it would be "somewhat important." Thus, education salience was high for 83 percent of likely voters. For African American voters, the proportion reached up to 90 percent.

Even more telling are the survey results from the election year. In 2005, 84 percent of all voters said that education would be a "very important" factor for them in the mayoral election, and 12 percent said it would be "somewhat important." Thus, *96 percent* of likely voters made education an important factor in the mayoral election. Although we do not have comparable data across other districts, these results suggest that even in the largest city in the nation—where any number of other policy areas (economic growth, crime, etc.) could confuse voters—education remains a central issue on which they form their opinion of the mayor.

UNDERSTANDING LEADERSHIP IN THE SCHOOL POLICY CONTEXT

A system of integrated governance places leadership demands on the mayor. It is thought that dynamic leadership from the top can improve organizational performance. Whether and how leadership can lead to management improvements has been the subject of much study. In an integrated governance system, the mayor must forge strong relationships with other city interests as well as school district management.[2]

The link between the mayor's office and the school board can facilitate political support for the school system. In the case of mayoral control in Chicago, Mayor Richard Daley has been visibly willing to invest his political capital in turning around low-performing Chicago schools. To restore public confidence, the new administration has projected an image of efficient, responsive, and "clean" government. The Chicago Public Schools use accountability-driven outcomes to measure performance. We know less, however, about the reengineering aspects that are less readily quantifiable—the more subtle changes in work climate, student morale, and characteristics of student of institutional resilience.

Charismatic Leadership

The pioneering sociologist Max Weber conceptualized three types of leadership: charismatic, bureaucratic, and traditional. Charismatic leadership is that of a transformer, what might be seen in modern business parlance as a "change agent." Weber's work also allows us to distinguish between "personal charisma" and "office charisma." Personal charisma is what the mayor brings to the office, and office charisma is what the mayor gains when he or she assumes control. We believe that mayor-appointed school boards will attach charisma to the office, regardless of who the mayor is. The mechanism may be one of sorting rather than transformation. In an integrated governance framework, the mayor's office now comes with jurisdictional authority and a new tradition of being accountable for the school district. When candidates are making their decision whether or not to run, they will know that the schools are a part of the package. In this new framework, individuals who wish not to be education mayors may be screened out (Weber 1947).

Even with the office charisma in place, mayoral control of school districts does not necessarily reach the full potential of the "integrated governance" reform model. Mayors may choose not to direct their full attention to educational improvement. Given the presence of competing interests, mayors are known to mediate and seek compromise. Some mayors may treat employment in the school district as their "spoils" to support a patronage-based machinery. Others may withhold their political capital in public education. Still others are reluctant to take direct intervention to turn around low-performing schools (Peterson 1981; Rich 1996).

No one can predict that there will be no crooks, and it remains difficult to say how much of this reform rests on the particular individual qualities of the mayor. But the office of the mayor does command a certain legitimacy. We further believe that the particular powers that come with the office will shape the person who takes it. Thus, the integrated governance theory targets the institutional building blocks that may make it easier for the mayor to grow into this role.

James MacGregor Burns has been a leading figure in scholarship on leadership, and he describes in his prologue where leadership must come from: "Moral leadership emerges from, and always returns to, the fundamental wants and needs, aspirations, and values of the followers . . . the kind of leadership that can . . . satisfy followers' authentic needs" (Burns 1978, 4). A leader who genuinely works for his or her city does not manufacture issues. Dahl's conception of the public's "indirect influence" on politicians' actions can help us understand this (Dahl 1961, 163). The rise of public education as an issue in the mayoral election of 1945, for example, is used by Dahl as a case to argue that the "leaders probably would have had neither the resources nor the skill to manufacture such a politically potent issue had there been no latent predispositions stemming from an accumulation of experiences neither created nor influenced by the leaders" (p. 163). In other words, the politicians could not independently manufacture an issue. The issue had to resonate with the predispositions of the followers.

Although the theoretical conception of this ideal, charismatic leader is easy to imagine, in practice no such person exists. One of Dahl's points in *Who Governs* is, after all, that there is a reciprocal and ambiguous relationship between politician and constituent, leader and follower. The ambiguity centers on the paradox that "leaders do not merely *respond* to the preferences of constituents; leaders also *shape* preferences." Thus, we cannot be so sure that issues must necessarily be validated by "experiences neither created nor influenced by the leaders" (Dahl 1961, 164). Theories of the second and third faces of power come to bear on precisely this point: Leaders may work subconsciously to shape followers' preferences and society/culture also plays a role shaping the leader–follower relationship. To sum up, we know that Mayor X will never be a perfect charismatic leader—the interesting question is to what extent leader X would manipulate the system.

Some believe that though the mayor may need voters' support, the happiness and fulfillment of the city's residents is not the mayor's primary goal. If conceptualized this way, residents have little "indirect influence" over this leader, and the leader is free to act as he or she wants. The mayor uses ideas such as "cover control and mobilization of bias" to further his or her own agenda without listening to the will of the people (Bachrach and Baratz 1975, 901).

The normative outcomes of an independent leader will depend on what the particular independent agenda looks like. In John Gaventa's *Power and Powerlessness* (1982), the agenda of the powerful is one that leads to disastrous consequences for the followers. But just because an idea does not originate from the followers does not mean that the leader's agenda will necessarily harm the followers. Innovative leaders, for instance, are given great praise when they introduce the public to new products or new ways of doing things. A may lead B to a place B was not planning to go, but B may end up quite happy.[3]

In the context of mayor-appointed school boards, this distinction is important. Cuban and Usdan have shown how the push for mayoral control has often been associated with local business and corporate interests. Shipps, too, has emphasized business partnerships with new mayor-led education regimes. Civic groups have also played an important role in promoting this reform.

In New York, Mayor Bloomberg has gained significant support from the Children First Initiative, which receives its funding from the Broad Foundation and the Robertson Foundation (Shipps 1997).

But does corporate involvement necessarily mean that mayoral control is at odds with the desires of city residents? We now turn to an investigation of what city residents see in the mayor and their city schools.

Public Opinion on Mayoral Control

As discussed by DeHoog, Lowery, and Lyons (2001), the field of public administration has struggled to develop studies that adequately identify the determinants of citizens' satisfaction with their local government. One of the factors that prevents more robust analysis is the lack of comparable measures across districts. Most local public opinion data are generated by local or regional news outlets or think tanks. These surveys are not comparable across districts and may even change their wording over time.

Many local polls also do not publicly publish their full results. An October 2005 *Boston Globe* poll, for instance, reported that "a majority" of respondents felt that Mayor Menino was only doing a fair, poor, or very poor job on the public schools (Estes 2005). The article reported that "the poll of 513 randomly selected Boston voters was taken by phone Oct. 15–20," and that "it has a margin of error of plus or minus 4.4 percentage points." But we are not given more information, for instance, about the background covariates of the respondents. It is very difficult to compare these one-time surveys of opinion over time or across cities. Moreover, general statements, such as "Grade the public schools," often mask more nuanced differences in respondents' thinking. A survey by Public Agenda found that surveys can overstate satisfaction when asked about overall satisfaction. When asked more detailed questions about whether children were safe, engaged, or challenged, far fewer parents in a national study gave public schools good marks (Public Agenda 2000).

In light of these data constraints, we are unable to conduct the sorts of comparative statistical analysis that we conducted in preceding chapters. We are not able to be as precise about the factors that influence the public's opinion. This field remains a contested one, as some argue that critical events rather than district performance are the most powerful predictors of public opinion of the schools (Pride 2002). What we do instead is to synthesize a number of different surveys, with an eye toward common themes that emerge. We are also able to take advantage of the excellent work of the Quinnipiac University Polling Institute. The institute regularly surveys New York City voters/residents on their political beliefs, including their attitudes toward education and Mayor Bloomberg's role in managing the school district.[4] Because of this data availability, New York becomes the focus of much of our discussion. We integrate results of surveys from other districts as well, but we do not have any cross-tab information from those other surveys and consequently are limited in what inferences we can make. We consider several themes that emerge from the public opinion data: (1) Education is a top priority for city voters; (2) support for mayoral control is mixed, (3) public support and satisfaction with mayoral control are mixed, and (4) there are racial differences in support for mayoral control.

Education a Top Priority for Voters

One of the most consistent findings across a diversity of polls on urban education is the sentiment that improving the public schools should be a top priority. In a 2005 poll of New York City residents, "out of 606 likely voters polled, improving public schools was the top priority of 32 percent of respondents, with 24 percent of respondents choosing increasing the amount of affordable housing" as their top priority. Similar results in New York City were seen in a November 2005 poll conducted by the Quinnipiac University Polling Institute. In another 2005 New York state poll, this time in Rochester, the concern for education was even more pronounced as "ninety-seven percent of respondents believe the quality of city schools is very or somewhat important to the county's well-being" (*Newsday* 2005).[5]

In Memphis, a 2000 survey found that improving the quality of education ranked as the most important issue on the public's agenda, with 91 percent of respondents considering the issue "very important." A 2001 poll in Los Angeles found that 51 percent of the general population and 70 percent of the African American population in the city "rated the quality of education provided by local public schools as inadequate or very poor." In Boise, education also was a top priority. City residents may also be making connections between the quality of their schools and the city's economic performance. In Cleveland, 84 percent of respondents in a 2005 survey agreed that "high-quality public schools are the absolute / high priority for creating a positive jobs environment" (Ethridge and Associates 2000).[6]

The priority of education may be related to demographics. Evidence from a 2000 survey in Akron provides some insight into these relationships. The report found that "respondents who were either single or between the ages of 18 and 24 identified crime and safety as their top concern while respondents with children and respondents with high school diplomas and above identified educational issues" (Marquette 2000, 3). Unfortunately, we do not have enough similar data sets to further explore this finding.

Attitudes versus Action

There is an important difference to note between attitudes about education policy and willingness to act to improve schools. In a 2001 national survey, the Public Education Network and *Education Week* asked voters what
would get them to give their time and energy for the improvement of public
education. A total of 53 percent of respondents said that they would be either
very or extremely likely to act in reaction to low scores on standardized tests.
Perhaps more telling for districts facing financial or academic "bankruptcy,"
81 percent of respondents said they would act in response to a "serious crisis"
(Public Education Network and *Education Week* 2005).

From a political science perspective, Kent Jennings long ago differentiated
between a simple "grievance" and the more developed "demand on the system." Although Jennings was studying parental grievances, a similar question
can be raised here: When does public dissatisfaction with the schools rise to
the level of a "demand on the system"? The answer of integrated governance
is that it is translated into a formal system demand when a vote is cast in the
mayoral election. This is, as education mayors attempt to articulate, a vote
on school performance (Jennings 1968, 373).

Support for Mayoral Control Is Mixed

An interesting finding that seems to be consistent across school districts is
mixed public support for mayoral control. In a 2005 poll in Rochester, only
43 percent of respondents said "it's a good idea for the mayor to play a more
hands-on role in running city schools." In a 2000 poll in Memphis, when
asked if the Memphis City Schools school board should be appointed instead
of elected, only 30 percent supported such a change. The other 60 percent
believed the board should remain an elected body. When later asked, however, about legislation that would allow a change from an elected board, 52
percent were supportive. A 2005 online poll in Los Angeles found that public confidence in the mayor was not very strong. When asked, "Do you think
the mayor will reform L.A.'s public schools?" 78 percent of respondents an-
swered, "No." A different piece found that "in a poll of 700 L.A. voters conducted in July for the California Teachers Assn.—an opponent of the idea—55
percent opposed mayoral control of schools. And 70 percent said school board
members should be elected" (McLendon 2005).

Strikingly, even in Boston, which is hailed nationally as a success, one recent poll finds that residents may desire a return to an elected school board.
In a poll released in November 2005 by the Political Research Center at Suffolk University, respondents were asked: "Would you support an elected
School Committee in Boston?" A total of 60 percent of respondents said yes,

24 percent said no, and 16 percent were undecided. Looking at support in New York, a year before mayoral control was implemented, only 21 percent of voters thought it was a good idea. A year later, this proportion had doubled, to 45 percent, suggesting that though the public is perhaps initially suspicious of mayoral control, over time it can be persuaded as to its efficacy. There is especially strong opposition from Democrats and the minority community.[7]

Public Support for and Satisfaction with Mayoral Control Are Mixed

In addition to mixed initial support for mayoral control, the survey data from New York do not show a significant rise in public satisfaction with the school system since mayoral control was implemented in 2002. If the Quinnipiac University polls are traced back to 1996, the satisfaction level with New York City schools overall remains flat. In 2004, satisfaction with the city schools remained at 12 percent, the same as it was in March 2002 and in 1997. Neighborhood schools are viewed more favorably, but the 27 percent satisfaction level in 2004 is lower than the 39 percent satisfaction expressed in 2002. One way to interpret these data is that in the face of a persistent underperformance, the public may come to expect a low-performing district and may be slow to embrace a new mayor's claims that education is improving.

Public support for New York Mayor Bloomberg and Chancellor Joel Klein's work on the schools is similarly low. Neither Klein nor Bloomberg have gained wide support for their efforts. In September 2005, Bloomberg reached 50 percent satisfaction for the first time since 2003. This may mark an improvement, but he has seen his satisfaction rate rise and fall in earlier periods, so it remains to be seen if he can maintain this higher level of public confidence and even expand on it. Klein's 40 percent satisfaction rating in September 2005 was still lower than his starting satisfaction rating of 46 percent in February 2003.

A final pair of questions offers insight into the potential for mayors to convince voters about school improvements. The first question asked New York voters in 2002 (before the mayoral control reforms were implemented) what their *expectations* were for Mayor Bloomberg's education regime. The second question, asked in 2004 after a year and a half of reforms, asked about *evaluations* of the mayor's performance. There is a sharp difference between responses to the two questions. Whereas 64 percent of respondents in 2002 expected Bloomberg to make substantial progress in improving the quality of education, only 29 percent of respondents in 2004 thought that substantial progress had actually been made. This contrast, and the overall low satisfaction rating for the mayor, are important in light of competing theories about mayors "spinning" the schools. With only one-third of the public believing that schools are making substantial progress, it seems hard to contend that the mayor is successfully making the schools appear better than they are. City residents seem cautious about reaching a positive judgment on school performance.

Racial Differences in Support for Mayoral Control

The data from New York offer us an opportunity to consider racial differences in support for, and evaluation of, mayoral control. Mayoral control, as we discussed in the opening chapters, has been opposed by some in the African American community. State takeovers of school districts have also raised racial questions. In both instances, there is a concern that systemwide control may reduce access and limit schooling opportunities for the minority community in the name of "efficiency." Beyond the context of mayoral control, there remain many underlying racial tensions in America's schools. Many districts have taken steps to try and address the race issue. In Austin in 2005, for instance, the city partnered with the school district to create two joint task forces "to address the quality of life, specifically education, of African American and Hispanic citizens."[8]

We can see significant racial differences in the New York data. In 2001, when 24 percent of white respondents thought mayoral control was a good idea, only 11 percent of the African American community felt similarly. In 2002, the split was greater—30 percent of African American respondents supported mayoral control, compared with 51 percent of whites. To explain these differences along racial lines, we turn to Henig's argument that for the African American community, the city school system is not simply an education production facility but also a source of solid, middle-class jobs. If a central, mayor-led administration took over the district, the security of those jobs could be threatened. Henig's argument is crystallized in a 1999 op-ed article by Anthony Jenkins (1999), who observed that "the D.C. mayoral race was about electing someone who could put the city back on its feet, someone who could get its services back to optimum efficiency. But to many African Americans, still the majority population in the city, that objective should not be accomplished at our expense."

EDUCATION AS A CITYWIDE PRIORITY

Education, more than any other factor in society, determines the ability of people to achieve their life goals, live well-adjusted and meaningful lives, share in the society's resources, and participate as responsible citizens in their community. The complexities of modern society have greatly expanded the responsibilities imposed on area educational systems. Central to these responsibilities is the need to generate better understanding among all who participate in and share the benefits of quality education. The schools are not only charged with providing basic skills, but also with an ever-growing range of social programs, ranging from identification of health problems to providing recreation and citizenship training. It is an awesome task. (Goals for the Greater Akron Area 1974)

As evidenced by this 1974 quotation from an Akron city report, city governments have for many years thought about the critical role they play in supporting the city school district. According to an analysis of the mayor's State of the City addresses in twenty-three cities across the nation, more than 90 percent showed a distinct interest in public education, even though most mayors currently do not hold a formal role in the school system (Wong and Jain 1999).

To explore the present relationship between cities and their school districts, we examined the websites of the city governments in our sample. We looked at both what was emphasized on the front pages of the sites and also what public postures the cities took toward the school districts. In our online supplement to the text, we present for each district the site that we visited and whether or not a city schools link (or a similar education link) was placed on the front page of the city's site.

Our analysis reveals a growing tension within city governments. On one hand, most cities maintain the traditional city / school district governance boundaries. On the other hand, we see much evidence of mayors who are interested in becoming more involved in the operation of their cities' school systems. We present both sides of this tension and discuss whether or not it is sustainable in the long run.

Maintaining Separate Systems of Information for the Citizenry

Most cities maintain traditional governance boundaries between the city and the school district. In some instances, these barriers are made prominent due to messages that pop up when a user visiting the city website clicks on a link to the school system. In Newport News, although "School Administration" is listed under the heading "City Departments," when you click on the link, you are not only sent to an external link but are also told by the city that it has no responsibility for what you are about to see: "You have requested a link that is external to our website. The City of Newport News neither has nor accepts control, responsibility, or liability over the information or services found on any external websites. The appearance of any hyperlink to an external website does not constitute endorsement by the City of Newport News of that or any other external website."

The same sort of message appears in Augusta, Georgia. "You are about to leave the Augustaga.gov web site: The City of Augusta is not responsible for the content or information on www.richmond.k12.ga.us." Just as these cities are not responsible for web content of the district, neither are they responsible for district governance.

The traditional barriers also arise in budgetary information. In Anchorage, before the Assembly, the mayor of Anchorage actually had to submit two separate budgets. "Because the mayor has no direct role in the school district budget, the administration will submit two separate tax setting ordinances to the Assembly Tuesday night. One will be for general government and one for the school district." Separate budgets and separate governance are the norm for these cities that have not adopted a system of mayoral control of schools.

If you browse the websites of the cities in our sample, for the most part you will not find prominent links to education. Presumably this is because those cities do not see education as the same type of service offered as police protection or public works. Education is sometimes lumped under "resources for citizens" and sometimes given a listing under related links. In Milwaukee, the link to the school district is listed under "Other Levels of Government." In Sugar Land, Texas, the Sugar Land Independent School District link is under "Non-City Services." An exception to this rule is the mayor-controlled district of New Haven, where the city identifies the school district as a city department.[9]

Cities Desire to Improve Educational Services

Despite maintaining traditional governance boundaries and not listing education as a core city service, cities nevertheless have made many attempts to improve city education. We find evidence that a number of the non-mayoral-control cities are attempting to develop joint projects with the district. In some cases, this partnership starts with regular meetings. In Abilene, Texas, there are regular special meetings of the Abilene City Council and Abilene Independent School District Board of Trustees.[10]

A set of case studies conducted by the National League of Cities as part of its Municipal Leadership in Education Project emphasizes the point that even when mayors do not have formal power over their cities' school districts, they can still be effective education partners. In both the State of the City addresses and in some additional speeches, we looked for examples of the same sentiment projected by mayors. For instance, in Savannah, Mayor Otis Johnson stated that the city, county, school district, and additional stakeholders engage in a collaborative effort to improve Savannah's education. He went on to argue that "if we do not willingly accept the responsibility for producing positive outcomes, we are expecting someone else to accept responsibility for the future of our children and to me, that's insane. Nobody is responsible for our children but us" (Johnson 2005, 10; also see Hutchinson and Van Wyngaardt 2004).

Many cities have a "Department of Youth Services" or its equivalent. These are frequently tied to programs such as tutoring and after-school enrichment. Some of these bodies have also moved in the direction of being advisory committees for the mayor. In Seattle, there exists an "Office for Education" that works on the Families and Education Levy, City/School Partnerships, Community Partnerships. In Saint Louis, Mayor Francis Slay has formed a "Mayor's Commission on Children, Youth and Families," on which he placed representatives from local government, education, philanthropic groups, business, and community agencies. The commission meets quarterly and offers recommendations for policy changes. Up the Mississippi River, Mayor Randy Kelly in Saint Paul has done a very similar thing in establishing the Capital City Education Initiative. The initiative is designed to "provide the framework for the Kelly administration to work with the school district and other public and nonpublic K–12 schools, Saint Paul's higher education institutions, teachers, parents, businesses, non-profits, arts organizations, foundations, and other stakeholders to meet Saint Paul's education needs."[11]

Many cities provide support services to the school district in the form of construction aid. In San Diego, for instance, "the San Diego Model School Development Agency's vision is to enhance the positive affect of building new schools in City Heights by developing—on at least one such site—not just an elementary school but also for-sale and for-rent homes, new or revitalized retail businesses, recreation areas, improved open space, and family services." In Huntsville, Alabama, where a former teacher is mayor, the city has made creative use of tax increment finance districts to help fund the city schools. In Syracuse, Mayor Matthew Driscoll worked with the state legislature to pass a $600 million School Facilities Renovation Project.[12]

In other cities, new liaison positions have been created. In Portland, the mayor assigns the "education advocate," and in Akron, a position has been created for a "deputy mayor for intergovernmental relations" to work with the school district more effectively. Akron has also been a leader in partnering with the school district to share revenues and jointly help the city's economic development.[13] In October 2001, the mayor of Akron jointly signed a "Contract with the Community" with the Akron public schools. The contract in Akron reflects many of the same principles we see in mayor-controlled districts. The primary difference is that this "contract" is not linked to electoral consequences (City of Akron 2001).

In Saint Louis, before the state decided to intervene in 2007, Mayor Francis Slay had attempted his own effort at reform by bringing in a corporate turnaround team. Without new formal governing arrangements, such as a mayor-appointed school board, the corporate turnaround vision failed to enact productive reform. As described in one newspaper article covering the city, after a year of the reform, "student enrollment continues to decline, teachers complain about poor morale and low pay, parents are unhappy about school closures, and voters are up in arms about high salaries paid to top administrators." Indeed, the state's decision in 2007 to step in was evidence that Mayor Slay's efforts were not enough. This example represents somewhat of a middle ground between the traditional, insulated understanding of the city–district relationship and the fully integrated mayor-control view. It remains to be seen if such a middle ground approach can be successful (Hardy 2003; Dobbs 2004).

The reasons for these forays into district governance are varied. In Nashville, Mayor Bill Purcell may have looked to the schools to establish his legacy. One expert observer noted that "if the test scores continue to improve, mayor [Purcell] would take credit for the good things that have happened. But his legacy as being the education mayor has a cloud over it right now." Mayor Purcell's political motives in this situation would seem to be aligned with school performance (Kerr 2005).

Portland mayor Vera Katz comes at the issue with a citywide interest and global competitiveness mindset: "The public schools system is truly the lifeline of the city. Without quality education, a city cannot create and sustain a workforce capable of being competitive in the global workforce of the 21st century" (Pittman 2002). As Saskia Sassen (2001) has argued in *The Global City*, it is now commonplace for local businesses to contract directly with corporations and governments in foreign nations. Research has found connections between "quality of life" and the attraction of new capital. Even cities such as Fargo, North Dakota, have put international business and global trade on their agenda. In its Legislative Agenda for 2005, the Fargo-Moorhead Chamber of Commerce included as a goal: "Support legislation that encourages entrepreneurship in the state and improves the state's (global) economic competitiveness, including tax incentives for (venture) capital formation." At the same time, the Chamber of Commerce saw the connection between this priority and education, noting its desire to support legislation that would "support adequate funding and programs that help to provide a contemporary workforce development system for the nation's business community." These goals are shared by city after city in the United States. Recognizing that they are now competing in a global marketplace, cities understand that addressing urban school district underperformance is not just a desire for redistributive justice: It is an effort to improve overall economic competitiveness of the city (Rogerson 1999).[14]

MAYORAL LEADERSHIP IN EDUCATION

To understand how mayors are positioning themselves in terms of leadership in the education sector, we look at their public pronouncements in State of the City addresses. This section discusses the collection, content analysis, and cross-district statistical analysis of these speeches.

Analyzing State of the City Speeches

To examine mayoral leadership more systematically, we analyze mayors' recent State of the City speeches. We were successful in gathering eighty-one speeches. More detailed information on the sources of these speeches is available in our online supplement to the book. Several preliminary notes can be made about these data. First, we recognize that the data are not complete (we are missing twenty-three districts), and more fundamentally that the data are only one "snapshot" in the life of the mayor's public life and the city's history. Some cities may have had one-time policy issues rise up in the year we examine. Because we have only one year of data, we are limited in the inferences we can make. Still, we code each speech and perform basic statistical analysis to examine the relationship between new-style mayors and public positions on education policy. Looking at the text of each speech, we constructed two indices to evaluate the interest level of mayors in exerting influence in the city school system.

First, we created a leadership index composed of three elements: prioritization of education, interest in playing an active role, and desire to actually engage in management of the school system. Following the procedure below, we coded each of these three dimensions as either a 1 or 0. Summing across the three dimensions produced an index with a 0–3 range, an average of 1.39, and a standard deviation of 1.29.

We asked first: In the State of the City speech, does the mayor communicate that education is a top priority for the city? Examples of this prioritizing can be found in a number of different cities, both with and without mayoral control. In Madison, Mayor David Cieslewicz stated that "even though public education is not part of City government, I believe that there is nothing more important to the health of our city than the quality of our public schools." In Rockford, Illinois, Mayor Doug Scott left no doubt about his position on the schools: "I will start today with education, because it is at the core of everything else we do. What we accomplish as a community is directly related to what goes on in our classrooms."

Second, we looked to see whether or not the mayor discusses an active role for the city in educating children (e.g., after-school programs). In Oakland, Mayor Jerry Brown announced some city initiatives: "In terms of young people, we've dedicated over a half a million dollars in the city's budget for after school programs. . . . We've also funded the middle school summer arts program in partnership with the Oakland Unified School District."

Third, we looked to see if the mayor expressed a desire to become involved in the *management decisions* of the school district. The clear examples here are the mayor-controlled districts, where mayors are talking about their accomplishments and plans for the future. Mayor Daley in Chicago pointed out that "last year we created 15 new schools. Twelve more were just announced and approved by the Board of Education, and a total of 18 will open next year as Renaissance 2010 schools." In Boston, Mayor Menino, too, offered a mix of accomplishments and looking ahead: "We were among the first school districts in the country to provide every child with access to full-day kindergarten. But that was not enough. To reach more of our children even earlier, we will add nearly 500 new seats for 4-year-olds in September. But let me tell you, even that will not be enough. I will direct the Boston Public Schools to provide all 4-year-olds in the city with full-day school within five years. Boston will be the first city in the nation to achieve this."

In addition to the leadership index, we also constructed a public confidence index. This index tracks three components of the mayor's speech: (1) an emphasis on accountability in the school system; (2) making explicit reference to test scores or standards; and (3) direct mention of the public confidence issue as related to the city schools. Assigning either a 1 (if the mayor mentioned accountability, test scores, or public confidence), or a 0 (if no mention was made), we produced an index with a range of 0–3, a mean of .68, and a standard deviation of 1.15.

In constructing the public confidence index, we first asked: Does the mayor emphasize accountability for the school system? In Albuquerque, for instance, Mayor Martin Chavez addressed the topic head on: "We need better accountability, we need a better relationship, and so this evening I want to call on APS [Albuquerque Public Schools] and all the public officials in the city for a new dialogue." In Baltimore, Mayor Martin O'Malley used similar language when he commented that "our school system is another area where increased transparency and accountability is critical to continuing reform—and still in great need."

We then asked: Does the mayor use test score data or make explicit reference to standards or other numeric data in his speech? In Providence, Mayor David N. Cicilline identified "two bottom lines in education—the achievement bottom line and the financial bottom line. In both cases, the Providence Schools are looking better and better." He then went on to note that, "as has been widely reported, our test scores are rising across the board." Finally, we asked: Does the mayor voice concern about improving public confidence in the school system? New Haven mayor John DeStefano Jr. spoke directly to the subject: "Without schools in which people have confidence, we cannot be a great city."

Specifying the Effects of Mayoral Control in Education Priority

Unlike earlier statistical analysis, here we have only one year of data. Our dependent variable is also different. Instead of a continuous variable such as the level of per-pupil revenues, our two dependent variables here are discrete, ordered indices. We therefore run an ordered logit regression model of the form

$$
\begin{aligned}
SPEECH\_INDEX_i = {} & \beta_0 + \beta_1 MAYORAL\_CONTROL_i \\
& + \beta_2 MAYOR\_COUNCIL_i \\
& + \beta_3 PCT\_SINGLE\_MEMBER_i + \beta_4 PCT\_PRIVATE_i \\
& + \beta_5 ENROLL_i + \beta_6 PCT\_HISPANIC_i \\
& + \beta_7 PCT\_AFR\text{-}AMERICAN_i \\
& + \beta_8 PCT\_KIDS\_POVERTY_i \\
& + \beta_9 PCT\_SPECIAL\_ED_i + \varepsilon_i
\end{aligned}
\tag{8.1}
$$

where $SPEECH\_INDEX_i$ is one of the two dependent variable indices just discussed for district i; $MAYORAL\_CONTROL_i$ is the summation of our NEW STYLE, MAJORITY, and FULL measures; $MAYOR\_COUNCIL_i$ is a dichotomous variable indicating whether or not the city uses a mayor–council form of government; $PCT\_SINGLE\_MEMBER_i$ is the percentage of city school board seats that are voted on in a single-member fashion; $PCT\_PRIVATE_i$ is the percentage of kindergarten through twelfth grade students in the city enrolled in private schools; $ENROLL_i$ is the district student enrollment; $PCT\_HISPANIC_i$ is the percentage of Hispanic students in the district; $PCT\_AFR\text{-}AMERICAN_i$ is the percentage of African American students in the district; $PCT\_KIDS\_POVERTY_i$ is the percentage of city residents, age three through eighteen, who were living below the poverty level in 2000; and, $PCT\_SPECIAL\_ED_i$ is the percentage of district students who have an individualized education plan.

New-Style Mayors Raise the Profile of Public Education

Looking at the overall picture, more than half the mayors either made education a top priority or mapped out an active role for the city in the provision of educational services. The details of the State of the City speeches are available in our online supplement. About a quarter of the mayors discussed accountability and outcomes measures, and nearly a third discussed ways in which the city might help to manage the school district. Approximately 17 percent of mayors directly addressed the issue of public confidence. When we run the statistical analysis, we find that greater mayoral control is positively and significantly related to our leadership index but not to our public confidence index (table 8.2). Though the analysis remains preliminary because of the smaller number of cities included in the sample, it suggests that mayors with more formal powers will desire to engage in greater leadership roles. At the same time, however, we do not find that increased mayoral control is related to express mentions of accountability, test scores, and public confidence. An important rhetorical distinction exists between these two indices, which may help to explain the divergent results. The language of leadership may more easily allow for generalization without firm commitments, whereas discussions of accountability systems and in particular standards and achievement tests are less amenable to mere platitudes. Mayors may see education reform as a part of their broad vision for their city, but without formal powers they are less likely to discuss issues that would involve or invite action over which they have little control. A mayor is not likely to propose specific new accountability measures, for instance, if he or she is not in a position to enact those measures.

Looking at the control variables, we see that being in a mayor–council city is significantly and positively related to the leadership index. The percentage of children enrolled in private school is also significantly and positively associated with the leadership index. This may suggest an added element of competition in the city, or the variable could be picking up some other social background noise.

Informal Mayoral Influence in Traditional Governance

We believe that the body of evidence, both qualitative and quantitative, suggests the conclusion that providing the mayor with greater formal powers over the school system will bring education policy to the forefront of a city's civic conversation. There are, however, alternative explanations that challenge our interpretation of mayors, formal powers over school affairs,

Table 8.2.   Results of Ordered Logit Regression Analysis of Education Content of State of City Speeches, City Governance, and Demographic Characteristics (coefficients and standard errors reported)

Variable	Leadership Index	Public Confidence Index
Mayor control index	0.724*	0.436
	(0.414)	(0.356)
Mayor–council	1.041*	0.455
	(0.536)	(0.675)
Achievement	–0.255	–0.231
	(0.353)	(0.454)
Percent single-member-elected	0.002	0.332
school board members	(0.657)	(0.780)
Percent in private school	15.995**	4.093
	(6.600)	(7.527)
Percent of revenues from state	–2.926	–3.916*
	(1.870)	(2.208)
Per-pupil expenditure,	0.074	0.130
current instruction	(0.154)	(0.181)
Enrollment (million)	7.200	3.852
	(6.052)	(2.814)
Percent Hispanic	–0.747	–0.526
	(2.462)	(3.353)
Percent African American	–1.376	0.139
	(2.161)	(2.722)
Percent of children living in poverty	7.857	6.048
	(5.243)	(5.718)
Percent special education	9.519	7.293
	(8.437)	(10.390)
N	81	81
Log likelihood	–78.55	–57.92

Note: Two-tailed significance denoted as $*p < .1$, $**p < .05$, $***p < .01$.

and public support. First, it can be argued that our focus on formal powers is misplaced. If a mayor has enough political capital or persuasive power, he or she may be able to significantly influence school district policy even without formal authority. One example of a mayor who may be able to do this is Richmond mayor Douglas Wilder. Wilder, a former governor of Virginia and one of the state's most powerful politicians, has shown inclinations that he may play a hand in school policy. In a 2005 op-ed article in the *Richmond Times-Dispatch*, he wrote that "I cannot merely say, 'Leave it to others to see the job through.' It is your job and mine." One description of the relationship between Mayor Wilder and the Richmond schools observed that, "technically, the superintendent reports to the school board, not the mayor, but Wilder isn't one to defer to bureaucratic flow charts." The article goes on to describe this scene where Mayor Wilder reacts to a truancy problem in the schools: "He had summoned the superintendent to his office to discuss the matter. 'I haven't been confrontational with her, but she has not been direct with me, and the whole purpose of the meeting today,' he said, as a mischievous smile spread across his face, 'is to find out how we're going to get along.'"

If every mayor had the power and political skill of Mayor Wilder, formal authority would be less necessary for mayors to affect school policy. But the reality is that most mayors do not have the political gravitas of Douglas Wilder. As the nation's first elected African American governor, Wilder drew much attention from beyond Virginia. Mayor Wilder, who won nearly 80 percent of the votes in his 2004 mayoral campaign, has statewide political power and national political connections unavailable to most municipal politicians. Most mayors need the additional leverage that formal powers provide to bring about systemic change in their city's school systems.

Traditional Governance and Periphery Programs

Although they are not vested with formal powers, traditional mayors have found ways to become involved in education. Most of the efforts to date have been in after-school programs. The prominence of after-school programs for urban areas is evident in a report on the issue from the National League of Cities. The report provides case study analysis across eight cities that implemented after-school programs as part of a thirty-month component of the Municipal Leadership for Expanded Learning Opportunities Program. The National League of Cities even created an "after-school action kit" designed to help districts develop their after-school options. Congress has become an active player as well, hearing testimony in 2003 from New Haven mayor DeStefano on the efficacy of after-school programs (Ouellette, Hutchinson, and Frant 2005).

Many nonmayoral-control mayors, in an effort to gain some leverage, have formed commissions or panels to study the city schools. In Pittsburgh, a 2003 task force produced a report that was very critical of the Pittsburgh city schools. In response to failing schools, the report's chairman on the subcommittee that studied district leadership voiced the opinion that "these core issues do not receive the priority of attention under the current governance structure." The report stated: "Vesting responsibility in the mayor will ensure that the schools are accountable to the city as a whole, rather than to small, well-organized interest groups." But since 2003, the governance structure has not changed (Lee 2003).

The reason for inaction may be the nature of commissions themselves. In an extensive study of education commissions from 1890 to the 1980s, Ginsberg and Wimpelberg (1987, 358) conclude: "Commissions respond to problems, raise issues, and offer solutions. It is beyond the scope of their ability, however, to make any changes in schools. Ultimately it is local school board officials, teachers, and parents who must undertake the difficult task of reform." Similarly, it is ultimately the mayor who must act if the recommendations of a blue ribbon panel are actually to be implemented.

THE PUBLIC CONFIDENCE CHALLENGE

This chapter has explored the public confidence and leadership dimensions of mayoral control of urban school systems. Along the way, it has uncovered a series of tensions related to mayors and schools. First, the public has a strong desire to see improved public schools, but at the same time it is skeptical of mayor-led reform and reluctant to credit mayors with school improvements. Second, and perhaps in light of the public's stance, the majority of mayors want to maintain traditional boundaries between school systems and city government. This desire to maintain boundaries is in tension with the rise of new-style mayoral leadership that challenges the mayor's office to expand its responsibilities in the domain of public education. Mayors in their speeches talk of education improvements, but they may be less likely actually to focus on specifics to back up their rhetoric.

In light of these tensions, we draw two conclusions. First, to improve public confidence in city schools, mayors must not only produce improved student achievement. They must also demonstrate to the city that they are genuinely behind the reform efforts for the long haul. Mayors are entering a policy domain where persistent underperformance has made the public cynical about the latest reform. Mayors, therefore, must convince city residents that mixing mayors and education is not just the latest educational fad. Mayors must demonstrate charismatic leadership if they are to overcome racial and political divides. This challenge is by no means an easy one.

Our second conclusion is an answer to the question: If public expectations are so high and the political challenges are so great, why would a mayor ever want to get into the education arena? Why not adhere to traditional governance barriers, while simply paying some rhetorical lip service to schools? The answer is that the public, for all its uncertainty about mayors, is hungry for improved public schools. A true "education mayor"—by which we mean a mayor who can bring about sustained improvement in city schools—would be delivering to the city's residents the public good they most desire: excellent education for every city student.

CHAPTER NINE

Mayorally Governed School Districts as Laboratories of Democracy

Our founding fathers set up the states as laboratories of democracy. That was a phrase used by James Madison and by other founders. And in so many ways, they are. I used to say when I was a governor I was much more proud of being the second state to do something than to be the first state to do something, because if we were the second state to do something it meant we were paying attention to the laboratories and we weren't embarrassed to take somebody else's good idea if it would help our people. I think today, more than any other single group of people, *the mayors embody that spirit.*
—President Bill Clinton (White House 1998)

FROM MAYORS WHO ARE IMPROVING STUDENT PERFOR-mance to those maintaining fiscal discipline and raising the profile of public education in their cities, the last decade has witnessed the rise of new-style mayors who are changing the face of urban education in the United States. The question for the future is: How will other cities learn from this first wave of mayoral control? On the basis of successes such as Boston and Chicago, and failures such as Detroit and Washington, how can mayors best help their city schools? As the last chapter illustrated, most U.S. mayors still find themselves isolated from their cities' school systems.

In this chapter we review the major findings of our study and discuss the implications of these findings for the future of the relationship between mayors and schools. As we have done throughout the book, we ground ourselves in the empirical results of our analysis. We do not advocate generally for all mayors to assume control of their cities' schools. Indeed, our results show that under certain conditions mayors may not find themselves in a favorable position to assume leadership. What we do argue for is the careful consideration of the available empirical evidence in determining the path of urban governance and education reform.

We believe the findings of our study can inform policy debates. We have considered the relationship between mayoral control and student achievement, financial, staffing, and public confidence outcomes. Summarizing the cross-district and multiyear analysis of achievement, we find:

- Even after factoring in strong structural forces such as poverty and a persistent racial achievement gap, moving from an old style of governance regime to a new, integrated governance framework will lead to statistically significant, positive gains in reading and mathematics, relative to other districts in the state (chapter 4).
- Mayor-led integrated governance is attempting to raise up the lowest-performing schools in the district, while at the same time avoiding a "brain drain" by improving schools at the top of the distribution as well (chapter five).
- In the case of Chicago, mayoral control provided a common structure for systemwide change. It facilitated curricular and instructional coherence by holding all schools to common standards of student achievement. At all levels, it focused district and school actors on a common goal and gave them the mechanisms to intervene and improve instruction (chapter six).
- New-style mayors are becoming more strategic in prioritizing their resource allocation and management. The data suggest that mayor-controlled districts focus on fiscal discipline by containing labor costs and reducing their bureaucratic spending (chapter seven).
- Mayors in integrated governance systems are more likely to stress accountability and outcome-based performance goals for the city's school districts. They are also more likely to advocate for a stronger city role in managing the school system (chapter eight).

Having done our best in the first eight chapters to lay out the theory behind and evidence in support of mayor-led integrated governance, in this final chapter we discuss the factors that may mediate the success or failure of mayoral control.

The chapter is organized into three sections. We first identify several prerequisites that must be in place before mayoral control can become a possibility. If these prerequisites are not met, mayoral control will not be an attractive policy option. Second, we discuss the importance of timing and partnership in determining mayors' likelihood of success. Finally, we conclude with suggestions for future lines of research and final thoughts on the future of mayors and schools in the United States.

THE CONTEXT FOR SUCCESSFUL MAYORAL CONTROL

We have recognized from the start that certain historical legacies in cities may make implementing mayoral control more difficult. As more cities, including smaller and midsized cities, try to learn from the first wave of reform, here we revisit the two most important factors that must be considered before mayoral leadership be successfully introduced:

1. the relationship between city and school district boundaries, and
2. the mayor's personal desire to lead district reform.

Coterminous City and School District Boundaries

In chapter three we discussed why the districts/cities in our sample for this study had to meet two 75 percent conditions: Districts receive at least 75 percent of their students from a principal city, and cities send at least 75 percent of their city's public school students to the same school district. Our decision rule recognized that jurisdictional boundaries (coterminous or not) are creatures of historic and other structural conditions at the time when the city and district were established. Though cities that are coterminous with school districts are the most natural locations for mayors to consider school leadership, the 75 percent rule reflects the modern enrollment reality that district and city boundaries are often overlapping. This preexisting spatial geography—both the boundary lines and the crossing of boundary lines as students flow to and from principal and neighboring cities—will affect the design of mayoral control.

When boundary lines significantly overlap, political problems arise because a mayor only has control over the part of the school district in his or her city. Changes are possible, but they may require the politically costly process of revising local charters and state codes. Even when mayoral control is not an issue, the process of realigning school district boundaries can be politically volatile. Omaha is an example of a city that recently wrestled with district boundaries (see Omaha Public Schools 2005; Saunders 2005). Competition and differing demographics between the districts further complicates the situation. A compromise can be reached, but it may take creative governance arrangements. The issue of multiple jurisdictions in Los Angeles was handled in the 2006 mayoral control plan with a Council of Mayors of nearby cities that are also served by the Los Angeles Unified School District (Helfand and

Blue 2006). This plan allowed for the leaders of other municipalities to gain a stake in school district governance.

A Mayor Who Wants to Lead District Reform

For a system of mayoral control to work, the mayor should have a strong desire to lead the city's schools. This is an obvious point, but one that must be emphasized. Our analysis of State of the City speeches in chapter eight suggests that not all mayors are interested in taking on this challenge. Indeed, some may wonder why a mayor, already burdened by many municipal responsibilities, would want to take on something as challenging as the city school district. In this view, there is little to gain from taking on an enterprise so difficult to turn around. This analysis is not entirely off the mark. When mayors decide to lead city school systems, they are taking on an enormous responsibility. Who would dare to take on such a project?

Integrated governance is a challenge, but it is also an opportunity for innovative, passionate mayors who are no longer willing to stand by and shrug off responsibility for their cities' schools. These mayors are marked by a vision that education is intimately related to the city's quality of life, so much so that it cannot be isolated from other core city services. If a city has a mayor who shares this vision, that city may be ready for a mayor-appointed school board. But if the mayor is wary of taking on the responsibilities of education policy, an appointed school board should not be on the table.

TIMING, PARTNERSHIPS, AND FLEXIBILITY

In this book we have discussed how different cities have experienced varying degrees of success with mayoral control. Two factors that shape the success of mayoral control are timing and partnership. In table 9.1, we present a sample of questions related to timing and partnership.

Timing

Timing is an issue in the planning, implementation, and review of mayoral control. For cities and mayors to have optimal timing requires that they remain sensitive to the many diverse interests that come to bear on urban education politics. City school boards may be more likely to adopt changes after sustained underperformance. If schools are showing improvement, the need for mayoral reform may not seem as pressing.

Also at issue is when it is best for a mayor to propose education governance. For instance, should a new mayor make it part of his or her campaign

Table 9.1 Questions of Timing and Partnership in Building Political Support for Mayoral Control

Factor	Timing	Partnership
School board opposition	When will the school board voice its strongest opposition? When might it be more amenable to change?	Are there any members of the school board who would support a governance change?
City politics	Should mayoral control be proposed as a campaign promise, an early priority once in office, or a program to embrace only after establishing power in other areas?	How does leadership in the minority community feel about mayoral control? Does the city council or board of aldermen support the reform?
State politics	When is it politically feasible to introduce legislation? Will the state legislature push its legislation before, after, or in conjunction with the mayor's pronouncements?	What allies does the mayor have in the state legislature? What portions of the state legislature will be more resistant to mayoral control?
Interest groups	When should the teachers' union be approached about mayoral control? What about other service employees' unions?	What discussions can be engaged in, in order to make the unions a partner in mayoral control reform?
Civic/business community	When should the civic leadership and business community be invited in to the process? Will civic leadership be brought on board later, or will they initiate the process?	How strong should the ties be between civic leadership and the mayor's office? When should the mayor's office act independently of the civic interests?
Local media	What information should be released to local media, and when in the process?	Are certain sections of the local media more favorable to mayoral control? Where is opposition likely to be published or broadcast?

platform? Or should a mayor establish herself or himself first before proposing such dramatic reform? Once mayoral control is in place, how much time
should a mayoral control regime be given before its success is judged? Mayors
will likely be thinking about election cycles.

Mayors and cities also need to consider their relationship with state legislatures. We have not delved into the city–state political dynamics that hover
in the background of mayoral control, but we have noted that mayoral control requires state legislation to be implemented. Mayors and city school districts must be aware of state political dynamics to know when the time is right
for proposing mayor-led education reform.

Partnerships

Partnerships are evident throughout the process. From the outset, the mayor
must recognize that he or she will depend mightily on the superintendent.
As discussed in chapter two, a "politics of partnership" can develop as the
mayor shields the superintendent from political pressures. Recent experiences
in Cleveland suggest that poor district performance may be correlated with a
disintegrating relationship between the mayor and superintendent. Superintendent Barbara Byrd-Bennett announced her resignation in 2005, and some
commentators saw her relationship with the mayor as a factor in that depar-
ture. The chief executive of the Greater Cleveland Growth Association observed that Byrd-Bennett and Mayor Jane Campbell "do not feel they are in
the same foxhole together. They were thrown together. In the Mike White
administration, they jumped into that foxhole together" (Okoben 2005). The
personal and professional dynamic between the mayor and superintendent is
at the core of integrated governance.

In practice, strong partnerships can be difficult to form in the context of
contentious histories. The 2006 experience of Los Angeles mayor Antonio
Villaraigosa, who was kept out of the superintendent hiring process, provides
an example of a strained partnership. Because the new state legislation would
not take affect until January 1, 2007, when Superintendent Roy Romer decided to retire in the fall of 2006, the question then was whether the mayor
would be able to help select the person to run the district. Though the mayor
campaigned to gain hiring and firing ratification powers, in the fall of 2006
he had to look on from the outside as the school board hired former Navy
vice admiral David L. Brewer III as the new superintendent (Associated Press
2006). A strong working relationship between Brewer and Villaraigosa is
essential for success in Los Angeles, but the rocky beginnings challenge the
establishment of a positive politics of partnership.

Partnerships must also be made with civic leaders and the minority community. As shown by Clarence Stone and his colleagues (2001), building "civic

capacity" is an essential element in successful education reform. Politically, deals must be struck with the teachers' union and the state legislature. Reformers who want to see an increased role for mayors must remember that mayors must rely on others at every stage.

Flexibility: Options for Reform

The conditions for timing and partnership will vary from city to city, and from year to year. In this dynamic context, it is important to remember that mayoral control is a *flexible reform* that can and should be adapted to particular local conditions. Integrated governance does not force policymakers to accept cookie-cutter regulations, but instead it allows for creative implementation that best matches what politicians and educators see in their district.

Cities interested in mayoral control have a range of options. In table 9.1, we present these options as they vary from low to high mayoral involvement in education. Looking at table 9.2, it is evident that cities must make two decisions: (1) How much involvement should the mayor have at this time? and (2) How much involvement is politically feasible at this time? We include the phrase "at this time" to emphasize the timing element—what may not be desired or politically feasible this year may be possible next year or five years down the road. What is possible in later years may actually depend on the reform options chosen this year. For instance, if a mayor forms a two-year commission to thoroughly study the school district, the findings of that commission may lead to more mayoral control down the line.

The options we lay out are not exhaustive, but they do span the possible range for cities and school districts. Moving from low to high mayoral involvement (left to right on table 9.2), these options are:

1. *Mayor-led "blue ribbon panel."* This is almost always a politically feasible option because the panel does not have any legal authority. Its recommendations are just that—recommendations. A panel may be a good way to get discussion going, but a concern is that the panel's recommendations will not be followed up with real action.

2. *Permanent mayoral office or department for education.* Because expert panels and commissions are typically dissolved after the release of their study, creating a permanent office or department within city government to look at education is more substantial. There may be some political resistance if the mayor's office is seen as encroaching on school district territory, but the mayor's office of education can focus on complementary efforts, such as after-school programs and facilities maintenance. Though an office such as this would not affect fundamental school district operations, it could provide the basis for a solid future

Table 9.2 The Range of Mayoral Involvement in Urban Education

Aspect	Low Involvement		Medium Involvement		High Involvement	
	Traditional Governance Arrangement	Mayor-Led "Blue" Ribbon Panel	Permanent Mayoral Office or Department for Education	Mayor-Supported School Board Slate	Partially Mayor-Appointed School Board	Fully Mayor-Appointed School Board
Description	Mayor responsible for city government; school district governance is wholly separate	Traditional governance system is not changed but mayor selects a blue ribbon committee to study the city's schools and produce a report; the report is not binding and the committee is not standing	Traditional governance system is not changed, but mayor establishes a standing office to promote city schools and advise the mayor's office on issues related to education	Mayor becomes more active in school governance by actively endorsing or campaigning on behalf of a slate of school board candidates	Traditional governance system is altered, and mayor is given power to appoint some of the school board members	Traditional governance system is replaced by a fully mayoral appointed school board
Example districts	Majority of U.S. school districts	Pittsburgh (Report issued by Mayor's Commission on Public Education in 2003)	Minneapolis (Capital City Education Initiative)	Saint Louis (Mayor Slay backed a slate of 4 candidates in 2003)	Oakland (minority-appointed) New York (majority-appointed)	Chicago Boston
Legal changes required?	No	No	Maybe	No	Yes	Yes

Major design considerations	Little to no mayoral involvement, so few design options available	Who should be on panel? How should they be selected? Scope of the panel's study Timeline for panel's work How involved should the school district be with this assessment? What outcome indicators will the panel look at? How will findings be presented?	What issues will the new office focus on? How will the office coordinate with the school district? Funding for the office? Who will lead the office?	How will school board candidates be identified for endorsement? Will mayor actively recruit the candidates? Will mayor give tacit endorsement, or actively campaign? Once on the board, what relationship will exist between mayor and supported school board members? What relationship with the rest of the school board? Should endorsements be made each school board election?	Should mayor appoint a majority or a minority of the board members? Should mayor be able to choose from any qualified candidate, or choose instead from a slate of candidates screened by independent commission? How long should mayor retain this power? Indefinitely? Limited number of years? How long will appointed members serve for? What additional checks and balances can be introduced to ease concerns about the transfer of power? Should an accountability and review panel be formed?	In addition to questions in the previous column: When should the mayor be given this power? Will appointing power be indefinite? Subject to vote? How large should the new school board be? How long should school board members serve for? How will the superintendent be selected?

partnership, demonstrating that the city is capable of successfully operating educational programs.

3. *Mayor-supported school board slate.* Mayor-supported school board slates are a twist on mayoral control. Rather than trying to *change* the system, in this reform approach, mayors try to *utilize* the system in a new way. Mayors can take advantage of low-salience school board elections and try to back a majority of the school board candidates. If successful, the mayor will have great informal influence over the board. Because of this increased informal influence, the strategy is likely to draw much resistance from entrenched interests. It may also create a schism on the board, between the mayor and non-mayor-supported candidates.

4. *Partially mayor-appointed school board.* Adopting the mayoral control notion, but taking a middle-of-the-road approach, this "hybrid" model allows for some, but not all, power to be shifted to the mayor. Depending on the specific proposal, the mayor may appoint a minority (e.g., Oakland) or majority (e.g., New York) of the school board. Because power is distributed, this option is more politically feasible. But for the same reason, the mayor may be more limited in what he or she can accomplish because there is potentially more opposition on the board to the mayor's vision.

5. *Fully mayor-appointed school board.* In this model, the mayor is given full power to appoint school board members. This type of reform has gained the most attention, despite the fact that it has only occurred in a few districts, because it involves an institutional restructuring of school system governance. It shakes up the status quo and demands real reform.

This broad range of reform options, taken together with the themes of timing and partnerships, leave many questions for cities, school boards, and mayors to consider. It is hoped that the research examined in this study will help policymakers as they answer those questions. But there is more for policy analysts to do, and we turn now to a future research agenda.

FUTURE RESEARCH AGENDA ON MAYORAL GOVERNANCE

Our study has covered much ground, from academics to finances to the salience of education as a city service. But there remains much to do. First and foremost, the databases that we employ should be updated to include the most recent years. We have set up our databases in a way that allows for integration of the new data as they become available. We can do this for achievement, finance, and staffing data, as well as for all our control variables.

Second, more work needs to be conducted on the relationship between "state takeovers" and the system of mayor-led governance on which we have focused in this study. In state takeovers, a state authority takes control of local school district operations for a specified period or until certain performance conditions are met. We have previously identified important distinctions between state takeover and cities implementing mayoral control. Though the state has a role in both actions, in mayor-led integrated governance, local control is maintained. City residents can vote for or against the mayor, but a state takeover board is not directly accountable to city residents. This is a very important distinction, and future research can investigate how this difference in governance is related to achievement, staffing, and financial outcomes (Wong, Langevin, and Shen 2004; Wong and Shen 2001).

Third, policies can be developed that address the issue of local boundaries and county governments. Given the politics of suburbia (see Oliver 2001), however, this may be an important policy arrangement to consider. Theoretically, many of the same principles should hold. Working with very different demographic background variables, however, may significantly alter the implementation of the reform.

Fourth, greater study can be made of the budgetary authority that mayors have over their city schools in both mayoral control and traditional governance arrangements. Research in this area can give us a better sense of actual mayoral influence by looking at the number of times mayors reject school budgets, the level of detail at which school budgets are reviewed, and the extent to which the mayor's office is involved in producing that budget. To the extent that even traditional mayors can use the school budget to leverage additional power, they may be able to increase their influence on the district even without appointing the school board.

MAYORS AND THE FUTURE OF URBAN EDUCATION

Whether they can appoint their school boards or not, many of America's major cities are governed by mayors who are passionate about improving their cities' school systems. Aware of the daunting task and the potential political risk, these mayors are forging ahead. They are not content to sit on the sidelines. Explaining his increased education involvement in 2003, Saint Louis mayor Francis Slay spoke from the heart, "It tears my heart to see neighborhoods laid to waste because parents have fled the city to educate their children. . . . If fighting for better education will somehow impact me politically, that's the price I am willing to pay. Doing nothing was not an option" (Wagman 2003).

Although many mayors share Mayor Slay's sentiments that "doing nothing" about their cities' schools is not an option, for many years it has not been clear that the answer is "doing something" in the form of a mayoral-appointed school board. On the basis of the analysis we have presented in this book, we believe that an answer has now emerged: Integrating city and school district governance can lead to improvements in student achievement and management efficiency.

Looking at the period 1999–2003, and evaluating the first wave of new-style mayoral leadership in education, we find that mayoral leadership is associated with higher elementary student achievement in reading and mathematics. Explaining these improvements are the macro–micro linkages that exist between governance and classroom changes. We find that mayors can change the nature of teaching and learning in ways that lead to student success. Looking at the longer period 1992–2003, we find that mayoral leadership is related to increased resources for instructional purposes and less spending on general administration. Taking a snapshot of the current crop of mayors, we find that new-style mayors make education a higher priority, raising public awareness about the need for school reform.

When we first set out to empirically assess the effects of mayoral control, we believed that many of these outcomes could result from mayoral control. But we did not have strong evidence to back it up, and we concluded in 2001 that it was "still too early to know" what changes mayoral control has brought about (Wong and Shen 2001, 20). After five years of research, however, with improved data, methods, and analysis, we are in a position to offer a strong conclusion.

The evidence we have presented in this book, which spans multiple years and districts across the entire country, suggests that the first wave of mayoral control has been a success. America's urban students are doing better now than they would be if mayors had not become more involved. Some districts' experiences with mayoral involvement have not been successful in raising student achievement, but the built-in safeguards kicked in and those cities were returned to an elected board. The reform's flexibility allowed for this return to traditional governance.

Mayors are not superheroes who can rescue school districts on their own. But mayors occupy a uniquely central institutional place in the urban political economy. They are not just another party in education decision making. The office of the mayor allows mayors to be leaders in education reform. Mayors can be the impetus for building civic capacity and establishing civic coalitions. Mayors can work with both local interests and state legislators. Mayors are in a position to respond to constituencies throughout the entire city.

Looking to the future, we believe that mayors will increasingly be asked to account for their cities' public schools. In a country where urban education continues to fail our most at-risk youth, mayors will have to change their traditional relationship with city schools or risk being challenged by those who will.

Achievement Analysis Methodology and Additional Findings for Chapter Four

THIS APPENDIX DISCUSSES THE MORE TECHNICAL DETAILS of the achievement analysis methodology we use to produce the results discussed in chapter four. We also provide the results of additional statistical models we analyzed using the "change in Z-score" dependent variable.

STATISTICAL MODEL: FURTHER DETAILS

We use an education production function approach to analyze the factors associated with student achievement in our sample of districts. The general form of the relationship is specified as

$$O_{it} = f(F_{it}, G_{it}, C_{it}, D_{it}) \qquad (A.1)$$

where outcomes (O_{it}) in district i in year t are understood to be a function of the vector of family background (F_{it}), vector of district governance arrangements (G_{it}), vector of city and community characteristics (C_{it}), and vector of district demographics (D_{it}). We assume a linear form of the production function, as other economists have done in this field (Hanushek and Raymond 2004). Our linear estimation initially takes the following form:

$$O_{it} = \beta_0 + \beta_F F_{it} + \beta_G G_{it} + \beta_C C_{it} + \beta_D D_{it} + \varepsilon_{it} \qquad (A.2)$$

This version of the model, however, fails to account for the fact that the outcome measures are constructed by states, and that state policies in the realms of funding, oversight, and accountability are likely to have an impact on achievement. Not accounting for these state effects would introduce significant bias into our estimates because we would be attributing to mayoral control changes that might actually be associated with state-level decisions. It could be the case, for instance, that the standardized test in State A is more favorable to urban students than the test in State B. If this is true, then districts in State A would see higher achievement not necessarily because of improved governance but simply because the test in State A is more amenable to their students.

Cleveland serves as a useful illustrative example of another methodological problem with equation A.2. The Ohio legislature took a large role in handing the Cleveland mayor control of the city schools. At the same time, the same legislature and the Ohio State Department of Education were working to make statewide improvements in education. The model specified in equation A.2 would not be able to separate out these two effects.

To untangle the effects of district governance from the possible biases of state tests and broader statewide efforts to boost student performance, we follow Hanushek and Raymond (2004) and add state fixed effects (δ_s):

$$O_{it} = \beta_0 + \beta_F F_{it} + \beta_G G_{it} + \beta_C C_{it} + \beta_D D_{it} + \delta_s + \varepsilon_{it} \tag{A.3}$$

As described by Hanushek and Rivkin (2004, 302), adding state fixed effects "effectively adds a linear trend in performance that is specific to each state. The growth formulation incorporate any state differences in policies, student and family characteristics, or other things that exert a constant influence on states performances over the relevant observation period. Adding the state fixed effect permits states to have policies that lead to trend differences in their student performance."

Adding state fixed effects controls for state factors that are constant over time, but this leaves open another set of questions about shocks in particular years. In 2002, for instance, after the passage of the No Child Left Behind Act, it is possible that districts (whether with mayoral control or not) changed practice to come into accordance with the act. This shock to the system would be independent of mayoral control, but equation A.3 would not be able to separate the two effects.

To address these time shocks, we introduce year fixed effects (γ_t). Including year fixed-effects controls for those year-specific factors that do not vary across districts. We are left with the equation:

$$O_{it} = \beta_0 + \beta_F F_{it} + \beta_G G_{it} + \beta_C C_{it} + \beta_D D_{it} + \delta_s + \gamma_t + \varepsilon_t \tag{A.4}$$

The year fixed-effects models essentially adds a series of dummy variables for each year, just as the state fixed-effects model adds a series of dummy variables for each state in the sample. Including these in the same model provides us with an equation that can better isolate the effects of the governance arrangements on student outcomes.

ANALYZING CHANGE IN Z-SCORE DEPENDENT VARIABLE

As discussed in chapter four, the changing of testing instruments by states from one year to another leaves us with some uncertainty about the nature of the constructed variable "change in Z-score from year $t-1$ to year t." Nevertheless, we believe it is important to consider the results of these models. The model for the analysis of change in Z-scores is:

$$
\begin{aligned}
CHANGE\_IN\_ACHIEVE_{it,t-1} = \ &\beta_0 + \beta_1 MAYORAL\_CONTROL_{it} \quad\quad (A.5)\\
&+ \beta_2 MAYOR\_COUNCIL_i \\
&+ \beta_3 PCT\_SINGLE\_MEMBER_{it} \\
&+ \beta_4 PCT\_PRIVATE_{it} \\
&+ \beta_5 PCT\_STATE\_REV_{it} \\
&+ \beta_6 PPE\_INSTRUCT_{it} + \beta_7 ENROLL_{it} \\
&+ \beta_8 PCT\_HISPANIC_{it} \\
&+ \beta_9 PCT\_AFR\text{-}AMERICAN_{it} \\
&+ \beta_{10} PCT\_KIDS\_POVERTY_{it} \\
&+ \beta_{11} PCT\_SPECIAL\_ED_{it} + \delta_s + \gamma_t + \varepsilon_{it}
\end{aligned}
$$

where $CHANGE\_IN\_ACHIEVE_{it,t-1}$ is the difference in a district's Z-score from year $t-1$ to year t, and all other variables are the same as defined in chapter 4. We present the results of these models in table A.1. The results are for elementary change outcomes only, because limitations in the high school data prevented us from considering change models for the high school grades.

These additional models confirm our findings that the presence of a new-style education mayor is positively associated with gains in standardized reading and mathematics at the elementary levels (table A.1). We also see the inverse relationship between full appointive power and standardized achievement. Most of the additional explanatory variables fail to rise to statistical significance, even those that were robust in the level of achievement analysis (e.g., the percentage of minority students in a

Table A.1 Results from Change in Z-Score Regression Models for Standardized Elementary Reading and Mathematics Achievement, 1999–2003 (with year and state fixed effects; coefficient and robust standard errors reported)

Variable	Reading		Mathematics	
	A	B	A	B
Mayor control index		0.009		0.002
		(0.024)		(0.018)
New-style mayor	0.136**		0.130***	
	(0.063)		(0.039)	
Majority appointment power	0.020		0.014	
	(0.049)		(0.033)	
Full appointment power	−0.180**		−0.178***	
	(0.086)		(0.057)	
Mayor–council	−0.042		−0.054**	
	(0.031)		(0.026)	
Percent single-member-elected school board members	0.035	0.033	0.090***	0.089***
	(0.025)	(0.027)	(0.024)	(0.028)
Percent in private school	−0.304	−0.253	−0.569**	−0.530**
	(0.233)	(0.222)	(0.256)	(0.253)
Percent of revenue from state	0.030	−0.013	−0.228*	−0.266**
	(0.141)	(0.132)	(0.132)	(0.123)
Per-pupil expenditure, current instruction	0.015	0.008	0.002	−0.005
	(0.013)	(0.011)	(0.015)	(0.014)
Enrollment (million)	0.030	0.006	0.033	0.012
	(0.050)	(0.055)	(0.044)	(0.054)
Percent Hispanic	0.044	0.061	0.023	0.041
	(0.097)	(0.097)	(0.106)	(0.093)
Percent African American	−0.065	−0.079	0.015	0.001
	(0.087)	(0.086)	(0.092)	(0.088)
Percent of children living in poverty	0.015	0.042	−0.169	−0.156
	(0.257)	(0.258)	(0.266)	(0.256)
Percent special education	−0.270	0.014	0.027	0.327
	(0.679)	(0.686)	(0.688)	(0.686)
Constant	−0.025	−0.021	0.156	0.157
	(0.131)	(0.122)	(0.133)	(0.123)
R^2	391	391	391	391
N	0.07	0.06	0.12	0.11

Note: Two-tailed significance denoted as *$p < .1$, **$p < .05$, ***$p < .01$. All models employ state and year fixed effects. Robust standard errors are produced by clustering on school districts.

district). We do not know with certainty why these models are not as powerful, but we suspect it may have to do with the issue we identified at the beginning: changing test instruments from year to year. It may also be the case that year-to-year fluctuations are adding significant noise to the change values.

Notes

INTRODUCTION

1. For more on San Diego, see Hess (2005). For more on Seattle, see Cuban and Usdan (2002), and for St. Louis see Wagman (2003).
2. See also the program website for more details: www.crss.org/tbisb.htm.
3. For more on Vallas, see LaRock (2003b) and Russo (2003).
4. The online supplement, which we refer to throughout the text, can be accessed through either Wong's website at Brown University (www.brown.edu/ Departments/Education/Education_Mayor) or the website maintained by Shen (www.Education Mayor.com).

CHAPTER ONE

1. See also Ravitch (2000). For background on how the field's understanding of school district politics has evolved, see Eliot (1959), Katz (1987), Callahan (1962), Peterson (1976), Bidwell (1965), Weick (1976), and Rogers (1968). To see how the older view was challenged, see Layton (1982), Burlingame (1988), Boyd (1983), Peterson (1976), Wirt and Kirst (1982), Mitchell (1988), Scribner (1977), and LaNoue (1982).
2. On the details of the budget cuts, see Mirel (1993, 100).
3. Evidence from a study by Hopkins (2004) suggests that mayoral control is more likely to arise in cities that are lagging in retail sales.
4. Zeigler cites Blau and Scott (1962) when drawing this distinction. In line with Zeigler's initial impressions, two types of models have dominated thinking about school board policymaking. The first—labeled at various times as "professional,

trustee, elite, and hierarchical"—emphasizes professional decision making and the authority of the superintendent. School board members see themselves as trustees who have been put in place to make decisions based on their own best judgment. The second model—known as "political, delegate, arena, or bargaining"—emphasizes the school board member's links to the citizens that voted him or her into office. In this second model, the board member sees his or her primary responsibility as being responsive to the demands of parents and other concerned citizens. Greene (1992) writes that "previous research suggests that a substantial majority of school boards adopt the professional orientation." His own conclusions, based on a study of New Jersey school boards, support this general conclusion. Numerous extensions have been suggested to augment these two models. E.g., Peterson and Williams (1972) conceptualize three models of decision making: an "organizational process" model, a "political bargaining" model, and a "rational decision maker." Rada (1988) offers a public choice framework for understanding board behavior.

5. In a more recent study, Moe (2005) analyzes survey data from California and finds that teachers' unions exert strong influence on school board elections and the attitudes of school board candidates. Taken together, these studies challenge the democratic nature of the traditional school board. Related to this body of research is another that has called into question the democratic nature of local council elections. Prewitt (1970) found that city council members are often selected as replacements to fill terms, thus circumventing a vote altogether. Prewitt and Ealau (1971) further called into question the democratic nature of local elections. From a public choice perspective, Weeres and Cooper (1992) have pointed out that urban school boards may engage in logrolling.

6. For a quick introduction to reform unionism, see Hardy (2005).

7. See also Portz (1996). The issue of race pervades all forms of local government, not just mayor–council cities. Moore (2002) studied black representation in council–manager cities and found that only slightly over 1 percent of all city managers in the country are black. The black community must have a critical mass of population and a share of the city council positions in order to get a black city manager put into place.

CHAPTER TWO

1. The bill was introduced as Ohio S. B. 146: "To amend section 3311.71 of the Revised Code to require that management and control of any school district that has an average daily membership exceeding forty thousand students, has a relatively high poverty index, and has been in academic emergency at least one of the four previous school years be assumed by a nine-member board of education appointed by the mayor of the municipal corporation containing the greatest portion of the district's territory." The text of the original bill can be found at www.legislature.state.oh.us/bills.cfm?ID=126_SB_46.

2. As we discuss in greater detail in chapter three, due to the smaller size of Harrisburg and Trenton, these districts are not included in the empirical analysis. We present small summaries here to alert readers to the governance changes that have taken place in each city.

3. For a more detailed discussion of Boston, see Usdan and Cuban (2003); Portz (1996, 2000); and Portz, Stein, and Jones (1999).

4. There is much research on reform in Chicago. See Wong (2001), Wong et al. (2001), and Shipps (1997, 2003a).

Although the 1995 legislation left intact some features of the previous decentralized arrangements, it reduced competing institutional authority and recentralized administrative authority. As a result of the 1995 reform, appointment decisions emanating from the mayor's office closely link the board, top administration, and the mayor's office. The law decreased the size of the fifteen-member board to five and put the mayor in charge of appointing board members, the board president, and the chief executive officer in charge of the schools. Daley picked Paul Vallas, his former budget director, to be the schools' first chief executive. The Vallas administration, with about 60 percent of the top managers coming from a noneducation career path, worked to restore public confidence and gained strong support from the media, businesses, and civic groups. In 2001, Mayor Daley appointed Arne Duncan to succeed Vallas. Duncan was a Harvard graduate who had played professional basketball before entering public education and serving as Vallas' chief of staff.

5. For more on Cleveland, see Rich and Chambers (2003).

6. For more on Harrisburg, see LaRock (2003a).

7. In *Harrisburg School District v. Zogby* (2003), the court explained: "Any city that adopts a mayor-council form of government under the Charter Law thus implicitly endorses the principle that, in addition to local ordinances, the city will be bound by applicable general laws subsequently enacted by the Legislature."

8. "Empowerment districts" are defined as "districts with a combined average of 50 percent or more of students scoring in the bottom-measured group of students statewide in math and reading for the previous two years." "News Release: Gov. Ridge Signs Education Empowerment Act," May 10, 2000; available at www.pde.psu.edu/.

9. For more on Oakland, see Gewertz (2000).

10. The legal authority comes from Miss. Code Ann. § 37-7-717 (2005), "Optional Methods of Selecting Trustees Pursuant to Agreement."

11. Cibulka (2003, 125). For more on Baltimore, see Orr (1999, 2001, 2004).

12. For a timeline of these financial difficulties, see *Baltimore Sun* (2004).

13. For more on Philadelphia, see Boyd and Christman (2003). For the background on and an analysis of the Philadelphia experience, see DeJarnatt (2004); Maranto (2005); and Gewertz (2005).

14. For more on Detroit, see Meinecke and Adamany (2001).

15. For more on Washington, see Henig (2004). The most comprehensive website tracking the District of Columbia Public Schools is DCPSWatch (www.dcpswatch.com), which is described as "an on-line magazine that covers education issues and news about the District of Columbia Public Schools. In addition to articles and columns about DCPS, DCPSWatch features resources for parents, students, teachers, DCPS employees, and civic activists."

16. This is discussed in *Shook v. District of Columbia Fin. Responsibility & Mgmt. Assistance Auth.*, 328 U.S. App. D.C. 74 (D.C. Cir. 1998): "In 1995, 22 years after the advent of home rule, Congress found that the District government was in the midst of a "fiscal emergency," plagued by "pervasive" mismanagement and "failing

to deliver effective or efficient services" to residents. District of Columbia Financial Responsibility and Management Assistance Act of 1995, Pub. L. No. 104-8, § 2(a)(1), (2) & (4), 109 Stat. 97, 98 (1995) (FRMAA). In response, it established what is popularly known as the Control Board. Composed of five members appointed by the President of the United States, the Control Board has been given wide-ranging powers to improve the District government's operations."

CHAPTER THREE

1. Michael Kirst has presented some of the most focused analyses of mayoral control and has raised important questions about specifying the relationship between mayors and actual school improvement. In synthesizing several relevant studies, Kirst finds that "it is not possible to link many changes in school policy and practice to changes in governance. Some major trends can be attributed in part to mayoral intervention, although there is no apparent relationship between level (low, moderate, or high) of mayoral influence and the impact on schools" (2002, 8).

Most researchers to date have acknowledged the importance of academic achievement to measure mayoral performance but have not provided extensive analysis of that achievement. E.g., Portz (2003, 112) writes that the "the key test in assessing school improvement is student academic achievement." Portz's ensuing analysis of Boston's academic improvements, however, lasts only a few pages and consists of summary achievement statistics. We point out this deficiency in the research not in a spirit of criticism, but in a spirit of recognition. We recognize that studying achievement across school districts is a difficult task. Indeed, in our own previous work, we have been unable to carry out the types of analysis we now present in this book. In Wong and Shen (2005, 83), we note: "Although student achievement outcomes dominate policy discussion, the data available at this time makes it quite hard to generalize across districts about mayoral takeover's effect on student achievement." We are pleased that no such note is necessary in this study.

Edited volumes by Jeffrey Henig and Wilbur Rich (2004) and by Larry Cuban and Michael Usdan (2003) provide the bulk of recent multidistrict research on mayoral control of schools. Both of these volumes employ case study methodology across a series of cities with mayoral control. They provide us with rich detail about the nature of mayoral control and in some cases track outcomes in particular districts. They do not, however, perform cross-district quantitative analyses. A related body of research is on state "takeovers" of school districts. As discussed in chapter 1, these two types of reforms are distinct from one another. Most studies of state takeovers suggest that it is far easier to clean up district-level finances and management practices than it is to make a dent in student achievement. In a study for the Reason Public Policy Institute, Seder (2000, 27) examines a sample of takeovers and finds that "from a financial-management standpoint, most of the different intervention strategies tend to be successful; . . . however, these intervention strategies have not consistently turned around academic results."

2. The special issue of the *Journal for Education for Students Placed at Risk* was volume 8, issue 1, in 2003.

3. Our determination of large school districts presents a version of Sorites's paradox about when a "heap" of stones becomes a heap, or evaluation of a color spectrum as to when orange becomes red. As with those cases, the problem is an intractable one that requires (as a practical matter) researchers to make reasoned assumptions. With regard to the midsized districts, Trenton has only twenty-four schools, and Harrisburg only fifteen schools. One additional district, Hartford, has thirty-three schools and is excluded from our sample. Hartford, however, was under partial state control for the entire duration of the period 1999 to 2003. Hartford did not return to full mayoral control until 2005. For the classic study of New Haven, see Dahl (1961).

4. The Department of Education uses seven codes for school districts: 1, regular school district; 2, component district; 3, supervisory union; 4, regional district; 5, state district; 6, federal district; and 7, other district. Our final sample consisted only of regular school districts, which is appropriate because the other types of school districts are atypical of standard school districts in the states.

5. Although we used the 2002–3 year of data, the size of the districts and their boundaries do not appear to change significantly over the five-year period (1999–2003) that we examine. All CCD files were accessed via the Internet from January through June 2005 (National Center for Education Statistics, http://nces.ed.gov/ccd/ccddata.asp). The three values the MSC variable can take are (1) primarily serves a central city of an MSA, (2) serves an MSA but not primarily its central city, and (3) does not serve an MSA.

6. The CCD provides data at both the school and district levels. We had to employ the school-level database here because we were making connections between individual schools and cities, not districts.

7. We proceeded in three steps to finalize our sample. First, for each regular school, the CCD database listed a city in which the school was located. This allowed us to aggregate up to the city level and create a measure of the "number of students in schools in City A." We excluded nonregular schools, such as "Governor's School of the Arts." Second, we also knew whether or not those schools in City A were in School District A (the corresponding major district associated with the city). This allowed us to calculate a measure of "number of students in schools in City A who are *not part of* School District A." Third, using these two measures, we calculated the ratio: the percentage of students going to school in City A who are actually a part of School District A. In some cases, the city listed for a school in the CCD file did not correspond to the political municipality the school was actually situated in. E.g., a school in the town of Webster Groves was listed (correctly) as being in the Webster Groves School District, but had "Saint Louis" listed as its location city. In fact, the school was located in Webster Groves. In these cases, we validated the school location by using the American Fact Finder address lookup tool. We looked at school addresses and the "place" listed to see if they were in fact part of the city, or if it was simply a case of mislabeling in the data set. We used the Census Bureau's online tools (http://factfinder.census.gov/servlet/AGSGeoAddressServlet) to look up each school individually and noted its actual location for verification purposes. Although they have not developed yet in many instances, it is possible that a regional planning board or committee might be formed in situations such as these. We consider this possibility in greater length in chapter nine.

8. Rule 4 led to the exclusion of the following districts (with cities in parentheses): Pinellas County School District (Largo), Charleston County School District (Charleston), Saint Lucie County School District (Fort Pierce), Richardson Independent School District (ISD) (Richardson), Orange Unified School District (Orange), Round Rock ISD (Round Rock), Guilford County Schools (Greensboro), Washoe County School District (Reno), Forsyth County Schools (Winston Salem), Carrollton-Farmers Branch (Carrollton), Lafayette Parish School Board (Lafayette), and Paradise Valley Unified District (Phoenix). Rule 5 led to the exclusion of the following districts: Spring Branch ISD (Houston), Alief ISD (Houston), North East ISD (San Antonio), San Antonio ISD, San Jose Unified School District, Northside ISD (San Antonio), Bakersfield City Elementary, Ysleta ISD (El Paso), Indianapolis Public Schools, Colorado Springs 11, El Paso ISD, Houston ISD, Kansas City 33, Oklahoma City, Stockton City Unified School District, Sacramento City Unified School District, Adams-Arapahoe 28j (Aurora), Omaha Public Schools, Riverside Unified School District, Tucson Unified School District, Corpus Christi ISD.

9. The American Institutes for Research continues to update the database and has plans to add data for 2004 and 2005. All data were downloaded in 2005 from http://208.253.216.16/assessment/default.asp.

10. For more on Baltimore, see Cibulka (2003).

11. The community power structure literature is synthesized well in two edited volumes: Aiken and Mott (1970) and Clark (1968).

12. The earlier study, with the alternative measure, is Wong and Shen (2005).

13. In an earlier study, we included a measure of duration, operationalized as the number of years since the mayor was given power to appoint the school board. Using this national sample, however, we are not at this time able to construct a comparable measure of duration for the other school reforms, e.g., in a non-mayoral-control city, how long their particular school reform has been in place. Even if we had the number of years, it is not clear that "one year of reform" leads to the same level of reform establishment in each district. In particular, we might think that in larger districts it may take longer for reforms to be established. For these two reasons, we do not include a simple duration measure in our models.

14. In its note to table 9 in its report on the 100 largest school districts, the NCES (National Center for Education Statistics 2002) writes: "Whereas table 8 deals with the number of schools in each district having a minority presence of any kind, table 9 presents the percentage of students in each district by specific racial/ethnic categories. This table illustrates that some school districts are made up of many minority groups while others have high concentrations of one minority group. For example, the New York City Public Schools have 38 percent Hispanic students and 35 percent Black students while the Philadelphia City School District has a much higher percentage of Black students (65 percent) than any other minority group. Also shown in table 9 is the number of students eligible for free or reduced-price lunch. Responses in this data category were available for 92 districts out of the 100 largest. Among these districts, the percentages of students eligible for free or reduced-price lunch under the National School Lunch Program varied greatly. Of the 92 districts that did report free and reduced-price lunch eligibility, 43 districts reported that over 50 percent of their students were eligible for free or reduced-price lunch."

15. Not every study finds that mayor–council governments are greater facilitators. Wheeland (2002) provides a caution: Handing the mayor too much direct power may have an adverse effect on his or her facilitative power.

16. The authors also identify two additional dimensions: The mayor may have veto power, but no appointment or budgetary authority; or the mayor may lack veto power, but have appointment or budgetary power.

17. The Dallas report is available at www.dallasnews.com/s/dws/spe/2004/dallas/letter.html.

18. See the discussion in Stone (2001, 124–28). In particular, their concern was that one might "characterize a system as a success simply because it is fortunate enough to draw its student body from among those already educationally advantaged."

19. Kain (2001, 3) reports that the "the UTD Texas Schools Microdata Panel (TSMP), currently includes individual data for more than 11 million students and more than 400,000 public school teachers and administrators for the period 1990 to the present."

20. National Center for Education Statistics (2005b). A distinction is made between three types of dropout rates: event rates, status rates, and cohort rates.

21. E.g., see Smith and Granberg-Rademacker (2003).

CHAPTER FOUR

1. Discussion of the model follows that by Davidson and MacKinnon (1993, 320–25). All regression analyses with fixed effects were carried out in Stata9, using the "xi: areg" command.

2. See the discussion in chapter seven for the details of inflation and regional cost adjustments.

3. We use Stata's "cluster()" command, as discussed at www.stata.com/support/faqs/stat/robust_ref.html. See Rogers (1993), Williams (2000), and Wooldridge (2002).

4. For more on the racial gap, see Caldas and Bankston (1998, 533–57), Jencks and Phillps (1998), Thernstrom and Thernstrom (2003), Kober (2001); Hallinan (2001), and Hanushek (2001, 24–28).

5. A study by Polsby (1994) found that Chicago's decentralized system of local school councils (LSCs) did not lead to systemwide improvement in student achievement. A more recent report, however, from Designs for Change finds some improvements linked to strong LSCs. See Moore and Merritt (2002).

CHAPTER FIVE

1. Jonathan Kozol's (1991) *Savage Inequalities* drew much attention in the popular press. In the academic literature, Diamond and Spillane (2004) have summarized much of the relevant literature surrounding inequality in urban schools.

2. For states that did not yet have achievement data in 1999, we used their first available year of data (e.g., 2000) as the starting point.

3. We weight our measures of inequality by the school enrollment. If student-level achievement data were available to us for every district, we could look at the spread in more detail.

4. We also considered combined models with dummy variables to distinguish between elementary and middle schools.

5. See the discussion in chapter seven for the details of these inflation and regional cost adjustments.

6. Peterson limits his use of the term "redistributive policies" to those policies "that have negative effects on local economies."

CHAPTER SIX

1. The mayor, board, and central office are significantly above the 2.5 threshold, which separates satisfactory from unsatisfactory performance. For a more detailed analysis, see Wong and Moulton (1996).

2. See the Chicago Public Schools website (www.cps.k12.il.us).

3. If these reforms sound familiar to the No Child Left Behind Act, it is not surprising. Chicago's accountability agenda was a model for the federal act and has been identified as part of the "first wave" of accountability standards and assessment reform (Mintrop and Trujillo 2004).

4. Probation managers tended to be highly regarded local principals of public, private, and parochial schools in the Chicago metropolitan region who acted as consultants to principals in sanctioned schools. External partners were usually university-based groups that provided a number of services to schools ranging from direct consultants to professional development service providers.

5. In his study of sanctioned schools in Maryland, Mintrop (2004) found that many teachers responded to this stigma of failure by leaving sanctioned schools.

6. We focused on mathematics and English because the district used scores on standardized tests in these areas to measure school and student performance and to place schools under probation and reconstitution.

7. We began classroom observations at Greene in the winter of 1997, at Reed in the winter of 1998, and at Weston in the fall of 1996. From 1996 to 1998, the ninth and eleventh grades were high-stakes grades for the TAP. The district used the percentage of students in these grades who scored at national norms on the TAP reading and mathematics tests to place schools on probation. From 1998 to 2000, the ninth and tenth grades were the high-stakes grades for both the TAP and the CASE.

8. *Test-taking* activities simulate test materials and conditions. *Reading/Test Skills Development* included two types of activities. The first involved teachers leading students through sample reading test passages. The second type of activities focused more specifically on reading strategies, such as Silent Sustained Reading and vocabulary development activities. *Other instruction* included those activities not directly related to the sanctioning policy.

9. In the classroom analysis, we compare the random sample of classes to classes in which teachers specifically taught the novel *To Kill a Mockingbird*. During the random sample of classes, teachers may or may not have taught to the TAP. Yet we are calling these "TAP" observations because teachers in all schools during these observations worked under school-level policies promoting TAP preparation, whether through activities such as weekly professional development or mandated instructional activities.

10. Classroom observations were coded with 80 percent reliability.

11. Table 6.3 describes what each type of question entails. After coding teacher questions, we grouped the questions into three broader categories: (1) Literal questions focus on the basic information stated in the text. These include basic stated information, key detail, and stated relationship questions. (2) Simple inferential questions require readers to make a generalization by connecting typically two pieces of information found in close proximity within a literary work. These include simple implied relationship questions. (3) Complex inferential questions require readers to connect several pieces of information across a literary text(s) to make conclusions and generalizations. These include complex implied relationship, authors' generalization, and structural questions. We grouped literary terms, general knowledge, vocabulary, and personal opinion into the "other" category.

CHAPTER SEVEN

1. The earlier study referred to is Wong and Shen (2005).

2. A business model of school governance will also emphasize efficiency in the educational production process, but we do not directly measure "efficiency" in our data set beyond the fiscal responsibility indicator.

3. Chicago is again illustrative of how this theory is put into practice. Once its members were appointed and granted new discretionary powers, the Chicago school board eliminated the Bureau of Facilities Planning in the central office (resulting in the elimination of 10 jobs), reduced the number of positions in the Department of Facilities Central Service Center by half (26 out of 50 positions were eliminated) and reduced the citywide administration of facilities from 441 positions to 34. Contracts for these services are now with private companies.

4. All staffing data are supplied by the U.S. Department of Education's Common Core of Data, which reports, for each district, the number of full-time equivalent employees in a number of positions: teachers, aides, instructional coordinators and supervisors, guidance counselors, librarians/media support staff, local education agency (LEA) administration, and school administration.

5. The data are actually presented in even smaller categories. The full set of seventeen categories is: prekindergarten teachers, kindergarten teachers, elementary teachers, secondary teachers, instructional aides, instructional coordinators and supervisors, elementary guidance counselors, secondary guidance counselors, librarians/media specialists, library/media support staff, LEA administrators, LEA administrative support staff, school administrators, school administrative support staff, student support services staff, and all other support services staff.

6. The measures are defined as: teachers (all prekindergarten, kindergarten, elementary, and secondary teachers); aides (all instructional aides); administration (LEA administrators plus LEA administrative support staff); supervisors (all instructional coordinators and supervisors); student support (all student support services staff); and guidance (all elementary and secondary guidance counselors). Additional discussion can be found on Wong's homepage at Brown University (www.brown.edu/Departments/Education/personnel.php?who=kwong) and at the website maintained by Shen (www.EducationMayor.com).

7. This is Series ID ECU12823I. We also used the general CPI-U inflator produced by the Bureau of Labor Statistics, but the results of the analysis remained substantively the same.

8. We ran one-year and two-year lagged models as well and found them to be similar to either the baseline or five-year lagged models. We present only the baseline and five-year lagged models in an effort to streamline the findings in this chapter. Summaries of all models, as well as descriptive statistics for all variables considered, are provided online via Wong's home page at Brown University.

9. Henig et al. (1999) also emphasize the time required for building sustainable partnerships.

CHAPTER EIGHT

1. For discussions on leadership turnover, see Jackson and Cibulka (1992).

2. For a summary of the relationship between leadership and management improvement, see Thomas (1988).

3. One could argue that such innovative leaders are only tapping into latent predispositions or fundamental preferences on behalf of the followers. Whether or not this is always the case leads to a larger debate over the extent to which leaders can ever change the preferences of their followers.

4. As described on its website, "The independent Quinnipiac University Poll regularly surveys residents in Connecticut, Florida, New York, New Jersey, Pennsylvania and nationwide about political races, state and national elections, and issues of public concern, such as schools, taxes, transportation, municipal services, and the environment" (www.quinnipiac.edu/x11358.xml). All the institute survey data we use are from surveys directed by Douglas Schwartz. They include: (1) Quinnipiac administration dates March 19–25, 2002; N = 1,038 New York City registered voters; random sample: yes; margin of error +/– 3 percent. (2) Administration dates July 8–15, 2002; N = 932 New York City registered voters; random: yes; margin of error +/– 3.3 percent. (3) Administration dates September 14–19, 2005; N = 1,504 New York City registered voters; random sample: yes; margin of error +/– 2.5 percent. (4) Administration dates February 19–24, 2003; N = 889 New York City registered voters; random sample: yes; margin of error +/– 3.3 percent. (5) Administration dates April 29–May 5, 2003; N = 757 New York City registered voters; random sample: yes; margin of error of +/– 3.6 percent.

5. The article states: "This telephone poll of a random sample of 1,102 New York City registered voters (including an oversample of Hispanic voters), yielding 606

likely voters, was conducted for NY1 News and *Newsday* by Blum and Weprin Associates, Inc., from October 30–November 4, 2005"; Quinnipiac University (2005). Also see McLendon (2005).

6. The executive summary, on which we base our analysis, is available at www.pipememphis.org/execsum.html. The survey, conducted by Ethridge and Associates, consisted of a representative sample of 401 registered voters in the city of Memphis. The PIPES Executive Summary reports that the maximum sampling error is +/– 4.9 percent at the 95 percent confidence level. See Richardson (2001); *Los Angeles Times* (2001); City of Boise (2005); poll conducted by Peter Hart and Bill McInturff for Council for Excellence in Government in partnership with Global Markets Institute at Goldman Sachs, www.gs.com/our_firm/our_culture/social_responsibility/gmi/docs/cleveland_pr.pdf.

7. The 2005 Suffolk poll had an $N = 400$.

8. For a discussion and brief analysis, see Reinhard (1998). See also Hoffman (2001) and Austin Independent School District (2005).

9. The typical listing of city departments included airport, accounting, animal control, central stores, civic center, code enforcement, community development, community relations, emergency management, engineering, fire, human resources, legal, library, municipal court, parks and recreation, planning, police, public health, purchasing, solid waste, street, traffic engineering, transit, utilities, utility billing, and vital statistics. This particular listing is from Amarillo (www.ci.amarillo.tx.us/citydepartments.htm) but is reflective of services listed by most cities; e.g., see www.ci.mil.wi.us/display/router.asp?docid=47 for Milwaukee; www.ci.sugarland.tx.us/ to Sugar Land, Texas; and www.cityofnewhaven.com/govt/gov18.htm for New Haven.

10. See minutes (2002), www.abilenetx.com/Minutes/Council/2002/2002-07-22.htm.

11. See www.cityofseattle.net/neighborhoods/education/, http://stlcin.missouri.org/education/commission.cfm, and www.stpaul4schools.org/actionplan.htm.

12. See www.sdmodelschool.net/, www.hsvcity.com/508/mayor_index.html, and www.syracuse.ny.us/mayorBio.asp.

13. In 1997, the city and school district made an agreement in which "the Akron school board agreed to allow the city's economic development office to offer TIF to new projects. The agreement also provides that Akron schools may not expand the school district into townships. In exchange for these commitments, Mayor Plusquellic agreed to share revenues received from the Joint Economic Development Districts (JEDDs) with Akron Public Schools" (City of Akron 2005).

14. Almost every city we looked at had resources for competing in the international economy or increasing trade.

References

Aiken, Michael, and Paul E. Mott, ed. 1970. *The Structure of Community Power.* New York: Random House.

Allinder, Rose M., Lynn S. Fuchs, Douglas Fuchs, and Carol L. Hamlett. 1992. Effects of Summer Break on Math and Spelling Performance as a Function of Grade Level. *Elementary School Journal* 92, no. 4 (March): 451–60.

American Educational Research Association, American Psychological Association, and National Council on Measurement in Education. 1999. *Standards for Educational and Psychological Testing.* Washington, D.C.: American Educational Research Association. www.apa.org/pubinfo/testing.html.

Anagnostopoulos, Dorothea, and Stacey A. Rutledge. 2003. The New Accountability, Student Failure, and Teachers' Work in Urban High Schools. *Educational Policy* 17:291–316.

———. 2007. Making Sense of School Sanctioning Policies in Urban High Schools: Charting the Depth and Drift of School and Classroom Change. *Teachers College Record* 109, no. 5:1261–1302.

Anderson, Steve E. 2003. *The School District in Educational Change: A Review of the Literature.* ICEC Working Paper 2. Toronto: International Centre for Educational Change.

Applebee, Arthur N. 1993. *Literature in the Secondary School: Studies of Curriculum and Instruction in the United States.* Urbana, Ill.: National Council of Teachers of English.

Associated Press. 2005. High School Senior Sworn In as Mayor. www.cnn.com/2005/POLITICS/11/22/teenmayor.ap/.

———. 2006. Navy Officer Tapped to Head L.A. Schools. October 13.

Attleboro Sun Times. 1997. Chicago's Schools Have Gone Back to Basics. July 13.

Austin Independent School District. 2005. City School District Create Two Task Forces to Address Quality of Life of African American and Hispanic Citizens.

Press Release, November 22, 2005. www.austinisd.org/newsmedia/releases/index.phtml?more=0971&lang=.

Bachrach, Peter, and Morton Baratz. 1975. Power and Its Two Faces Revisited: A Reply to Geoffrey Debnam. *American Political Science Review* 69, no. 3:900–4.

Baker, Brian. 2006. Stephen Reed: Mayor of Harrisburg. *City Mayors.* www .citymayors.com/mayors/harrisburg_mayor.html.

Baker, William Ernest. 2001. The Limitations of Mayoral Appointing Authority and Their Effects on Quality of Life in Alabama's Largest Cities. PhD diss., Department of Political Science and Public Administration, Auburn University.

Ball, Stephen J., and Richard Bowe. 1992. Subject Departments and the "Implementation" of the National Curriculum Policy: An Overview of the Issues. *Journal of Curriculum Studies* 24:97–115.

Baltimore Sun. 2004. Timeline of City Schools' Financial Troubles. April 4. www.baltimoresun.com/news/education/bal-te.md.timeschools04apr04002654, 1,6123692.story?coll=bal-local-utility.

Baquir, Reza. 1999. *Districts, Spillovers, and Government Overspending.* World Bank Policy Research Working Paper 2192. Washington, D.C.: World Bank.

Barr, Rebecca, and Robert Dreeben. 1983. *How Schools Work.* Chicago: University of Chicago Press.

Berry, Jeffrey M. 1999. *The New Liberalism: The Rising Power of Citizen Groups.* Washington, D.C.: Brookings Institution Press.

Bersin, Alan D. 2005. Making Schools Productive. *San Diego Union Tribune,* June 5.

Bidwell, C. 1965. The School as a Formal Organization. In *Handbook of Organziations,* ed. J. March. Skokie, Ill.: Rand McNally.

Blau, Peter M., and W. Richard Scott. 1962. *Formal Organizations: A Comparative Approach.* San Francisco: Chandler.

Bloomberg, Michael R. 2002. School Reform: Putting Our Kids First. July 10. www.ci.nyc.ny.us/html/om/html/2002a/weekly/weekly_061002.html.

Blume, Howard. 1999. The Best School Board Money Can Buy. *L.A. Weekly,* April 7. www.laweekly.com/news/politics/the-best-school-board-money-can-buy/6706.

Boyd, W. L. 1983. Rethinking Educational Policy and Management: Political Science and Educational Administration in the 1980's. *American Journal of Education,* November, 1–29.

Boyd, William Lowe, and Jolly Bruce Christman. 2003. A Tall Order for Philadelphia's New Approach to School Governance: Heal the Political Rifts Close the Budget Gap, and Improve the Schools. In *Powerful Reforms with Shallow Roots: Improving America's Schools,* ed. Larry Cuban and Michael Usdan. New York: Teachers College Press.

Brimmer, Andrew F. 1998. Statement of the Chairman. District of Columbia Financial Responsibility and Management Assistance Authority, Washington, February 12.

Brown, Mike. 1996. Boston: Menino Says Mayors Key to Better Publish Schools. Press Release, United States Conferences of Mayors. www.usmayors.org/uscm/us_mayor_newspaper/documents/10_28_96/documents/Boston_Daley_Menino_Say_Mayors_Key_to_Better_Public_Schools_111396.html.

Burlingame, M. 1988. The Politics of Education And Educational Policy: The Local Level. In *Handbook of Research on Educational Administration*, ed. N. J. Boynan. New York: Longman.

Burns, James MacGregor. 1978. *Leadership*. New York: Harper & Row.

Burns, Nancy. 1994. *The Formation of American Local Governments*. New York: Oxford University Press.

Burtless, Gary., ed. 1996. *Does Money Matter? The Effect of School Resources on Student Achievement and Adult Success*. Washington, D.C.: Brookings Institution Press.

Bushweller, Kevin. 1998. Do State Takeovers Work? *American School Board Journal*, August.

Caldas, Stephen J., and Carl Bankston. 1998. The Inequality of Separation: Racial Composition of Schools and Academic Achievement. *Educational Administration Quarterly*, October, 533–57.

California Department of Education. 2003. State Schools Chief O'Connell Names Seasoned Administrator to Lead Oakland Unified School District. www.cde.ca.gov/nr/ne/yr03/yr03rel29.asp.

Callahan, R. 1962. *Education and the Cult of Efficiency*. Chicago: University of Chicago Press.

Campbell, Jo. 1994. Interpreting Scores from Standardized Tests. *Clearing House* 67, no. 6 (July/August).

Cardwell, Diane, and Mike McIntire. 2005. Mayor Accuses His Opponent of Wavering on Education Policy Over the Years. *New York Times*, September 26.

Carr, Sarah. 2004. Mayoral Ties to Schools Called Vital. *Milwaukee Journal Sentinel*, March 24. www.jsonline.com/news/metro/mar04/217123.asp.

Catalyst. 1997. www.catalyst-chicago.org/arch/03-97/037main.htm.

Cella, Matthew. 2004. Williams' Plan for Schools Rejected. *Washington Times*, April 20. www.washtimes.com/metro/20040420-112716-2277r.htm.

Census Bureau. 2005. Financial Data. www.census.gov/govs/www/school.html.

Chambers, Stephanie. 2002. Urban Education Reform and Minority Political Empowerment. *Political Science Quarterly* 117, no. 4 (Winter): 643–65.

———. 2006. *Mayors and Schools: Minority Voices and Democratic Tensions in Urban Education*. Philadelphia: Temple University Press.

Chambers, Jay G. 1998. *Geographic Variations in Public School Costs*. Washington, D.C.: National Center for Education Statistics, U.S. Department of Education.

Chicago Sun-Times. 1997. High Schools Rebound: Daley Hails Surge in Reading, Math Test Scores. May 1.

Cibulka, James G. 2003. The City-State Partnership to Reform Baltimore's Public Schools. In *Powerful Reforms with Shallow Roots: Improving America's Schools*, ed. Larry Cuban and Michael Usdan. New York: Teachers College Press.

City of Akron. 2001. Press Release, October 15. http://ci.akron.oh.us/News_Releases/2001/101501.html.

———. 2005. Mayor Brings $2 Million to Weekly News Conference. Press Release, March 25. www.ci.akron.oh.us/News_Releases/2005/0325.html.

City of Boise. 2005. Poll Shows a Strong Majority of Boise Residents Think Their City Is on the Right Track. Press Release, June 9. www.cityofboise.org/Departments/Mayor/NewsReleases/2005/page823.aspx.

Clark, Burton. 1968. Interorganizational Patterns in Education, *Administrative Science Quarterly* 10, no. 3:224–37.

Clark, Nicolas, and Vincent Hoffman-Martinot. 1998. *The New Political Culture.* Boulder, Colo.: Westview.

Clingermayer, James C., and Richard C. Feiock. 1997. Leadership Turnover, Transaction Costs, and External City Service Delivery. *Public Administration Review* 57, no. 3 (May): 231–39.

Clotfelter, Charles T. 2001. Are Whites Still "Fleeing"? Racial Patterns and Enrollment Shifts in Urban Public Schools, 1987–1996. *Journal of Policy Analysis and Management* 20 (Spring): 199–221.

Coburn, Cynthia. 2001. Collective Sense-Making about Reading: How Teachers Mediate Reading Policy in Their Professional Communities. *Educational Evaluation and Policy Analysis* 23:145–70.

———. 2004. Beyond Decoupling: Rethinking the Relationship between the Institutional Environment and the Classroom. *Sociology of Education* 77:211–44.

Coburn, K. Gwyne, and Pamela A Riley. 2000. *Failing Grade: Crisis and Reform in the Oakland Unified School District.* Report prepared for Pacific Research Institute for Public Policy. Available at www.pacificresearch.org.

Cohen, David K. 1989. *Teaching Practice: Plus a Change.* East Lansing, Mich.: National Center for Research on Teacher Education.

Coleman, James S., Ernest Q. Campbell, Carol J. Hobson, James McPartland, Alexander M. Mood, Frederic D. Weinfield, and Robert L. York. 1966. *Equality of Educational Opportunity.* Washington, D.C.: U.S. Government Printing Office.

Collins, James. 2002. City Ponders Major Changes to Charter, *Yale Daily News,* January 31.

Connecticut General Assembly. 1999. *State Board of Trustees for the Hartford Public Schools: Final Report.* Legislative Program Review and Investigations Committee. www.cga.ct.gov/pri/archives/1999sbfinalreport1overview.htm.

Cooper, Bruce S., and Marie-Elena Liotta. 2001. Urban Teachers Unions Face Their Future: The Dilemmas of Organizational Maturity. *Education and Urban Society* 34, no. 1:101–18.

Cronin, Joseph M. 1973. *The Control of Urban Schools: Perspective on the Power of Educational Reformers.* New York: Free Press.

Cuban, Larry, and Michael Usdan, eds. 2003. *Powerful Reforms with Shallow Roots: Improving America's Urban Schools.* New York: Teachers College Press.

Dahl, Robert A. 1961. *Who Governs? Democracy and Power in an American City.* New Haven, Conn.: Yale University Press.

Daigneau, Elizabeth. 2006. Deficit Discipline: Elected Leaders Focus on Results, *Governing,* January, 6–57.

Daley, Richard M. 2005. Address at the Delivering Sustainable Communities Summit. www.odpm.gov.uk/stellent/groups/odpm_communities/documents/page/odpm_comm_036922.hcsp.

Davidson, Russell, and James G. MacKinnon. 1993. *Estimation and Inference in Econometrics.* New York: Oxford University Press.

Dean, M. 2006. More City Public Schools Meet State's Yearly Progress Report. *Phila-delphia Daily News*, September 1.

DeHoog, Ruth H., David Lowery, and William E. Lyons. 2001. Citizen Satisfaction with Local Governance: A Test of Individual, Jurisdictional, and City-Specific Explanations. *Journal of Politics* 52, no. 3 (August): 807–37.

DeJarnatt, Susan L. 2004. The Philadelphia Story: The Rhetoric of School Reform. *University of Missouri at Kansas City Law Review*.

DeSantis, Victor S., and Tari Renner. 2002. City Government Structures: An Attempt at Clarification. *State and Local Government Review* 34, no. 2:95–104.

Detroit Free Press. 2000. School Chief Says He's Ready. May 6.

Diamond, John B., and James P. Spillane. 2004. High-Stakes Accountability in Urban Elementary Schools: Challenging or Reproducing Inequality. *Teachers College Record* 106, no. 6 (June): 1145–76.

Dobbs, Michael. 2004. Corporate Model Proves an Imperfect Fit for School System. *Washington Post*, December 5.

Dotinga, Randy. 2005. Who Will Be Left to Govern San Diego? *Christian Science Monitor*, July 20.

Dusseau, Deborah, David Hurst, and David Bitter. 2003. The Numbers Game. *Princi-pal Leadership*, September, 49–54. www.ncacasi.org/enews/enewsoct03.

Edelstein, Fritz. 2004. Mayors and School Districts. *School Planning & Management*, March. www.peterli.com/archive/spm/626.shtm.

———. 2005. Ohio Mayors' Education Roundtable Meets for Fifth Time. *U.S. Mayors Newspaper*. www.usmayors.org/USCM/us_mayor_newspaper/documents/09_12_05/add_roundtable.asp.

Eliot, T. 1959. Toward an Understanding of Public School Politics. *American Political Science Review* 82:1065–87.

Emanski, Joe. 2004. Q and A with Doug Palmer, Part 2 of 2, *Trenton Downtowner*, August.

Ennis, Michael. 2005. What's the Matter with Dallas? Why the City's Timid Political Culture Doesn't Live Up to Its Brash Image, *Texas Monthly*, July.

Estes, Andrea. 2005. Poll Suggests a Solid Lead for Menino. *Boston Globe*, October 23.

Ethridge and Associates. 2000. Executive Summary. Summary of report prepared for Partners in Public Education. Memphis. www.pipememphis.org/execsum.html.

Fantini, Mario, and Marilyn Gittell. 1973. *Decentralization: Achieving Reform*. New York: Frederick A. Praeger.

Field, Michael W. 2002. Re: *Montiero v. Providence School Board Nominating Com-mission*, Letter to Mr. Clifford R. Monteiro, December 13. www.riag.ri.gov/civil/open_gov/oma/2002/OM%2002-25.php.

Firestone, William A. 1989. Using Reform: Conceptualizing District Initiative. *Edu-cational Evaluation and Policy Analysis* 11, no. 2:151–65.

Fowler, William J., Jr. and David H. Monk. 2001. A Primer for Making Cost Adjustments in Education: An Overview. In *Selected Papers in School Finance, 2000–01*. Washington, D.C.: National Center for Education Statistics, U.S. De-partment of Education.

Frederickson, H. George, and Gary Alan Johnson. 2001. The Adapted American City: A Study of Institutional Dynamics. *Urban Affairs Review* 36, no. 6:872–84.

Fung, Archon. 2004. *Empowered Participation: Reinventing Urban Democracy.* Princeton, N.J.: Princeton University Press.

Gamoran, Adam. 1988. Resource Allocation and the Effects of Schooling: A Sociological Perspective. In *Microlevel School Finance: Issues and Implications for Policy—Ninth Annual Yearbook of the American Educational Finance Association*, ed. D. H. Monk and J. Underwood. Cambridge, Mass.: Ballinger.

Gates, Bill. February 2005. www.gatesfoundation.org/MediaCenter/Speeches/BillgSpeeches/BGSpeechNGA-050226.htm.

Gaventa, John. 1982. *Power and Powerlessness: Quiescence and Rebellion in an Appalachian Valley.* Champaign: University of Illinois Press.

Gewertz, Catherine. 2000. In Jerry We Trust. *Teacher Magazine*, May/June.

———. 2005. State-Run Pa. District Battles Host of Woes. *Education Week*, March 2.

Ginsberg, Rick, and Robert K. Wimpelberg. 1987. Educational Change by Commission: Attempting "Trickle Down" Reform. *Educational Evaluation and Policy Analysis*, Winter, 344–60.

Gittell, Marilyn. 1969. Professionalism and Public Participation in Educational Policy-Making: New York City, A Case Study. In *The Politics of Urban Education*, ed. M. Gittell and A. G. Hevesi. New York: Praeger.

Giuliani, Rudolph W. 1999. We Must Reform Our School System Aggressively and Without Delay. Mayor's WINS Address, May 30. http://home2.nyc.gov/html/records/rwg/html/99a/me990530.html.

Goals for the Greater Akron Area. 1974. www.ci.akron.oh.us/2025/GGAA-1974.html.

Gonzalez, Ron. 2004. 10 Ways a Mayor Can Help Improve Public Education. *New York Times*, May 4.

Gottlieb, Rachel, and Oshrat Carmiel. 2005. Mayor Appoints Himself, Expects to Be Chairman. *Hartford Courant*, December 6. www.courant.com/hc-biged1206.artdec06,0,313545.story?track=mostemailedlink.

Greene, K. R. 1990. School Board Members' Responsiveness to Constituents. *Urban Education* 24, no. 4:363–75.

Grimshaw, William J. 1979. *Union Rule in the Schools: Big-City Politics in Transformation.* Lexington, Mass.: D. C. Heath.

Grossman, Pam, and Susan Stodolsky. 1998. Content as Context: The Role of School Subjects in Secondary School Teaching. *Educational Researcher* 24:5–11.

Hallinan, Maureen T. 2001. Sociological Perspectives on Black-White Inequalities in American Schooling. *Sociology of Education* 74 (Extra Issue: Current of Thought: Sociology of Education at the Dawn of the 21st Century), 50–70.

Hanover, Larry. 2005. Lytle Quits, Stunning District, *Times of Trenton*, November 22.

Hanushek, Eric A. 1979. Conceptual and Empirical Issues in the Estimation of Educational Production Functions. *Journal of Human Resources*, Summer, 351–88.

———. 1986. The Economics of Schooling: Production and Efficiency in Public Schools. *Journal of Economic Literature*, September, 1141–77.

————— 2001. Black-White Achievement Differences and Governmental Interventions. *American Economic Review* 91, no. 2:24–28.

Hanushek, Eric A., and Margaret E. Raymond. 2004. The Effect of School Accountability Systems on the Level and Distribution of Student Achievement, *Journal of the European Economic Association*, MIT Press, 2(2–3): 406–15.

Hardy, Lawrence. 2003. The Urban Challenge: Against the Odds in City Schools. *American School Boards Journal*, December. www.asbj.com/specialreports/ 1203Special%20Reports/S2.html.

—————. 2005. Public Interest vs. Self Interest. *American School Boards Journal*, July. www.asbj.com/2005/07/0705newsanalysis.html.

Harrisburg City Schools. 2001. *School District Improvement Plan: Establishing a Culture of Excellence*. www.hbgsd.k12.pa.us/204375111393230/lib/204375111393230/ empowermentplan.pdf.

Helfand, Duke, and Howard Blue. 2006. Gov. Signs Mayor's Dream Into Law. *Los Angeles Times*, September 19.

Helms, Ann Doss. 2003. Vote Will Drive CMS Future: School Board Struggling with Crowding, Staffing, New Construction. *Charlotte Observer*, October 12.

Henig, Jeffrey R. 2004. Washington, DC: Race, Issue Definition, and School Board Restructuring. In *Mayors in the Middle: Politics, Race, and Mayoral Control of Urban Schools*, ed. J. Henig and W. Rich. Princeton, N.J.: Princeton University Press.

Henig, Jeffrey R., Richard C. Hula, Marion Orr, and Desiree S. Pedescleaux. 1999. *The Color of School Reform: Race, Politics, and the Challenge of Urban Education*. Princeton, N.J.: Princeton University Press.

Henig, Jeffrey R. and Wilbur C. Rich, eds. 2004. *Mayors in the Middle: Politics, Race, and Mayoral Control of Urban Schools*. Princeton, N.J.: Princeton University Press.

Herszenhorn, David M. 2006. City Considers Plan to Let Outsiders Run Schools. *New York Times*, October 5.

Hess, Frederick M. 1999. *Spinning Wheels: The Politics of Urban School Reform*. Washington, D.C.: Brookings Institution Press.

—————. 2002. *Revolution at the Margins: The Impact of Competition on Urban School Systems*. Washington, D.C.: Brookings Institution Press.

—————. 2005. *Urban School Reform: Lessons from San Diego*. Cambridge, Mass.: Harvard Education Press.

Hightower, Amy M., Michael S. Knapp, Julie A. Marsh, and Milbrey W. McLaughlin. 2002. The District Role in Instructional Renewal: Making Sense and Taking Action. School Districts and Instructional Renewal. In *School Districts and Instructional Renewal: Opening the Conversation*. New York: Teacher College Press.

Hill, H. 2001. Policy Is Not Enough: Language and the Interpretation of State Standards. *American Educational Research Journal* 38:289–318.

Hill, Paul T., Christine Campbell, and James Harvey. 2000. *It Takes a City: Getting Serious about Urban School Reform*. Washington, D.C.: Brookings Institution Press.

Hill, Paul T., and Marguerite Roza. 2004. *How Within-District Spending Inequities Help Some Schools to Fail*. Brookings Paper on Education Policy. Washington, D.C.: Brookings Institution.

Hillock, G. and L. H. Ludlow. 1984. A Taxonomy of Skills in Reading and Inter-preting Fiction. *American Educational Research Journal* 21, no. 1:7–21.

Hoffman, Kevin. Black Group Opposes State Takeover of Schools. *Kansas City Star*, March 3.

Honig, Meredith I., and Thomas C. Hatch. 2004. Crafting Coherence: How Schools Strategically Manage Multiple, External Demands. *Educational Researcher* 33, no. 8:16–30.

Hopkins, Dan. 2004. Risky Business: The Role of Economic Insecurity in Fostering Mayoral Control of Schools. Working Paper, Harvard University. www.people.fas.harvard.edu/~dhopkins/.

Hurwitz, Sol. 2001. The Outsiders. *American School Board Journal*, June.

Hutchinson, Audrey M., and Denise Van Wyngaardt. 2004. *Stronger Schools, Stronger Cities*. Institute for Youth, Education and Families, National League of Cities. www.nlc.org/content/Files/IYEF-StrongerCitiesReport.pdf.

Inglehart, Ronald. 1990. *Culture Shift in Advanced Industrial Society*. Princeton, N.J.: Princeton University Press.

Jackson, Barbara L., and James G. Cibulka. 1992. Leadership Turnover and Business Mobilization: The Changing Political Ecology of Urban School Systems. In *The Politics of Urban Education in the United States*, ed. James Cibulka, Rodney Reed, and Kenneth Wong. Washington, D.C.: Falmer Press.

James, Sheryl. 2002. Schools Chief Put to the Test. *Detroit Free Press*, January 22.

Jencks, Christopher, and Meredith Phillips. 1998. *The Black-White Test Score Gap*. Washington, D.C.: Brookings Institution Press.

Jenkins, Anthony. 1999. Black Enough: Some People Wonder Whether DC's Mayor Really Is One of Them. *Washington Post*, January 17.

Jennings, M. Kent. 1968. Parental Grievances and School Politics. *Public Opinion Quarterly*, Autumn, 363–78.

Jennings, N. 1996. *Interpreting Policy in Real Classrooms: Case Studies of State Reform and Teacher Practice*. New York: Teachers College Press.

Johnson, S. M., and S. M. Kardos. 2001. Reform Bargaining and Its Promises for School Improvement. In *Conflicting Missions? Teachers Unions and Educational Reform*, ed. Tom Loveless. Washington, D.C.: Brookings Institution Press.

Johnson, Otis. 2005. Education Rituals in the Savannah Community: A Position Paper. City of Savannah Town Hall Meeting on Public Education, July 25. www.ci.savannah.ga.us/cityweb/townhallmtgs/schoolreform/town_hall_school_speech_final.pdf.

Joyner, Chris. 2005. Attorney: Mayor Can't Ax Panelists. *Clarion-Ledger*, July 29.

Kain, John F. 2001. The UTD Texas Schools Microdata Panel (TSMP): Its History, Use and Ways to Improve State Collection of Public School Data. Paper pre-pared for meeting on the Secretary's Forum on Research and Value-Added Assessment Data. www.utdallas.edu/research/tsp/pdfpapers/paper28.html.

Kane, Thomas, Douglas Staiger, and Jeffrey Geppert. 2002. Randomly Accountable. *Education Next*, Spring, 57–61.

Katz, M. B. 1987. *Reconstructing American Education*. Cambridge, Mass.: Harvard University Press.

Keller, Edmond J. 1978. The Impact of Black Mayors on Urban Policy. *Annals of the American Academy of Political and Social Science*, September, 40–52.

Kerr, Gail. 2005. Purcell Has Two Years Left to Shape His Legacy. *Tennessean*, November 6. www.tennessean.com/apps/pbcs.dll/article?Date=20051106&Category =COLUMNIST0101&ArtNo=511060390&SectionCat=&Template=printart.

Kilpatrick, Kwame. 2002. Inaugural Address. www.ci.detroit.mi.us/mayor/speeches/ speeches_inaug.htm.

King, Gary, Robert Keohane, and Sydney Verba. 1994. *Designing Social Inquiry*. Princeton, N.J.: Princeton University Press.

Kirst, Michael W. 2002. *Mayoral Influence, New Regimes, and Public School Governance*. CPRE Research Report RR-049. Philadelphia: Consortium for Policy Research in Education, University of Pennsylvania Graduate School of Education.

Kleine, Robert, Philip Kloha, and Carol S. Weissert. June 2003. Monitoring Local Government Fiscal Health. *Government Finance Review* 19, no. 3:18.

Kober, Nancy. 2001. *It Takes More than Testing: Closing the Achievement Gap*. Washington, D.C.: Center on Education Policy.

Koretz, Daniel M. 2002. Limitations in the Use of Achievement Tests as Measures of Educators' Productivity. *Journal of Human Resources*, Autumn, 752–77.

Kozol, Jonathan. 1991. *Savage Inequalities*. New York: Crown.

Kuo, Wen H. 1973. Mayoral Influence in Urban Policy Making. *American Journal of Sociology* 79, no. 3 (November): 620–38.

Lanoue, G. R. Political Science. In *Encyclopedia of Educational Research*., vol. 3, ed. H. E. Mitzel et al. Washington, D.C.: American Educational Research Association.

LaRock, J. D. 2003a. Harrisburg: A Mayor Making Strides in Public Education, *US Mayors Newspaper*, July 14. www.usmayors.org/uscm/us_mayor_newspaper/ documents/07_14_03/harrisburg.asp.

———. 2003b. Mayoral Leadership on Education. *US Mayors Newspaper*, February 3. http://mayors.org/uscm/us_mayor_newspaper/documents/02_03_03/education1.asp.

Layton, D. 1982. The Emergence of the Politics of Education as a Field of Study. In *The Management of Educational Institutions*, ed. H. L. Gray. Lewes, U.K.: Falmer Press.

Lee, Carmen J. 2003. Mayor's Panel Concludes Problems Are So Severe Big Changes Are Needed. *Pittsburgh Post-Gazette*, September 23.

Levine, Arthur. 2000. Make Giuliani the Education Mayor Abolish the Board of Education. *New York Times*, January 8. www.tc.columbia.edu/newsbureau/ article.htm?id=2737.

Lewis, Dan A., and Kathryn Nakagawa. 1995. *Race and Educational Reform in the American Metropolis: A Study of School Decentralization*. Albany: State University of New York Press.

Lipsky, Michael. 1980. *Street-Level Bureaucracy: Dilemmas of the Individual in Public Services*. New York: Russell Sage Foundation.

Lopate, Carol, Erwin Flaxman, Effie M. Bynum, and Edmund W. Gordon. 1970. Decentralization and Community Participation in Public Education. *Review of Educational Research* 40, no. 1:135–50.

Los Angeles Times. 2001. Poll Analysis: Los Angeles Ready to Break Up School District, But Not City. March 5.

Louis, K. Seashore, Karen Febey, and R. Schroeder. 2005. State-Mandated Accountability in High Schools: Teachers' Interpretations of a New Era. *Educational Evaluation and Policy Analysis* 27, no. 2:177–204.

Loveless, Tom, ed. 2000. *Conflicting Missions?: Teachers Unions and Educational Reform.* Washington, D.C.: Brookings Institution Press.

———. 2003. *Brown Center Report on American Education 2003.* Washington, D.C.: Brookings Institution Press.

Loyola Marymount University. 2005. Exit Poll Study, Center for the Study of Los Angeles, March 8. www.lmu.edu/csla/press/releases_2005/Election.html.

Lutz, F. W. 1980. Local School Board Decision-Making: A Political-Anthropological Analysis. *Education and Urban Society* 12, no. 4:452–65.

MacPherson, Karen. 2003. DC Schools Still Struggling after Starting "Hybrid" Board. *Pittsburgh Post-Gazette*, April 28. www.post-gazette.com/neigh_city/20030428clevelandsidecity8p8.asp.

Mabeus, Courtney. 2006. New York School Takeover Gets Mixed Reviews. *Examiner.* www.examiner.com/a-339086-New_York_school_takeover_gets_mixed_reviews.html.

Maranto, Robert. 2005. A Tale of Two Cities: School Privatization in Philadelphia and Chester. *American Journal of Education*, February, 111.

Marquette, Jesse F. 2000. *Imagine.Akron: 2025 Household Survey.* Prepared by Center for Policy Studies, September.

Marschall, Melissa, and Paru Shah. 2005. Keeping Policy Churn Off the Agenda: Urban Education and Civic Capacity. *Policy Studies Journal* 33, issue 2:161–80.

Marsh, Julie A. 2002. How Districts Relate to States, Schools and Communities: A Review of Emerging Literature. In *School Districts and Instructional Renewal,* ed. Amy Hightower, Michael A. Knapp, Julie A. Marsh, and Milbrey W. McLaughlin. New York: Teachers College Press.

Martinez, Michael. 2000. City Schools Gain in 2nd Test Iowa Exam Shows Small Improvement. *Chicago Tribune*, May 16.

Massell, Diane, and Margaret E. Goertz. 2002. District Strategies for Building Instructional Capacity. In *School Districts and Instructional Renewal,* ed. Amy Hightower, Michael A. Knapp, Julie A. Marsh, and Milbrey W. McLaughlin. New York: Teachers College Press.

McAdams, Donald R. 2002. The New Challenge for School Boards. *ECS Governance Notes*, February.

McDonald, Brent. 2003. Oakland's "Strong Mayor" Reconsidered. *National Civic Review*, Fall.

McLendon, Gary. 2005. No "Us vs. Them" on City Schools: All Agree They're a Top Priority. *Rochester Democrat and Chronicle*, October 13.

Meinecke, Derek W., and David W. Adamany. 2001. School Reform in Detroit and Public Act 10: A Decisive Legislative Effort with an Uncertain Outcome. *Wayne State University Law Review* 47, no. 9.

Meyer, Wayne, ed. 1999. *Clinton on Clinton.* New York: HarperCollins.

Mintrop, Heinrich. 2004. *Schools on Probation: How Accountability Works (and Doesn't Work).* New York: Teachers College Press.

Mintrop, Heinrich, and Tina Trujillo. 2004. Corrective Action in Low-Performing Schools: Lessons for NCLB Implementation from State and District Strategies in First-Generation Accountability Systems. Center for the Study of Evaluation, National Center for Research on Evaluation, Standards, and Student Testing, Graduate School of Education and Information Studies, University of California, Los Angeles.

Miranda, Rowan A. 1994. Explaining the Privatization Decision among Local Governments in the United States. *Research in Urban Policy* 5:231–74.

Mirel, Jeffrey. 1993. *The Rise and Fall of an Urban School System*. Ann Arbor: University of Michigan Press.

Mitchell, D. E. 1988. Educational Politics and Policy: The State Level. In *Handbook of Research on Educational Administration*, ed. N. J. Boynan. New York: Longman.

Moe, Terry M. 2005. Teacher Unions and School Board Elections. In *Besieged: School Boards and the Future of Education Politics*, ed. William G. Howell. Washington, D.C.: Brookings Institution Press.

Moore, Cherise G. 2002. *Blacks in City Management*. Ph.D. diss., Public Administration, Arizona State University.

Moore, Donald R., and Gail Merritt. 2002. *Chicago's Local School Councils: What the Research Says*. Designs for Change, Chicago, January.

Morgan, David R., and Sheilah S. Watson. 1992. Policy Leadership in Council-Manager Cities: Comparing Mayor and Manager. *Public Administration Review*, September, 438–46.

National Center for Education Statistics. 2005a. School District Demographics System. http://nces.ed.gov/surveys/sdds/index.asp.

———. 2005b. A Recommended Approach to Providing High School Dropout and Completion Rates at the State Level. http://nces.ed.gov/pubsearch/pubs info.asp?pubid=2000305.

National School Boards Foundation. 1999. *Leadership Matters: Transforming Urban School Survey*. Alexandria, Va.: National School Boards Association.

New Haven Public Schools. 2006. *About NHPS: Dr. Reginald Mayo*. www.nhps.net/admin/drmayo_2.asp.

Newsday. 2005. NY1/Newsday Poll Shows Schools Are Top Concern. December 1. Online. www.ny1.com/ny1/NY1ToGo/Story/index.jsp?stid=3&aid=54804.

NewsHour with Jim Lehrer. 2005. School Reform in New York City. Special Report, September 28. www.pbs.org/newshour/bb/education/july-dec05/nyc_9-28.html.

Nichols, John. 2005. Urban Archipelago. *Nation*, June.

Nystrand, Martin. 1997. *Opening Dialogue: Understanding the Dynamics of Language and Learning in the English Classroom*. New York: Teachers College Record.

Okoben, Janet. 2005. Byrd-Bennett a Victim of Plummeting Image. *Cleveland Plain Dealer*, August 6.

Oliver, J. Eric. 2001. *Democracy in Suburbia*. Princeton, N.J.: Princeton University Press.

Olszewski-Kubilius, Paula, and Lee Seon-Young. 2004. The Role of Participation in In-School and Outside-of-School Activities in the Talent Development of Gifted Students. *Journal of Secondary Gifted Education* 15:107–23.

Omaha Public Schools. 2005. Questions & Answers Concerning One City, One School District. www.ops.org/Revised%20Questions%20for%20Commu.pdf.

Orfield, Gary, 2001. *Schools More Separate: Consequences of a Decade of Resegregation.* Cambridge, Mass.: The Civil Rights Project at Harvard University.

Orr, Marion. 1999. *Black Social Capital: The Politics of School Reform in Baltimore, 1986–1998.* Lawrence: University Press of Kansas.

———. 2001. *Black Social Capital: The Politics of School Reform in Baltimore.* Lawrence: University Press of Kansas.

———. 2004. Baltimore: The Limits of Mayoral Control. In *Mayors in the Middle: Politics, Race, and Mayoral Control of Urban Schools,* ed. J. Henig and W. Rich. Princeton, N.J.: Princeton University Press.

Ouellette, Mark, Audrey Hutchinson, and Nina Frant. 2005. The Afterschool Hours: A New Focus for America's Cities. National League of Cities. Institute for Youth, Education & Families. www.nlc.org/content/Files/IYEF-Lessons%20Learned%20Afterschool.pdf.

Palmer, Douglas H. 2005. Mayor Palmer Launches School Reform Coalition to Build On New Education Law Center Report. Press Release, June 20. www.edlawcenter.org/ELCPublic/AbbottIndicators/AbbottIndicatorsPressRelease_Trenton.pdf.

Parker, L. A. 2006. School Board Hires New Superintendent. *Trentonian,* June 28.

Peterson, Paul E. 1976. *School Politics, Chicago Style.* Chicago: University of Chicago Press.

———. 1981. *City Limits.* Chicago: University of Chicago Press.

Peterson, P. E., and T. Williams. 1972. Models of Decision Making. In *State, School, and Politics: Research Directions,* ed. M. W. Kirst. Lexington, Mass.: Lexington Books.

Pierce, Margo. 2005. A City That's Good for Kids: Mayoral Candidates Discuss Education and Youth. Cincinnati City Beat. www.citybeat.com/2005-08-03/news2.shtml.

Pittman, Alan. 2002. Child Support, *Eugene Weekly,* February 7. www2.eugeneweekly.com/2002/02_07_02/coverstory.html.

Polkinghorne, Donald E. 1995. Narrative Configuration in Qualitative Inquiry. *Qualitative Studies in Education 8,* no. 1:3–23.

Polsby, Daniel. 1994. Chicago School Reform: First Annual Evaluation. Heartland Policy Study, Heartland Institute, October 31.

Portz, John. 1996. Problem Definitions and Policy Agendas: Shaping the Education Agenda in Boston. *Policy Studies Journal* 24:371–86.

———. 2000. Supporting Education Reform: Mayoral and Corporate Paths. *Urban Education,* November.

———. 2003. Boston: Agenda Setting and School Reform in a Mayor-Centric System. In *Mayors in the Middle: Politics, Race, and Mayoral Control of Urban Schools,* ed. J. Henig and W. Rich. Princeton, N.J.: Princeton University Press.

Portz, John, Lana Stein, and Robin Jones. 1999. *City Schools and City Politics: Institutions and Leadership in Pittsburgh, Boston, and St. Louis.* Lawrence: University Press of Kansas.

Pressman, Jeffrey L., and Aaron Wildavsky. 1973. *Implementation: How Great Expectations in Washington Are Dashed in Oakland; Or, Why It's Amazing That Federal*

Programs Work At All, This Being a Saga of the Economic Development Administration As Told by Two Sympathetic Observers Who Seek to Build Morals on a Foundation of Ruined Hopes. Berkeley: University of California Press.

Prewitt, Kenneth. 1970. Political Ambition, Volunteerism, and Electoral Accountability. *American Political Science Review* 74:999–1006.

Prewitt, Kenneth, and Heinz Eulau. 1971. Social Bias in Leadership Selection, Political Recruitment, and Electoral Context. *Journal of Politics* 33, no. 2:293–315.

Pride, Richard A. 2002. How Critical Events Rather Than Performance Trends Shape Public Evaluations of the Schools. *Urban Review*, June, 159.

Providence Schools. 2005. Mayor Announces Search for School Board Members Application deadline Extended to October 28th. Press Release. www.providence schools.org/dept/board/nomination.html.

Public Agenda. 2000. National Poll of Parents of Public School Students. www.public agenda.org.

Public Education Network and *Education Week*. 2001. *Action for All: The Public's Responsibility for Public Education.* April. www.publiceducation.org/pdf/ Publications/National_Poll/April_2001_Action_for_All.pdf.

Quinnipiac University. 2005. Bloomberg Approval Tops 2-1 among All Groups, Quinnipiac University Poll Finds; More New Yorkers Say Make Education Top Priority. Press Release, November 17. www.quinnipiac.edu x1302.xml? ReleaseID=850.

Rada, R. D. 1988. A Public Choice Theory of School Board Member Behavior. *Educational Evaluation and Policy Analysis*, Fall 1988, 225–36.

Ravitch, Diane. 2000. *Left Back: A Century of Failed School Reforms.* New York: Simon & Schuster.

———. 2005. Every State Left Behind. *New York Times*, November 7.

———. 2007. *Will mayoral control save our schools?* Presentation at the Hoover Institution, Stanford University. April 24, 2007. Online: www.hoover.org/ multimedia/events/7559467.html.

Ravitz, Jason, John Mergendoller, and Wayne Rush. 2002. What's School Got to Do With It? Cautionary Tales about Correlations between Student Computer Use and Academic Achievement. Paper presented at annual meeting of American Educational Research Association, New Orleans, March.

Reinhard, B. 1998. Racial Issues Cloud State Takeovers. *Education Week*, January 14. www.edweek.org/ew/ewstory.cfm?slug=18minor.h17.

Rich, Wilbur C. 1996. *Black Mayors and School Politics.* New York: Garland.

Rich, Wilbur C., and Stefanie Chambers. 2003. Cleveland: Takeovers and Makeovers Are Not the Same. In *Mayors in the Middle: Politics, Race, and Mayoral Control of Urban Schools*, ed. Jeffrey Henig and Wilbur C. Rich. Princeton, N.J.: Princeton University Press.

Richardson, Jill Darling. 2001. Poll Analysis: Los Angeles Ready to Break Up School District, But Not City. *Los Angeles Times*, March 5.

Rogers, William H. 1993. Regression Standard Errors in Clustered Samples. *Stata Technical Bulletin* 13:19–23.

Rogerson, Robert J. 1999. Quality of Life and City Competitiveness. *Urban Studies*, May 1. www.fmchamber.com/government/update.html.

Russell, Scott. 2005. Schools Become Big Issue in Mayor's Race. *Southwest Journal*, September 23. www.swjournal.com/articles/2005/09/23/news/news13.txt.

Russo, Alexander. 2003. Political Educator. *Education Next*, Winter, 38–43.

Sassen, Saskia. 2001. *The Global City: New York, London, Tokyo*. 2nd ed. Princeton, N.J.: Princeton University Press.

Saulny, Susan. 2005. Higher Student Test Scores Mean Progress? Council Wants Proof. *New York Times*, June 28.

Saunders, Michaela. 2005. Senators Have Final Say on Schools. *Omaha World-Tribune*, July 26. www.omaha.com/index.php?u_pg=1640&u_sid=1468510.

School Code of Illinois. 1996. Section 34-18, paragraph 30.

School District Takeover. *Peabody Journal of Education* 78, 1, 5–32.

Schumaker, Paul. 1991. *Critical Pluralism, Democratic Performance, and Community Power*. Lawrence: University Press of Kansas.

Scribner, J. D., ed. 1977. *The Politics of Education*. Seventy-Sixth Yearbook of National Society for the Study of Education. Chicago: University of Chicago Press.

Seder, Richard C. 2000. *Balancing Accountability and Local Control: State Intervention for Financial and Academic Stability*. Policy Study 268. Los Angeles: Reason Public Policy Institute.

Shen, Francis. 2003. Spinning the Schools: Political Incentives and Mayoral Takeover of Urban Schools Districts. Paper presented at 2003 Annual Meeting of American Educational Research Association, Chicago.

Shipps, Dorothy. 1997. The Invisible Hand: Big Business and Chicago School Reform. *Teachers College Record*, Fall, 99.

———. 2003a. The Businessman's Educator: Mayoral Takeover and Nontraditional Leadership in Chicago. In *Powerful Reforms with Shallow Roots: Improving America's Urban Schools*, ed. Larry Cuban and Michael Usdan. New York: Teachers College Press.

———. 2003b. Chicago: The National "Model" Reexamined. In *Mayors in the Middle: Politics, Race, and Mayoral Control of Urban Schools*, ed. J. Henig and W. Rich. Princeton, N.J.: Princeton University Press.

———. 2004. Chicago: The National "Model" Reexamined. In *Mayors in the Middle: Politics, Race, and Mayoral Control of Urban Schools*, ed. J. Henig and W. Rich. Princeton, N.J.: Princeton University Press.

Siemers, Erik. 2005. Should City Control APS?, *Albuquerque Tribune*, November 4. www.abqtrib.com/albq/nw_education/article/0,2564,ALBQ_19857_4212399,00.html.

Siskin, Leslie S. 1994. *Realms of Knowledge: Academic Organizations in Secondary Schools*. Washington, D.C.: Falmer Press.

Smith, Kevin B., and J. Scott Granberg-Rademacker. 2003. Money Only Matters If You Want It to? Exposing the Normative Implications of Empirical Research. *Political Research Quarterly* 56, no. 2 (June): 223–32.

Snyder, Susan. 2006. New Challenges Ahead for Dallas. *Philadelphia Inquirer*, August 20.

Spillane, James P. 1996. Districts Matter: Local Education Authorities and State Instructional Policy. *Education Policy* 10:63–87.

Spillane, James, Brian Reiser, and Todd Reimer. 2002. Policy Implementation and Cognition: Reframing and Refocusing Implementation Research. *Review of Educational Research* 72:387–431.

Stone, Clarence Nathan. 1989. *Regime Politics: Governing Atlanta 1946–1988*. Lawrence: University Press of Kansas.

Stone, Clarence, Jeffrey R. Henig, Bryan D. Jones, and Carol Pierannunzi. 2001. *Building Civic Capacity: The Politics of Reforming Urban Schools*. Lawrence: University Press of Kansas.

Sutton, Marsha. 2005. The Push for Mayor-Appointed School Boards Bypasses San Diego—for Now. *Voice of San Diego*, June 15. www.voiceofsandiego.org/site/apps/s/content.asp?c=euLTJbMUKvH&b=291837&ct=1010937.

Svara, James H. 1987. Mayoral Leadership in Council-Manager Cities: Preconditions versus Preconceptions. *Journal of Politics*, February, 207–27.

———. 1990. *Official Leadership in the City: Patterns of Conflict and Cooperation*. New York: Oxford University Press.

———. 2001. Do We Still Need Model Charters? The Meaning and Relevance of Reform in the Twenty-First Century. *National Civic Review* 90, no. 1:19–34.

———. 2003. Effective Mayoral Leadership in Council-Manager Cities: Reassessing the Facilitative Model. *National Civic Review*, Summer.

Taebel, D. A. 1977. The Politics of School Board Elections. *Urban Education* 12, no. 2:153–66.

Talbert, Joan E., and Milbrey W. McLaughlin. 1994. Teacher Professionalism in Local School Contexts. *American Journal of Education* 102, no. 2:123–53.

Tennessean. 2005. Editorial: Say No to Sales Tax Hike—and Age-Based Subsidies. www.nashvillescene.com/Stories/News/2005/05/26/Say_No_to_Sales_Tax_Hike_amp_15/index.shtml.

Thernstrom, Abigail, and Stephan Thernstrom. 2003. *No Excuse: Closing the Racial Gap in Learning*. New York: Simon & Schuster.

Thevenot, Brian. 2004. School Board Fate in Voters' Hands. *New Orleans Times Picayune*, June 13.

Thomas, Alan Berkeley. 1988. Does Leadership Make a Difference to Organizational Performance? *Administrative Science Quarterly* 33, no. 3 (September): 388–400.

Thompson, Edward, and David M. Brodsky. 1997. Structure and Mayoral Roles: A Research Note. *Urban Studies*, November.

Thompson, J. Phillip. 2005. Seeking Effective Power: Why Mayors Need Community Organizations. *Perspectives on Politics* 3:301–8.

Traub, James. 2000. What No School Can Do. *New York Times Magazine*, January 16, 52–53.

Tyack, David B. 1974. *The One Best System: A History of American Urban Education*. Cambridge, Mass.: Harvard University Press.

Usdan, Michael, and Larry Cuban. 2003. Boston: The Stars Finally Align. In *Powerful Reforms with Shallow Roots: Improving America's Schools*, ed. Larry Cuban and Michael Usdan. New York: Teachers College Press.

Van Lier, Piet. 2001. Boston's Menino: "Judge Me Harshly" If Reforms Fail. *Catalyst Cleveland*, May/June.

Vance, Paul L. 2006. Personal letter. October 6. www.k12.dc.us/dcps/home.html.

Wagman, Jake. 2003. Power Brokers Play Role in Campaign for School Reform. *Saint Louis Post-Dispatch*.

Weaver, R. Kent. 1986. The Politics of Blame Avoidance. *Journal of Public Policy* 6, no. 4:371–98.

Weber, Max. 1947. *Max Weber: The Theory of Social and Economic Organization*, trans. A. M. Henderson and Talcott Parsons. Glencoe, Ill.: Free Press.

Weeres, J. G., and B. Cooper. 1992. Public Choice Perspectives on Urban Schools. In *The Politics of Urban Education in the United States: The 1991 Yearbook of the Politics of Education Association*, ed. James Cibulka, Rodney Reed, and Kenneth Wong. Washington, D.C.: Falmer Press.

Weick, K. 1976. Educational Organizations as Loosely Coupled Systems. *Administrative Science Quarterly* 21:1–89.

Wheeland, Craig. 2002. Mayoral Leadership in the Context of Variations in City Structure. In *The Future of Local Government Administration: The Hansell Symposium*, ed. G. Frederickson and J. Nalbandian. Washington, D.C.: International City/County Management Association.

White House. 1998. President Clinton Discusses Education Issues with Mayors Conference. Press Release, May 7.

Whittle, Chris. 2005. The Promise of Public/Private Partnerships. *Educational Leadership*, February.

Wikstrom, Nelson. 1979. The Mayor as a Policy Leader in the Council-Manager Form of Government: A View from the Field. *Public Administration Review* 39, no. 3 (May): 270–76.

Wilder, L. Douglas. 2005. Our Job: Are We Satisfied Where We Are?" *Richmond Times-Dispatch*, August 7.

Williams, Rick L. 2000. A Note on Robust Variance Estimation for Cluster-Correlated Data. *Biometrics* 56:645–46.

Wilson, William J. 1987. *The Truly Disadvantaged: The Inner City, the Underclass, and Public Policy*. Chicago: University of Chicago Press.

Wirt, F. and M. Kirst. 1982. *Schools in Conflict*. Berkeley, Calif.: McCutchan.

Wohlstetter, Priscilla, and Karen McCurdy. 1991. The Link between School Decentralization and School Politics. *Urban Education* 25, no. 4:391–414.

Wolman, Harold, John Strate, and Alan Melchior. 1996. Does Changing Mayors Matter? *Journal of Politics* 58, no. 1 (February): 201–23.

Wong, Kenneth K. 1990. *City Choices: Education and Housing*. Albany: State University of New York Press.

———. 1991. The Politics of Urban Education as a Field of Study: An Interpretative Analysis. In *The Politics of Urban Education in the United States: The 1991 Politics of Education Association Yearbook*, ed. James G. Cibulka, Rodney J. Reed, and Kenneth. K. Wong. London: Falmer Press.

———. 1999. *Funding Public Schools: Politics and Policy*. Lawrence: University Press of Kansas.

———. 2000. Big Change Questions Chicago School Reform: From Decentralization to Integrated Governance. *Journal of Educational Change* 1, no. 1 (January): 95–103.

Wong, Kenneth K., and D. Anagnostopoulos. 1998. Can Integrated Governance Reconstruct Teaching? Lessons Learned from Two Low-Performing Chicago High Schools. *Educational Policy* 12:19–30.

Wong, Kenneth. K., Dorothea Anagnostopoulos, Stacey Rutledge, and Claudia Edwards. 2001. *The Challenge of Improving Instruction in Urban High Schools: Case Studies of the Implementation of the Chicago Academic Standards.* Report Submitted to U.S. Department of Education.

Wong, Kenneth K., Dorothea Anagnostopoulos, Stacey Rutledge, Laurence Lynn, and Robert Dreeben. 1999. *Implementation of an Educational Accountability Agenda: Integrated Governance in the Chicago Public Schools Enters Its Fourth Year.* Chicago: Department of Education and Irving B. Harris Graduate School of Public Policy Studies, University of Chicago.

Wong, Kenneth K., Robert Dreeben, Laurence Lynn Jr., and Gail L. Sunderman. 1997. *Integrated Governance as a Reform Strategy in the Chicago Public Schools.* Chicago: Department of Education and Irving B. Harris Graduate School of Public Policy Studies, University of Chicago.

Wong, Kenneth K., and Pushpam Jain. 1999. Newspapers as Policy Actors in Urban School Systems: The Chicago Story. *Urban Affairs Review* 35, no. 2:210–46.

Wong, Kenneth K., Pushpam Jain, and Terry N. Clark. 1997. *Mayoral Leadership in the 1990's: Fiscally Responsible and Outcome Oriented.* Paper presented at 1997 Annual Conference of Association for Public Policy Analysis and Management, Washington.

Wong, Kenneth K., Warren E. Langevin, and Francis X. Shen. 2004. When School Districts Regain Control: The Political Economy of State Takeover of Local Schools and Its Withdrawal. Paper prepared for 2004 Annual Meeting of American Political Science Association.

Wong, Kenneth K., and Mark H. Moulton. 1996. Developing Institutional Performance Indicators for Chicago Schools: Conceptual and Methodological Issues Considered. In *Advances in Educational Policy, Volume 2: Rethinking School Reform in Chicago,* ed. Kenneth K. Wong. Greenwich, Conn.: JAI Press.

Wong, Kenneth K., and S. A. Rutledge, eds. 2006. *Systemwide Efforts to Improve Student Achievement.* Greenwich, Conn.: Information Age Publishing.

Wong, Kenneth. K., and Francis X. Shen. 2001. *Does School District Takeover Work? Assessing the Effectiveness of City and State Takeover as a School Reform Strategy.* Paper prepared for 97th Annual Meeting of American Political Science Association, August 30–September 2.

———. 2002. Does School District Takeover Work? Assessing the Effectiveness of City and State Takeover as a School Reform Strategy. *State Education Standard,* Spring, 19–23.

———. 2003. Measuring the Effectiveness of City and State Takeover as a School Reform Strategy. *Peabody Journal of Education* 78, no. 4:89–119.

———. 2005. When Mayors Lead Urban Schools: Assessing the Effects of Mayoral Takeover. In *Besieged: School Boards and the Future of Education Politics,* ed. William G. Howell. Washington, D.C.: Brookings Institution Press.

Wong, K. K., and G. L. Sunderman. 2000. Implementing Districtwide Reform in Schools with Title I Programs: The First Two Years of Children Achieving in Philadelphia. *Journal of Education for Students Placed at Risk* 5, no. 4:355–81.

Woodall, Martha. 2006. For Dallas, a Raise and 3-Year Extension. *Philadelphia Inquirer*, August 24.

Wooldridge, Jeffrey M. 2002. *Econometric Analysis of Cross-Section and Panel Data.* Cambridge, Mass.: MIT Press.

Yin, Robert K., R. James Schmidt, and Frank Besag. 2006. Tracking Student Achievement Trends across Different Tests: Using Standardized Slopes as Effect Sizes. *Peabody Journal of Education.*

Young, Beth. 2002. *Characteristics of the 100 Largest Public Elementary and Secondary School Districts in the United States: 2000–01.* Washington, D.C.: National Center for Education Statistics. http://nces.ed.gov/pubs2002/100_largest/btables.asp#9.

Zeigler, L. Harmon. 1975. School Boards Research: The Problems and Prospects. In *Understanding School Boards: Problems and Prospects*, ed. Peter J. Cistone. Lexington, Mass.: Lexington Books.

Ziebarth, Todd. 2002. *State Takeovers and Reconstitutions Policy Brief.* Paper prepared for Education Commission of the States. www.ecs.org.

Index

Note: Page numbers followed by the letter "t" indicate tables in the text.